M000250677

THE VEGAN
BUTCHER

ZACCHARY BIRD

THE VEGAN BUTCHER

Smith
Street
Books

Welcome to the ultimate guide to plant-based meat: how to turn everything that exists vegan! This beast of a book is dedicated to all the dishes you thought you'd given the boot to once you went vegan. It turns out that you – and the animals! ... and the planet! – really can have it all.

So, first things first. Why would a vegan want to eat something that tastes and looks like meat? Because – duh – it's yum! Vegans aren't vegan because they hate flavour, that's animal cruelty you're thinking of. These days, choosing vegan food doesn't mean giving up your culinary traditions or really making much personal sacrifice at all. There's now no reason not to recreate the flavours, textures and (if you're into it) appearance of the food you've always enjoyed.

Guess what the big secret is? Making plants taste and look like cooked meat is suspiciously similar to the process it takes to make meat taste and look like meat! Blogger and author Lauren Toyota of Hot for Food fame gets it. She sums it up best when she says: 'To make your substitutes like meat, use all the familiar herbs, seasonings and umami-rich flavour boosters – don't skimp! Then use all the traditional cooking techniques available to bring out those flavours – marinade, roast, sear, sauté, grill and braise. Go wild, and transform these plants into something succulent and drool-worthy.'

So many of the flavours assumed to be exclusive to meat are created through technique and seasoning. Liberate yourself from outdated ideas: the same effort applied to plant-based food can achieve some seriously impressive results, which are as good as, if not better than, their meaty counterparts.

The recipes and guides within these pages are here to hold your hand as you cook your way from easy substitutes to advanced analogues. Learn how to master

the classics like seitan (that doesn't suck) and a good tofu turkey. Breathe new life into old veg' with clever cooking tricks before trying your hand at cutting-edge plant-based food science, which will allow you to make pure plant-based magic in your own kitchen.

A HISTORY OF MOCK MEAT

Mock meat is no newcomer and much of it has remained the same for a long time. Seitan, originating from China, is over a thousand years old and tofu is at least double that in age. Vegetables served as pork, and stuffed bean curd sheets served as mock duck or sausages are dishes from centuries-old Buddhist vegetarian cuisine. In the western world, Seventh Day Adventists have been promoting and inventing meat alternatives since the mid-19th century. Places like Battle Creek Sanitarium sold products such as Protose, made from wheat gluten and peanuts, which have become the precursors to many commercial modern meat alternatives.

Turn of the 20th-century vegetarian cookbooks show recipes calling for novel aesthetic touches like adding macaroni bones to a vegetable cutlet – another devastating blow to the persistent myth that mocking meat is a fresh concept! By the 1940s, the term 'vegan' had been coined by Donald Watson and the collaborative, concentrated movement to find ways to make living animal-free possible was fully underway. The slow trickle of initial choices: veggie burgers, the discovery of *Fusarium venenatum* (a high-protein microfungus used to make mycoprotein: later to become Quorn) and Tofurky products have since turned into a deluge of alternatives that seem to update more quickly than a social media feed. As Seth Tibbott, founder and chairman of the Tofurky company says: 'The Tofurky Company, founded in 1980, is thrilled to be a part of the breathtaking growth in vegan foods that is now happening all over the world. This shift is one of the biggest and most needed changes in earth's history. Let's do this!'

The commercial world of vegan food is constantly evolving with the assistance of the very latest scientific discoveries, and my job helping to develop mass-produced, plant-based meats looks a lot more like lab work than it does home cooking. The home cook doesn't need to be kept out of the loop, though, because I've broken down how to utilise some of these in your own kitchen: methylcellulose, konjac, gums and pure gluten will leap from the ingredients lists on the back of packets and into your pantry and fridge.

Some specifically modified ingredients, carefully chosen proteins and fibres, and curated flavour compounds are out of reach for the home cook, but only so far as having to use them yourselves. Grocery store shelves are readily lined with products that have done the finicky finessing of these ingredients into analogues that can be cooked just like meat and subbed into recipes. The dishes in this book will come out fabulous whether you fashion them from scratch, swap them out for beans or vegetables, or just grab a packet off the shelf to skip ahead.

I don't miss meat, nor do I miss the confines it restricted my cooking to, so it follows that this book is all about embracing invention and cancelling convention. No two real animals, drumsticks, steaks, roasts or nuggets look the same, which means you're totally in control of whether your food looks hyper-realistic, imaginative or like a delicious, featureless blob (meatloaf, anyone?). You've been granted full creative licence and a limit does not exist: these recipes aren't just replacements for meat, they're its successors. Not eating fake meat saves exactly zero extra animals. It's high time we put absolutely everything back on the menu and eat some bloody good food.

HOW TO USE THIS BOOK

The recipes in this book teach you how to recreate classically vegan-unfriendly dishes, showcasing the sheer volume of replacements that plant-based cuisine has in its arsenal. However, don't let that limit you: substitutions are definitely allowed on this menu; in fact, that's the whole spirit!

Many recipes offer several choices for the base protein, so you can use what's available to you or cook your way through the options to find your personal favourite. (Tried rice paper bacon? How about mushroom bacon? Or even spawn of seitan bacon? Coconuts? Carrots? Eggplant?! Oh my!) Off-the-shelf meat alternatives are more than welcome substitutions for an endless array of savoury inspiration. I invite you to use your favourites and take advantage of what you can find on sale or what's in season, as being out of one ingredient is a hell of a good excuse to test out a different one.

Give my recommendations a go, then take the training wheels off by using what you've learned to substitute the substitutions themselves! Throw some TVP chunks into your bourbon chicken instead of cauliflower; use shredded ham seitan to stuff char siu bao if you're not game to try banana peel pork; or even make up your own combos using multiple dishes.

Each chapter holds techniques that range from easy to advanced so that you can get stuck in straight away, no matter what level of expertise you're at. Under the title of each recipe, find one (easy) to three (advanced) stars, which indicate the complexity of the dish. You can try new ideas at your own pace, then graduate through the levels, or stick to the simpler ones when you want to get dinner on the table in 30 minutes, leaving the advanced recipes for special occasions (think vegan turkducken for Thanksliving!).

For those wanting to truly master the art of vegan butchery, it's all here for you. We've got undercover footage from a plant-based meat factory, so there are photographs and step-by-step guides scattered throughout to help you get comfortable turning fresh ingredients into meat doppelgangers: fresh banana blossom blossoming into fish; watermelon reared into a ham; and jackfruit hatching into chicken are all caught on camera in each respective chapter for you to replicate.

But first up, we're going back to the very beginning and learning the basics! Classic meat alternatives tried and tested over hundreds of years, like fresh seitan, tofu, bean curd sheets and konjaku are broken down into methods you can achieve at home today. There are cooking techniques that have been banished from vegan menus for too long (deep-frying, barbecuing and smoking) that you might need a refresher course on. Plus you'll be all the better the cook after reading up on how to harness the power of synergistic umami (savoury flavour) and fat to make your fake food taste real AF. There's a whole new world of meat made out of plants for you to learn about, so let's get started.

LET'S

GET

STARTED

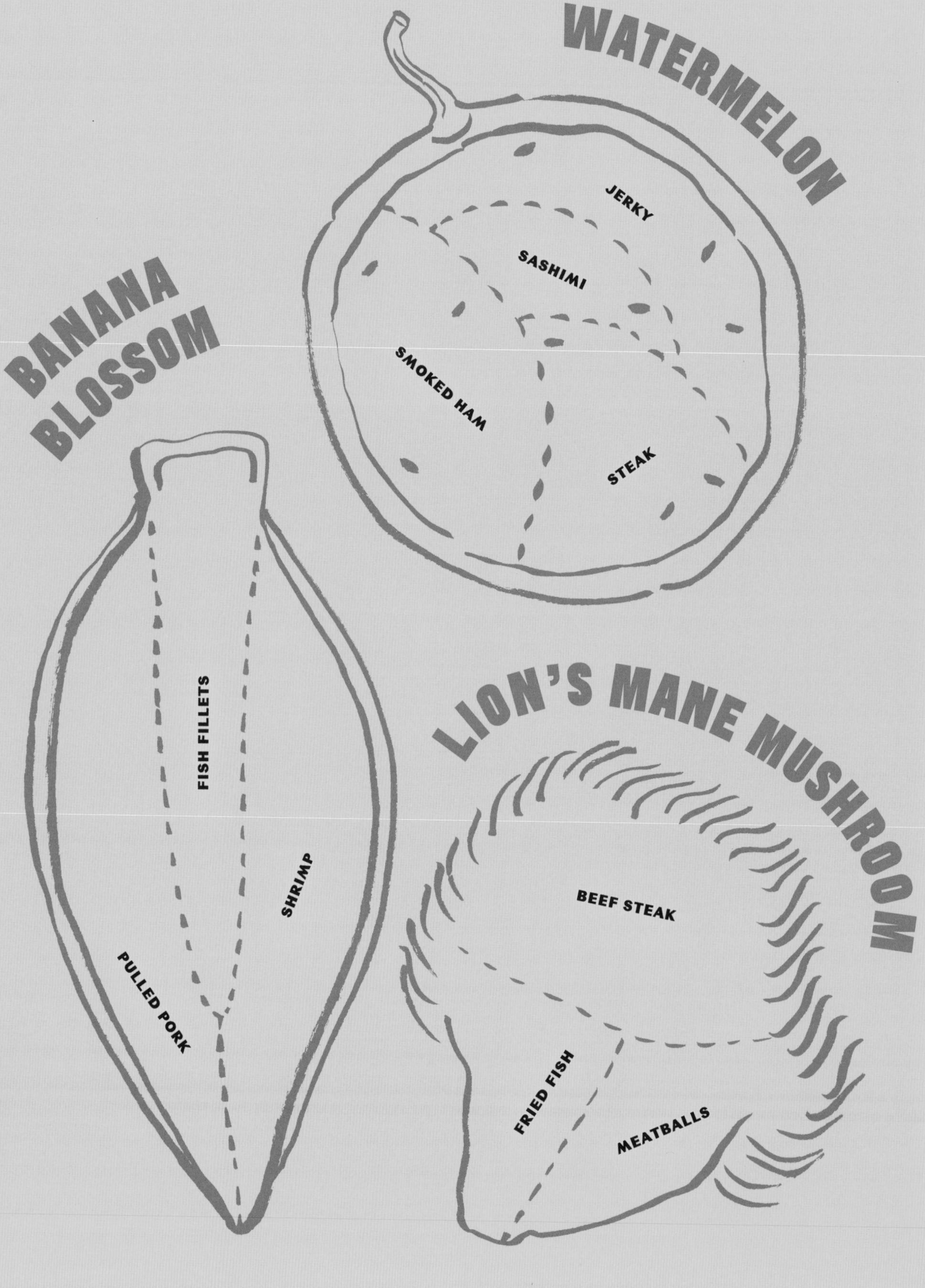

WATERMELON

- JERKY
- SASHIMI
- SMOKED HAM
- STEAK

BANANA BLOSSOM

- FISH FILLETS
- SHRIMP
- PULLED PORK

LION'S MANE MUSHROOM

- BEEF STEAK
- FRIED FISH
- MEATBALLS

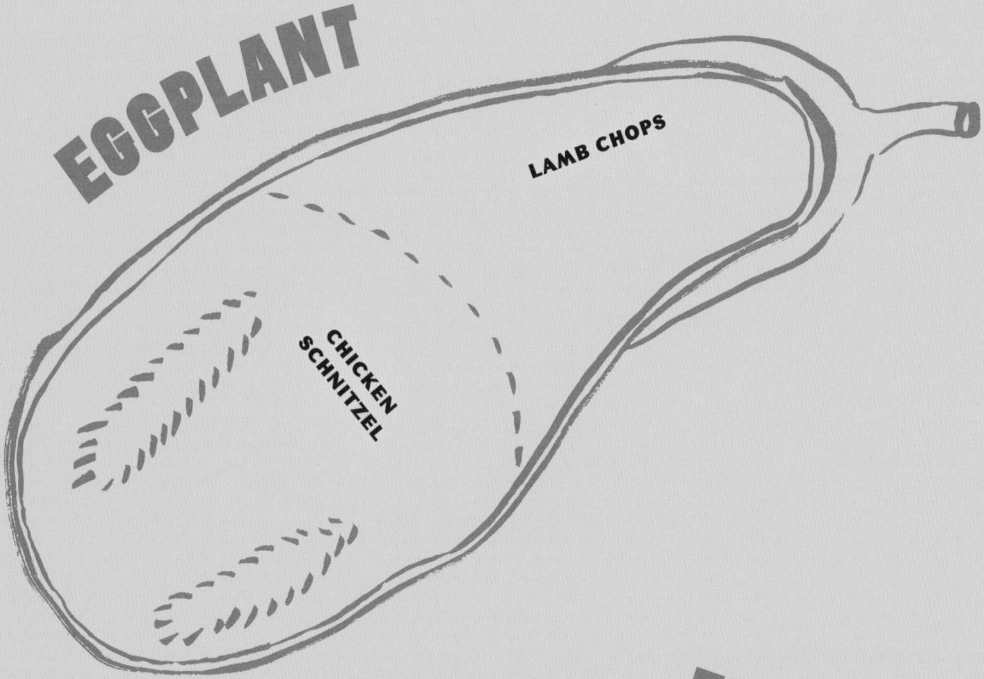

EGGPLANT

LAMB CHOPS

CHICKEN
SCHNITZEL

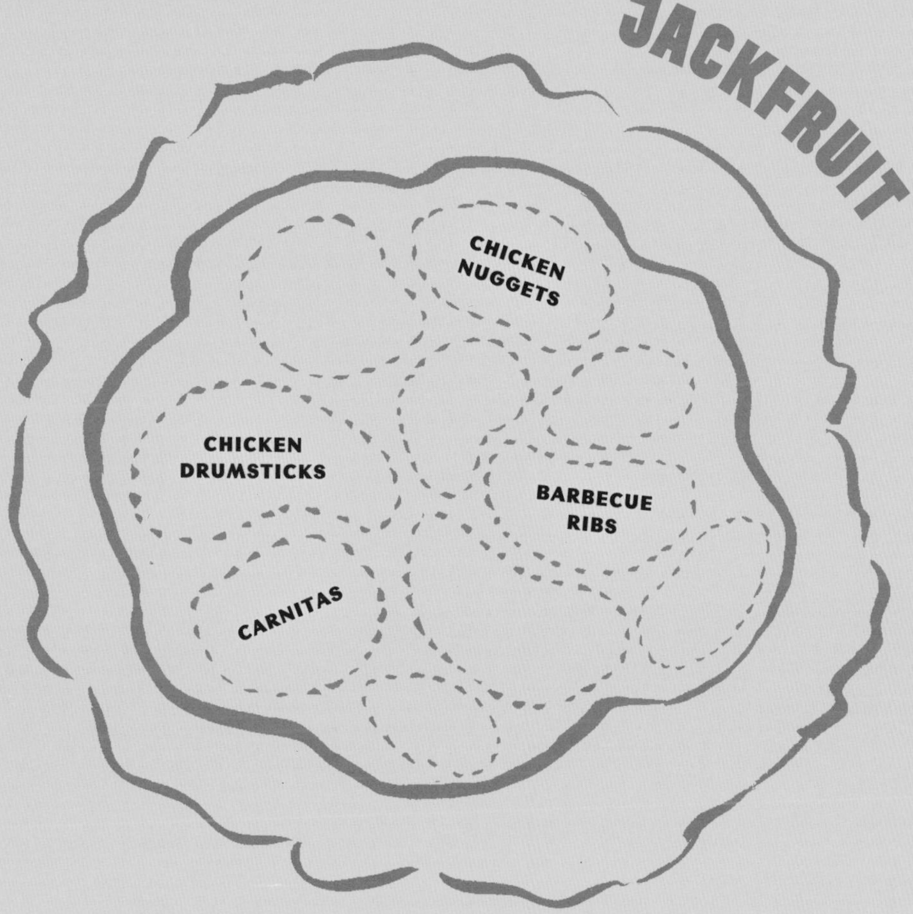

JACKFRUIT

CHICKEN
NUGGETS

CHICKEN
DRUMSTICKS

BARBECUE
RIBS

CARNITAS

UMAMI

Umami – or moreish savoury flavour – is a deal-breaker when it comes to making rich and satiating meat alternatives that can compete with the traditional versions. Cooked animal products tend to be very high in umami, so any attempt at imitating them will be lacking without it. Adding umami to your food using MSG (monosodium glutamate) is like the savoury counterpart to sprinkling in sugar to sweeten a dish. It's easy, effective and will significantly improve the taste of meat analogues. It's not cheating at all to make use of the wonderful modern ingredients we have available, but with that said, it isn't the only way to invite the umami army into your kitchen.

SYNERGISTIC UMAMI

Umami comes in two main forms: basal (free glutamate) and secondary (nucleotides such as inosinate and guanylate), which can be found in many plants. Glutamate is made available in food through processes, such as ripening, fermenting, drying, aging and roasting. For example, fresh mushrooms are naturally high in umami, but become much richer in flavour when dried or fermented – dried shiitake mushrooms especially so, as they are high in nucleotides. Tomatoes, like mushrooms, are also a reliable vegan source of umami, which is amplified in pastes or after drying. Toasting nuts coaxes out their flavours and also boosts their umami. Nori, as it is a seaweed, is already rich in umami and in its dried form this is only increased.

Synergistic umami is activated when you combine basal and secondary umami-rich ingredients in the same recipe. By their powers combined, free glutamate (basal) with just a small amount of nucleotides (secondary) added will intensify the umami by more than seven times! That's a whole lotta extra savoury. A real-life example of this is one of the foundations of umami-rich Japanese cooking: awase dashi. Bonito flakes, being dried fish, are very high in the nucleotide inosinate and when combined with dried kombu, which is high in glutamate, the resulting umami is much more powerful than either ingredient could be by itself. We employ a similar collaboration in the vegan Awase dashi (see page 118) in this book, which uses the guanylate in dried shiitake mushrooms to replace the dried fish. Try combining sundried tomatoes, tomato paste (concentrated purée), dried mushrooms or dried seaweed in dishes built from basal umami ingredients to achieve the teamwork that makes the savoury dream work.

VEGAN BASAL INGREDIENTS WITH FREE GLUTAMATE

SEAWEED • MUSHROOMS • WALNUTS • BEANS OR BEAN PASTE • VEGETABLES AND FRUIT SUCH AS: ONION, GARLIC, TOMATOES, CARROTS, CELERY, ASPARAGUS • FERMENTED FOODS SUCH AS: MISO, SOY SAUCE, KIMCHI/SAUERKRAUT, VEGAN OYSTER/FISH/WORCESTERSHIRE SAUCE, PLUM OR BALSAMIC VINEGAR • EXTRACTS AND YEASTS SUCH AS: MSG, VEGEMITE/MARMITE, NUTRITIONAL YEAST, TORULA YEAST

VEGAN SECONDARY INGREDIENTS WITH NUCLEOTIDES OR GUANYLATE

DRIED SEAWEED • SEMIDRIED AND SUNDRIED TOMATOES • DRIED MUSHROOMS
FRESH MUSHROOMS (SHIITAKE, ENOKI, PORCINI)

FURTHER FLAVOUR NOTES

Flavoured salts, such as smoked salt and kala namak (Indian black salt), are another way to introduce complex flavours and the saltiness inherent in meat products. They tend to reduce in flavour as they cook: smoked salt is best used as a finishing salt, so the smokiness is maximised; whereas kala namak is great used in meat alternatives as the sulphuric 'eggy' flavour that is generally unrecognisable once it is cooked.

Miso is fermented and shouldn't be overcooked – many traditional recipes avoid adding miso to boiling water. To use, massage the miso into liquid with your fingertips to properly incorporate it.

The compound 2-methyl-3-furanthiol is responsible for the aroma of cooked meat products. It can also be found in vegan products like fermented soy sauce and yeast extracts. The intensity only increases upon cooking. Brine or oil from jarred sundried tomatoes, capers, olives, artichokes or capsicums (bell peppers) is another way to pack in flavour and additional umami.

Mirepoix and sofrito (a base of onion, carrot and celery) or the Cajun holy trinity (onion, celery and capsicum/bell pepper) are common combos used to kickstart the flavour profile of many dishes from around the world. Celery enhances the presence of both umami and sweetness in the final flavour, carrot adds sweetness, and onion, as it caramelises, adds a rich complexity through both umami and sweetness. Together, these ingredients make for a fragrant and rounded base to add your meaty flavours.

FAT

Fat-free cooking has its time and place, but you'll be hard pressed to capture the authenticity of many animal products without it. It's no big secret that fat is key to making food taste delicious. Fat carries flavour, changes mouthfeel and is a primary ingredient in most real animal products, so shouldn't be skimped on. Put simply, flavours won't be nearly as accessible to your tastebuds and you'll never achieve the satiation that comes from meat products without fat. Meat alternatives tend to be naturally high in protein and/or carbohydrates, so don't be afraid to add in some fat.

Refined coconut oil, vegetable suet or vegetable shortening are all great ways to add fat without adding flavours that will detract from the dish. Extra virgin olive oil is suitable for serving with seafood dishes and salads, whereas deep-frying calls for refined oils, such as vegetable, rice bran or canola.

SEITAN

TRADITIONAL SEITAN FROM FLOUR

Seitan is formed from wheat protein and it is one of the most versatile meat-alternative bases available. It's pure gluten! The original method of creating seitan is to make a dough of flour and water, knead it into a ball to develop the gluten (just like other doughs), then you wash it to rinse away the starches leaving you with a mass of mostly gluten protein. This method takes just three ingredients: flour, water and elbow grease. It also gives you the most control over the texture of your final product, as you can stop the washing process at various points, leaving in starches to interrupt the gluten and give inconsistent and meatier textures to your seitan (as opposed to the infamous, one-note rubbery texture seitan can take on that doesn't do it many favours as a meat substitute). And that's not the only way! Once washed, you can braid, twist, knot, flatten, layer and stretch out the individual strands of gluten to form them as you please.

This washing method makes it far more difficult to disperse other ingredients or flavours throughout the seitan, so it is best used when simmering in flavoursome stock or serving with lots of marinade or sauce. Hand-washed seitan is one of the cheapest ways to produce incredible meat alternatives, thanks to the relatively low cost and accessibility of flour and water. Another advantage is you tend to work off any associated calories in the dish you're making by the time you manage to get it on the table. That's true guilt-free cuisine!

The case for lazy seitan-making is a strong one. You get to zone out and totally forget what you are doing and your seitan will be all the better for it. Autolysing the dough (allowing the flour and water to rest before kneading) reduces the effort required, and resting the kneaded dough before cooking allows the gluten to continue to develop. Plan ahead or get completely distracted between steps; either way, if you take your time you'll reap the rewards.

A rich colour in seitan and other animal analogues can be achieved in a number of ways: pink or red food colouring without cochineal (colour 120) gives the illusion of rare meat; whereas beetroot (beet) powder becomes grey as it bakes, imitating cooked meat. Fresh beetroot or beetroot juice creates a deep pink colour but also introduces flavour. Red yeast rice powder has little flavour and is a very effective colourant. In sauces and gravies, browning liquid and red wine help boost the richness.

BASIC WASHED SEITAN

✶ ✶

MAKES 360-600 G (12½ OZ-1 LB 5 OZ)

As this method makes it more difficult to incorporate flavours into the inside of the seitan, I prefer to use washed flour for smaller pieces and shreds. If you'd like to make a larger roast, refer to the vital wheat gluten recipe on page 66 or follow the method in the preparing seitan as ham recipe on page 176.

INGREDIENTS

plain (all-purpose) flour or bread flour (at least 11% protein)	1 KG (2 LB 3 OZ)

① Combine the flour and 600 ml (20½ fl oz) of water in a large bowl and mix until a dough ball forms. Knead the dough for 3-4 minutes in a stand mixer fitted with a dough hook. Alternatively, knead by hand for 10 minutes by pushing the dough away from you with the heel of your hand, then folding the dough over and pulling it back towards you. Repeat this push-pull method until the dough springs back when you press down on it. Kneading the dough lines up the messy gluten proteins and creates the folds and texture that will mimic meat.

② Rest the dough ball for 1 hour submerged in cold water.

③ Change the water in the bowl with more cold water, then get to know your dough. Draw the curtains, light some candles and get intimate. Begin to massage and knead the dough under the water to wash the starches out. When the water becomes thick and milky, change it out with warm (not hot!) water and reserve the milky liquid.

④ Continue to wash, mangling the dough as the strands of gluten form. Reserve the starch water from the second wash and add it to the first batch of milky liquid. Transfer to a large container and use it to make Spawn of seitan (see page 26).

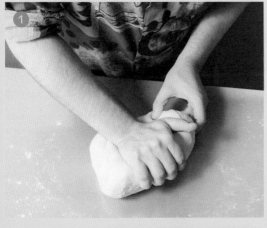

⑤ Repeat this process, rinsing with alternating warm water (to relax the gluten and release starch) and cold water (to contract the gluten and firm up) until the dough volume is halved.

⑥ Once the water running from the seitan is no longer slimy, you can finish washing and kneading under running water as the gluten will have firmed up enough - refer to When to stop washing (see page 24) for more information. Finish with a rinse of cold water, squeeze out any excess, then transfer the droopy seitan to a colander for 1 hour to drain off more starchy liquid.

Make sure your flour has at least 11% protein to be suitable for this method. Bread flour, or any strong flour with a higher protein content will yield slightly more of the final product.

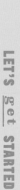

FATTY WASHED SEITAN

✳ ✳ ✳

MAKES 1 KG (2 LB 3 OZ)

If making beef- or pork-inspired seitan, add food colouring (pink or red) to the water. This is also a good idea for your first-time hand washing the dough, as it will help you see the difference between the starch (light clumps) and gluten protein in the dough as you wash.

INGREDIENTS

plain (all-purpose) flour	2 KG (4 LB 6 OZ)
boiling water	500 ML (2 CUPS)
vegan-friendly red food colouring (or more for darker meat)	3-4 DROPS

① You'll need to begin this recipe at least 2 days before serving. Place the flour in a very large bowl. Drizzle the boiling water over the flour and mix in with a fork. Combine the red food colouring with 750 ml (3 cups) of cold water and stir into the dough.

② Use your hands to knead the dough into a ball. Knead the dough for 3-4 minutes in a stand mixer fitted with a dough hook. Alternatively, knead for up to 10 minutes by hand. Cover with water and rest overnight.

③ Change out the water in the bowl with more cold water. Begin to massage and knead the dough under the water to wash the starches out.

④ When the water becomes thick and milky, change it out with warm (not hot!) water and reserve the thick sludgy starch water. Continue to wash, mangling the dough as the strands of gluten form.

⑤ Change out the water again (this time for cold water) and add the milky liquid to the sludgy starch water. Use the liquid to make Spawn of seitan (see page 26). Continue to wash the dough, rinsing with alternating warm water (to relax the gluten and release starch) and cold water (to contract the gluten and firm up). If it begins to look like a brain, you're well on your way.

⑥ Once the water draining from the seitan is no longer slimy, remove one-quarter of the dough and set aside. Continue to knead the dough and rinse out the starches under running water. Wash until just before mid-washed (see page 24), then knead in the reserved dough. Your dough ball will weigh around 1 kg (2 lb 3 oz) when it is ready. Drain the seitan in a colander for 1 hour to remove excess liquid.

⑦ Place the seitan in a bowl, cover and rest at least overnight in the fridge. Right before cooking, knot, braid or mangle further to create more connections and interesting texture within your seitan. Use in the seitan ham basic recipe (see page 176), large roasts or the beef mince on page 236.

WHEN TO STOP WASHING

Many seitan recipes call for a complementary base ingredient to dilute the texture (such as tofu, jackfruit, beans). This same softer effect can be achieved by washing less and leaving some starch in the gluten. As you become comfortable with washed seitan, you can easily adapt the texture by stopping washing at various stages of the preparation.

Within the online seitan community, rock stars are born when a new method for exciting textures is offered up by a mad home scientist. One such notable seitanist is Oncle Hu who builds meat alternatives from seitan that is 'Not That Washed'. The washing method still calls for thorough mangling and washing in every part of the dough, with the aim to leave small pockets of starch throughout to create fattiness and tender texture. Aim to stop your washing around the early or mid-point with no large visible starch blobs for this signature 'melt in your mouth'-style seitan.

Early washed: 500–600 g (1 lb 2 oz–1 lb 5 oz) remaining dough.
Remaining liquid: looks like soy or oat milk.
Makes: fatty meat; sausages.

Mid-washed: 360–500 g (12½ oz–1 lb 2 oz) remaining dough.
Remaining liquid: looks like almond milk.
Makes: poultry.

Mostly washed: 360 g (12½ oz) or less remaining dough.
Remaining liquid: looks a little cloudy.
Makes: steak; brisket.

COOKING SEITAN

Once washed, seitan should be treated like raw meat: stored in the fridge and cooked properly before serving. You can rest it covered in water for a more tender texture or simply cover for a day or two in the fridge to improve before cooking. Also, like meat, you can cook it any which way you desire to encourage even more insane textures. Once you fully sell your soul to seitan, the wicked beasts you can summon will be limitless. The most dramatic effect you can have on the quality of your seitan comes from technique and cooking correctly. When it comes to cooking, what generally works the best is to set and simmer your seitan before reheating and serving.

SETTING

Forming a crust helps the seitan hold whatever shape you've prepared it in. Searing two sides, baking for a brief initial period, or in some cases microwaving, will achieve this effect.

SIMMERING

Get the inside of the seitan cooked through by simmering it in a flavoured stock. This method requires fairly constant monitoring as liquid above a low simmer will make the texture spongy or even produce the dreaded rubberiness that puts people off seitan too often. It will absorb the liquid and swell up, so make sure your stock is well seasoned. Alternatives for this step include wrapping the seitan and steaming, soaking in marinades for recipes that involve baking, slow cooking or low and slow smoking or pressure cooking. Large roasts and dense blocks of seitan require up to 2 hours of pressure cooking/steaming; for smaller pieces you can get away with 30–60 minutes.

FINISHING

Once the simmering step is complete and the seitan has cooled, most seitan recipes are ready to be heated and served. You can fry, sear, smoke, use a butane torch or bake to finish off the dish. If you've pressure cooked or steamed your seitan, you'll want to add flavour so choose a method like smoking, baking or grilling in a rich sauce, or crumbling and frying.

SPAWN OF SEITAN

The starchy water that runs from a ball of dough as it is washed has its own properties that you'll want to take advantage of. Allow the thick starch water to sit for over an hour and the liquid will separate into clear water and a thick, plaster-like white starch that will settle on the bottom. Pour out the water and reserve the thick sludge, otherwise known as 'spawn of seitan', to use in making meat alternatives. (Plus, spawn of seitan is an incredibly fun phrase to regularly throw around the kitchen.) Pour it back into or onto seitan to introduce textural variety (as in the Smoked ham roast on page 210), mix it with

flavours and fry it up to make crispy pan-fried bacon, microwave in thin layers to make deli-style meats (see Prosciutto on page 227) or add even more starch to make pork crackling (see Chicharrones on page 204). Alternatively, add water or flavoured liquid back into the sludge to thin it out for uses such as a buttermilk substitute when crumbing ingredients or even making an impromptu omelette. The devil can tolerate a lot of atrocities but wasting a versatile ingredient like this is too much even for them. Save your spawn!

QUICK SEITAN FROM VITAL WHEAT GLUTEN

Vital wheat gluten (VWG), not to be confused with frivolous wheat gluten, aka gluten flour or wheat gluten, is the pure, dried form of flour protein. It requires much less kneading than traditional seitan as the gluten begins to form when wet. Over-kneading VWG can lead to rubberiness, which won't feel much like a successful animal analogue. The main benefit to this ingredient is the speedy process it makes of mixing flavours, fats and starches to mimic various animal products.

Tofu is a popular feature artist with this form of gluten. The pre-eminent Tofurky brand roast uses a combination of seitan and tofu, selected

by founder Seth Tibbott because, 'they are very different to the industrial proteins, isolates and powders found in many meat alternatives today. Tofu or tempeh are lightly processed traditional soy foods that, along with seitan, have a long history of providing nutrient-dense, healthy protein throughout the world for centuries.' This means that not only can gluten, tofu or tempeh do all the hard work in making tried-and-tested meat alternatives, they also won't let you down when assigned a group project. The recipes in this book also remix vital wheat gluten with jackfruit, beans, mushrooms or even plain (all-purpose) flour to tweak the protein sources and resulting texture of the final product.

SOYBEANS

The vast majority of soybean crops grown the world over are fed to livestock raised for human consumption. Any concern for the environmental impact of soy alternatives within a plant-based diet is negated by the fact that you consume dramatically less soy by not feeding it to something else first. Soy milk has done a bang-up job of putting dairy milk out of a gig, but that's only the beginning of the humble soybean's potential.

Prepared soy protein alternatives include tempeh, tofu, TVP, natto and more. To employ this protein bean at home, simply master how to make fresh soy milk and most of the hard work is done for making okara, yuba (bean curd sheets) and your own homemade tofu ... all at once!

Okara is the leftover soy pulp from making soy milk. It is high in fibre and calcium and can be used immediately while wet. Alternatively, leave it to dry into crumbs (this form can also be purchased at Asian supermarkets). Use the dried form as breadcrumbs or in baking. Both the fresh and dried forms can be used as fibre in plant-based meat.

Yuba is a sheet of bean curd that forms on soy milk when it's heated to 70–80°C (160–175°F). It works wonderfully as skin in vegan poultry-inspired dishes or it can be layered to make denser plant-based meat. As a natural by-product of soy-milk production, yuba features heavily in Buddhist cuisine and early meat alternatives, such as 'vegetarian duck', which is formed by wrapping layers of yuba around a stuffing to create a denser fake meat. It's stunningly breezy to wrap nuggets, roasts, mince or vegetables in yuba to hold everything together.

And then there's tofu. Whether it's silken, soft, medium, firm, semi-firm, extra-firm, super-firm, thawed, scrambled, raw, fried, baked or steamed; flaccid or half-mast to fully erect, the variety of tofu textures available is extensive, and the ways that you can further change it are even more expansive. It's even more inexpensive if you make it yourself. Tofu really can do it all!

To become a master of making tofu at home all you need is soybeans, a coagulant and a tofu mould. If you don't have a mould, you can fashion one out of two deep plastic takeaway containers. Cut slits in the bottom and sides of one container and line with muslin (cheesecloth). Use the other container to fit on top to hold weights for pressing. You can control the firmness of your tofu by using different coagulants (see page 32) or by pressing your tofu for less (for softer) or more (for firmer) time.

FRESH SOY MILK

MAKES 3.5-4 LITRES (118-135 FL OZ)

What's a dairy alternative recipe doing in a book about vegan meat? Soy milk is delicious and easy to make at home, but it's far from the only trick soybeans can perform. Using one 500 g (1 lb 2 oz) batch of dried soybeans, you should be able to produce one yuba sheet as it heats, your choice of 3.5–4 litres (118–135 fl oz) of fresh soy milk or 300–420 g (10½–15 oz) of tofu, plus a heap of fresh okara left over to use as breadcrumbs or in the okara chicken mince on page 67. What a yield!

INGREDIENTS

dried soybeans	500 G (1 LB 2 OZ)

For homemade tofu, you should use freshly made soy milk as store-bought varieties don't usually have enough protein content and won't make the process cost-effective.

① Soak the soybeans in plenty of cold water for 12 hours. Check that they have fully soaked by splitting one between your fingers. If the inside is yellow and it splits easily, you're ready to go. Strain and reserve the soaking water. Leaving plenty of room in your blender (the mixture will thicken and froth up towards the end), add the soybeans and 1 litre (34 fl oz) of reserved soybean water and blend for 3 minutes until creamy.

② Prepare two stockpots. Place one pot over medium heat and add the remaining reserved soybean water and enough extra water to make up 3 litres (101 fl oz). When bubbling, pour in the soybean purée and stir for 5 minutes. Switch off the heat. Stir and abruptly stop your spatula halfway around the pot to fold the foam into the liquid. Repeat this stirring and folding motion to incorporate the foam. Watch closely as it can rise rapidly towards the end of the cooking time. Allow to cool for 30 minutes.

③ Place a nut milk bag in the second pot. Pour the soybean mixture through the bag. Squeeze the bag to extract the milk from the soy pulp (called okara or lees). Spread out the okara within the bag and set aside to dry out. Simmer the filtered soy milk over medium heat for 10 minutes to thicken up.

④ To use as soy milk, thin out with up to 500 ml (2 cups) of water (or more to achieve your desired consistency), then mix in a pinch of salt and vanilla extract to taste and store in a glass jar in the fridge. To use as okara, you're done! Simply transfer the dry pulp to an airtight container and keep in the fridge until needed. To make yuba, keep the heat on and read on. To make tofu, turn the page.

YUBA

MAKES I SHEET

To make yuba at home, you'll need patience and loads of passive time on your hands as each sheet needs to individually form on the surface of the milk before the next one can begin. You may like to make a single sheet for coating ingredients when preparing your fresh soy milk or tofu. Or you may prefer to buy it. Thankfully, good-quality frozen, refrigerated or dried yuba sheets can be purchased easily and cheaply from almost all Asian supermarkets – so you can save your time and fresh soy milk. All forms benefit from a good soak in a flavoured stock before using.

INGREDIENTS

fresh Soy milk (see opposite)	2 LITRES (8 CUPS)

Using a thermometer will take the mystery out of this recipe and ensure you're on the right track.

① Pour the soy milk into a large saucepan and heat to 70-80°C (160-175°F) - the 'yuba zone'. Adjust the heat to maintain this temperature. Do not agitate the pan from this point at all. The surface of the milk will begin to subtly transform and become tacky.

② After a few minutes, a skin will form over the milk. Allow it to extend over the entire surface and visibly firm up. Depending on the consistency of your heat and the pan size, a full skin can take 15-45 minutes.

③ Place a wooden spoon over a stockpot to create somewhere for the finished yuba to hang. When satisfied with your yuba, slice around the pan with a chopstick or knife to separate the yuba from the side, manoeuvre the chopstick under it and fish it out of the pan, draping it over the wooden spoon. If it bunches up, allow it to cool slightly before gently prying it apart with your fingertips. It may take a few goes to perfect this motion.

④ Spread the yuba carefully on a sheet of baking paper and allow it to dry out for several hours before attempting to move it. Use while damp to wrap around loose meat alternatives, such as jackfruit, or allow to fully dry and rehydrate as needed. Store in an airtight container in the fridge.

FRESH TOFU

MAKES 300-420 G (10½-15 OZ)

> LITTLE MISS MUFFET SAT ON HER TUFFET EATING HER
> CURDS AND WHEY. ALONG CAME A SPIDER WHO SAT DOWN
> BESIDE HER AND SAID, 'HUN, I THINK YOU'VE MISSED A
> PRETTY BIG STEP IN THIS RECIPE.'

Those who hate tofu are just telling you their favourite marinade is air. Tofu, being little more than soybeans and coagulant, relies on user input in the form of marinades, choosing the correct texture and applying techniques to help coax out its full potential. When you reach a certain level of veganism, you'll find yourself scoffing tofu straight out of the packet, but until you get there, marinating and cooking properly is critical to a good soy-based snack.

Squeezing or pressing out tofu liquid makes room for flavour to be absorbed (except for silken tofu, which should not be pressed lest you destroy the whole block). To boot blandness in any tofu dish, sit your tofu in flavoured stock first, then squeeze out any excess liquid. You can also smoke fresh tofu by placing a whole pressed block on a barbecue away from direct heat and smoking for a few hours to infuse the tofu with flavour. Check out my smoking tips on pages 50–53.

INGREDIENTS	
fresh Soy milk (see page 30)	3.5 LITRES (118 FL OZ)
COAGULANT	
nigari water OR	1 TBSP
nigari crystals OR	3¼ TSP
gypsum powder	12.5 G

① Pour the soy milk into a large saucepan, place over medium heat and bring to just under 80°C (175°F) or around the 'yuba zone' (see page 31). Stir the soy milk at regular intervals to prevent yuba from forming.

② Mix your coagulant of choice with 3 tbsp of water. If using nigari crystals, allow to sit for 10 minutes to dissolve.

③ Lay two layers of muslin (cheesecloth) over a tofu mould or prepared container and place on a tray or in the sink to catch excess water spillage.

You'll need a thermometer for this recipe.

④ Ensuring the soy milk is still just under 80°C (175°F), mix one-third of the coagulant water in a figure-eight motion into the soy milk to disperse it. Be very gentle and only make a couple of passes to preserve the large curds. Cover the pan for 3 minutes, then stir the coagulant water and add another one-third to the pan. Cover again for 3 minutes.

⑤ Stir the remaining coagulant and add it to the pan, gently stirring to separate the 'curds and whey'. Allow the curds to settle to the bottom of the pan, then carefully pour out most of the whey from the top.

⑥ Ladle out the soy curds with a mesh sieve and transfer to the prepared mould. Fold over the muslin and cover with the top of the mould or a matching-sized container.

LET'S get STARTED

CONTINUE ☞

⑦ Add weights (such as two tins of beans) and press for at least 15 minutes to achieve soft tofu. Increase the weights on top and press for 20-30 minutes to achieve firmer tofu.

⑧ Fill a large container with cold water. Open the muslin and gently lower the prepared tofu into the cold water to lock it into shape.

Carefully unwrap the rest of the muslin, leaving the tofu in the water. Eat fresh, or store in water or reserved tofu whey until ready to use. Use within 5 days or freeze to evolve the texture. You can cut your tofu up and steal any of the marinades or glazes in this book. Tofu is only as boring as your imagination and marination!

FREEZING TOFU

Tofu can be made chewier and meatier before you even open the packet. The pockets of water in tofu expand when frozen, making larger 'pores' for flavour to seep into. To achieve this, keep your tofu in its packet (or in water if it is homemade), then freeze overnight or for longer. Fully thaw the tofu when you're ready to go (in boiling water, the microwave, on the bench, take a long hot bath together), then crack the packet, press out the excess liquid and it's ready for action.

Take a look at the transformations! The image opposite shows four kinds of tofu - fresh on the left, and after being frozen and defrosted on the right.

① Hard or extra-firm tofu, which has most of its liquid pressed out already, gains the least textural transformation through the freezing and defrosting process, as there's not much liquid to expand.

② Homemade tofu varies in water content, depending on how long you press it for. This block of tofu was pressed for 15 minutes before being locked into shape in a cold-water bath. Storing homemade tofu in the freezer prior to use means you don't need to worry about it going bad, plus it is a fail-safe method for making sure it's nice and firm when you're ready to cook.

③ Firm or medium tofu really starts to evolve after the freezing and thawing process. When frozen and defrosted once, it becomes spongy and chewier - working perfectly in chicken-inspired recipes, such as the Nashville-fried chicken on page 74. Freezing and thawing this tofu twice creates an edible soy-based sponge that is best used for drinking up marinades, such as the delicious General Tso's sauce on page 80, which calls for double frozen and defrosted firm tofu.

④ Silken to classic-medium tofu, when frozen and thawed once, becomes flaky and can be used to mimic white fish. I recommend freezing silken tofu twice to achieve the gorgeously flaky final texture you'll want for the Fillet no fish on page 284 or the Fish fillets on page 122.

Use this as a guide and experiment with the brands local to you - the water content in tofu packets varies and in this process it's the amount of liquid that will affect your final product. Note that some tofus will adopt a spongy texture after freezing, but all the better to soak the flavour up with. Next time you unpack your groceries, get those tofu blocks straight in the freezer and take control of your tofu texture!

KONJAKU

Konjaku (from the konjac root, pronounced 'konn-yak-u') is a vegetable and the holy grail of plant-based seafood alternatives, available for use in recipes as powdered glucomannan. It is also available at Asian supermarkets prepared as a Japanese seaweed-flavoured firm jelly slab. This ingredient is the primary agent in commercial vegan shrimp and scallops as well as shirataki noodles (zero-calorie konjac noodles). To make konjaku yourself, you will need glucomannan powder (from health-food stores and online) and slaked lime (food-grade calcium hydroxide – available from brewery shops and online). The results will have you accused of being a liar who's served up real seafood as some sort of sick joke, which is seen as high praise in the meat-alternative community.

To prepare store-bought konjaku for recipes, it should be cut up and boiled for 3 minutes to reduce the scent. It can immediately be used in Takoyaki (see page 132) or Duck fried rice (see page 82). Freezing and thawing konjaku so that, like tofu, the water inside it expands, can help improve its chewiness. For a simple vegan shrimp substitute, purchase shirataki noodles that come pre-packed in small bundles. Drain the liquid and separate the noodles on baking paper. Freeze and thaw in the microwave twice, sprinkle over lemon juice and spices, then crumb and fry.

BASIC KONJAKU

MAKES 1 KG (2 LB 3 OZ)

After following the preparation method below, konjaku can be further mixed with ingredients, such as tofu, cooked rice, starches and more. It can be set by boiling (best for preserving shape and a softer end-product), or for some recipes you can quickly microwave (much quicker and results in a firmer texture) the konjaku on a plate or in moulds to prepare it for cooking. Setting the konjaku reduces the fishy smell and taste you'll notice once you fold in the slaked lime.

INGREDIENTS
PLAIN KONJAKU

glucomannan powder	25 G (1 OZ)
slaked lime	1.5 G
boiling water	200 ML (7 FL OZ)

SEAWEED KONJAKU (OPTIONAL)

dulse flakes or aonori seaweed flakes	1 TBSP

SEAFOOD KONJAKU (OYSTERS, SHRIMP AND BAKED FISH)

Awase dashi (see page 118)	500 ML (2 CUPS)
chicken-style stock powder	2 TSP
garlic cloves, minced	4
lemon, juiced	1/2
vegan fish sauce	2 TSP

A thermometer will be necessary for success in this recipe.

① For plain konjaku, heat 800 ml (27 fl oz) of water to 50°C (120°F) in a saucepan, then pour into a large bowl.

② If making seaweed konjaku, combine the water and the dulse or seaweed flakes in a saucepan, heat to 50°C (120°F), then transfer to a bowl.

③ If making seafood konjaku, combine all the ingredients in a saucepan, add 300 ml (10 fl oz) of water and heat to 50°C (120°F). Transfer to a bowl.

④ Continuously whisk the liquid in the bowl, gradually add in the glucomannan to make a gel, then set aside to cool for 15 minutes.

⑤ With gloved hands, knead the gel as though it were the ghost of a dough ball for 3 minutes or until the mixture whitens.

⑥ Whisk the slaked lime into the boiling water. Slowly add to the glucomannan gel, kneading it in with a gloved hand. Continue to mix for 2 minutes or until the mixture firms up. Allow to sit for 10 minutes.

⑦ If using seafood konjaku to make oysters (see page 167), shrimp (see page 162) or baked fish (see page 164), turn to the relevant page and follow the instructions for cooking.

⑧ For plain or seaweed konjaku, prepare a saucepan of boiling water. Using wet hands, shape the gel into five or six balls and place in the boiling water. Boil for 25-30 minutes, then remove and drain. Slice up and use in recipes, or store for a week in the fridge or freeze to make the texture chewier.

TVP

TVP (Textured Vegetable Protein) is like a colouring-in book for flavour. It comes in a huge array of shapes and sizes for you to use as the textural foundation in dishes, just BYO seasoning! TVP is made using an extrusion process that isn't available to home cooks, but it's cheap and well stocked at Asian grocery stores and large chain supermarkets. All forms of TVP hold up very well during long bouts of cooking and will happily soak up flavour while maintaining all that awesome texture.

'IT COMES IN ALL SHAPES AND SIZES, IT'S SHELF STABLE FOR A LONG TIME AND CAN BE READY TO COOK IN MINUTES! TVP IS THE REAL MVP, WHICH OBVIOUSLY STANDS FOR MOST VERSATILE PROTEIN!'

Richard Makin,
School Night Vegan

TVP should be rehydrated fully prior to use in recipes, with the exception of fine mince pieces. These finer forms of TVP can be mixed into recipes dry, partially hydrated or fully hydrated for different textural effects like gristle, fatty meat and more or less chewiness.

A common mistake when using finer TVP is drowning it in too much liquid to hydrate it before use, which leaves it oversaturated and not very chewy in the final product. For burgers, I use partially hydrated TVP mince so that the TVP soaks up some of the flavour from the other ingredients in the recipe. Large pieces need to be cooked in rapidly boiling water until fully hydrated before being used in dishes such as Schnitzels (see page 84) or Sweet 'n' sour pork (see page 186), as they won't soften further when fried. Stocks are an effective way to add flavour directly into TVP and should be used in preference to water where possible. Note: acidic liquid hydrates TVP more quickly.

The dynamic properties and different sizes, shapes and even base ingredients (pea-based TVP is becoming more popular) mean TVP will continue to be innovated. In this book, we use the most common varieties: TVP mince (most common, very small pieces); slices, strips, chunks or soy curls (bite-sized pieces); and large pieces (also often billed as slices or strips, but are several bites' worth).

MUSHROOMS

Mushrooms, when not ruining most vegans' claim to eating 100% plants, are one of the best weapons in our arsenal against bland meat alternatives. Of the few raw vegan umami sources, mushroom diversity gives a vegan butcher so many options to vary the taste, texture and intensity of your mock meat. When in doubt, and if opting for the most flavour, a medley of different mushroom varieties cooked together will always produce a richer experience.

On the next page I explore popular mushroom varieties that shine when used as different meat alternatives. Some varieties are utilised in the recipes that follow. If you have a trusty guide to lead you to wild-picked mushrooms, then I encourage you to forage; simply peel or cut off dodgy bits, or give the mushrooms a quick rinse under water before cooking. Check out which varieties are available near where you live and, in the worst case, seek out farmers' markets for local producers who grow the harder-to-find varieties (and not just bags of Swiss browns and button).

PREPARING MUSHROOMS

It's a long-held myth that you should avoid wetting your mushrooms. Mushrooms are more than 90% water and have a unique cellular structure that holds up well through long cooking processes. Improve your texture and flavour by using the wet-fry method taught to me by Jim Fuller, mycologist from Fable Food Co:

> 'FIRST, BOIL TO PERFECTION – YOU CAN KEEP ADDING WATER UNTIL THIS IS ACHIEVED. REMEMBER YOU CAN'T OVER-BOIL A MUSHROOM BECAUSE OF THEIR UNIQUE CELLULAR STRUCTURE. THEY WILL LET THEIR OWN WATER OUT SO DON'T PUT TOO MUCH WATER IN AT ONCE. WHEN PERFECTLY TENDER, LET THE WATER EVAPORATE UNTIL THE PAN IS BASICALLY DRY. THEN ADD OIL OR FAT AND YOUR AROMATIC STUFF. QUICK SAUTÉ OR STIR-FRY AND SEASON TO TASTE WITH SALT.'

Shrooms prepared this way undergo more of the maillard reaction (to brown and develop flavour) and absorb less fat due to the collapsed structures.

Another method to properly brown mushrooms is to press them as they cook. They will collapse quickly, scream dramatically, then give up and sizzle in their own juices. The unique structure of mushrooms means that when compressed they still hold together and brown up rapidly once their liquid has been forced out. Using large mushrooms, such as maitake or lion's mane, means you can create hunks of browned meat using only a sandwich press or by using another pan to press down on the mushroom in a frying pan. Try out this method in the Mushroom steak frites on page 260. Smaller mushrooms aren't excluded either – press fresh shiitake to make perfectly round pepperoni slices (see page 225) or press clustered mushrooms for instant shreds that are a real treat in the Chimichurri steak tacos on page 257.

BUTTON/CUP, CREMINI AND PORTOBELLO

These are all the same mushroom at different stages of its life: baby buttons/cups evolve into pubescent cremini before becoming adult portobellos. These three are usually the easiest to source and are a reliable choice for adding flavour. Portobello can also serve as a structure for stuffing and providing texture.

SHIITAKE

Ooh, mami. Savoury royalty! Fresh shiitake have flavour, but when dried these bad boys become super potent. A must-have in your kitchen for adding meatiness.

KING OYSTER

Its stalks make this mushroom uniquely brilliant as perfectly round scallops, thick strips of bacon, long shreds or heaps of shapes that other mushrooms don't have the real-estate space available to carve out.

OYSTER

Grow in clusters so that you can shred or tear into chunks of whatever size you need. The flavour is addictive: you could batter and fry them for the rest of your life and still crave them the next day. At least that's how it goes for me. Great fried and served as calamari.

SAFFRON MILK CAP/PINE

Found seasonally as a wild-picked mushroom, the saffron milk cap has a delicious flavour and bright orange colour. Goes particularly well in Paella (see page 160) and other seafood-inspired dishes.

LION'S MANE

A big fluffy mushroom that sort of resembles a lion's mane. Absolutely legendary results either pressed into a dense steak (see page 260) or as fried fish that flakes (see page 122). The Hannah Montana of mushrooms. You truly do get the best of both worlds.

PORCINI

Fresh porcini can be used in medleys or wherever you'd use button or cremini mushrooms. Porcini powder is another source of guanylate so can be used to achieve synergistic umami.

SLIPPERY JACK

With pores on its underside instead of mushroomy gills, the slippery jack lives up to its name with its sticky, slimy caps. Don't be put off by its unfortunate exterior, as this is a champion mushroom, perfect for adding to mushroom medleys.

LOBSTER OF THE WOODS

Does what it says and tastes like lobster. Chop it up, cook and replace the TVP in tuna salad for a lobster salad version. Alternatively, try it in Paella (see page 160), Squid ink pasta (see page 146) or pre-cook and add to a Hearty fish pot pie (see page 156) to get that unique flavour into your seafood dishes.

CHICKEN OF THE WOODS

The natural flavour of this mushroom has been described as a cross between chicken and lobster. It's bright orange, has a similar texture to chicken and is easier to catch than a real one. Switch it in as the chicken in the Caesar salad on page 95 or thread it onto skewers in the Lamb shish kebab on page 252 for a chicken-style variant.

MAITAKE/HEN OF THE WOODS

Comes in a large cluster that does well under pressure. Track down this mushroom to try in the Mushroom steak frites on page 260 or press the cluster into browned folds and shred.

SAFFRON MILK CAP/PINE

DRIED SHIITAKE

SLIPPERY JACK

OYSTER

LION'S MANE

KING OYSTER

USING STORE-BOUGHT MEAT ALTERNATIVES

Commercial meat alternatives have the very latest in science at their disposal, and employ exciting compounds to mimic particular flavours, as well as modified starches and other unique ingredients that are generally unavailable for the home cook to play with. You can creatively incorporate these products into your recipes, and you'll notice the closer realism in flavour and texture. For the most part, the recipes in this book will work if you want to swap in the corresponding commercial alternatives in the dish to save yourself some time. Without these particular ingredients, the home cook's technique is their friend to drawing out the savoury, smoky and umami flavours that will make meat feel mocked.

Vegan varieties of chicken-style, beef-style and pork-style stock powders are fairly easy to come by. These help you sneak in flavours that will taste far more real than a blend of herbs could ever achieve, so do try to incorporate them into your cooking wherever possible.

The latest innovation in fake meat available to the home cook, comes in the form of methylcellulose. Even if you can't get your hands on it, reading the notes on page 276 on how this ingredient works will help you understand and be more inventive with store-bought mock meats that use it.

SMOKING

Many recipes in this book use liquid smoke, which is simply smoke passed through water so you can add flavour. It's an easy hack to make food taste like it's been smoked for hours without having to go to the effort; still, nothing beats the flavour that comes from actually smoking food for hours. Smoking your meat alternatives has the most profound impact on making show-stopping substitutes that don't taste like regular old veg (no offence to regular old veg but this book isn't about you).

My personal meditation comes in the form of an afternoon sitting next to a smoker with a beer and absolutely nothing else to do except wait for the most incredible mock meats of my life. For regular enthusiasts, dedicated smokers or kettle/barrel smokers take a lot of the constant monitoring out of smoking.

Offset smokers that attach to a barbecue are another way to smoke meat alternatives. However, for beginners, jury-rigging your own grill or barbecue into a makeshift smoker is as easy as using a cheap smoker box or even foil, as outlined below.

Simon Toohey, a plant-food pioneer who has had his own vegetable-based smokehouse, elaborates on how anyone can tap into the benefits:

'COOKING YOUR VEG OVER CHARCOAL MAKES IT TASTE SO MUCH BETTER BY ADDING THAT WONDERFUL SMOKY FLAVOUR. IF YOU HAVE A BARBECUE, WHEN USING YOUR CHARCOAL, ADD A LOG OF WOOD TO THE OUTER EDGE. THIS WILL SMOKE SOFTLY BUT NOT BURN, MEANING YOU WILL GET A BEAUTIFUL FLAVOUR OF WOOD SMOKE. HOWEVER, IT'S NOT ALWAYS EASY TO SMOKE VEG ALL THE TIME, SO A CLASSIC SMOKING GUN IS A GREAT WAY TO IMPART BEAUTIFUL COLD-SMOKE FLAVOURS.'

No matter your budget or commitment issues, anyone can tap into the benefits of that primal, smoky, 'this-food-has-been-properly-cooked' flavour everyone loves.

USING A SMOKER BOX

When meat is smoked, barbecued or grilled, much of the flavour comes from the fat dripping off the meat onto the hot grill, barbecue or pan, then vaporising and in turn coating the meat in smoky flavour. Frequently basting your fake meat with marinades mimics this process, while adding a tray of water to your smoker, barbecue or grill produces steam and helps cook your ingredients.

WOOD CHIPS

Wood chips can be soaked in water or flavoured liquid (try apple juice, shiitake dashi, bourbon, beer or wine if you're willing to share your tipple with your wood chips!) to delay their smoke release and add extra flavour. In my smoker box, I like to use a combination of wood chips soaked for several hours and dry wood chips for a gradual, constant stream of smoke. Wood chips in a smoker box can last for 2–4 hours and need to be replenished every now and then. Wood chunks are also available for long smokes over several hours, as they release smoke more slowly and don't need to be changed as often. Check the manufacturer's instructions on your wood chips or chunks for best usage tips. Aim for a low, steady stream of pale smoke for delicious results.

Different wood chips produce different flavours that can complement your food. Don't be afraid to choose a blend, experimenting with which flavours you like best, or simply combine whatever you can find.

WOODCHIP FLAVOURS	
Apple	SEAFOOD, POULTRY, PORK
Cherry	PORK, POULTRY, LAMB, BEEF
Hickory	PORK, BEEF
Maple	POULTRY, PORK
Mesquite	BEEF, PORK
Oak	SEAFOOD, POULTRY, LAMB, BEEF
Pecan	BEEF, POULTRY, LAMB, PORK
Walnut	PORK, BEEF

① Soak a few handfuls of wood chips in water or flavoured liquid for at least 2 hours. Preheat your barbecue in a well-ventilated outdoor location. The smoking temperature inside your barbecue when closed should be around 110-120°C (230-250°F) to ensure your food won't cook too quickly.

② To use a smoker box, half-fill the box with soaked wood chips on one side and add dry wood chips to the other side. Add the lid to the smoker box and place on the barbecue grill plate, directly above the heat, then close the barbecue lid.

③ To use foil, place half a handful of soaked wood chips in the centre of a large square of foil and seal to enclose. Poke a few holes in the top of the foil packet to allow airflow and for the smoke to escape, then place on the barbecue, directly above the heat, and close the barbecue lid. Repeat with a handful of dry wood chips. Foil packets need closer monitoring and more frequent replenishing than other methods.

④ Wait for the smoker box or foil packet to begin emitting a small amount of smoke, then add your ingredients to the barbecue, away from the heat or suspended above the grate if needed. Close the barbecue, leaving the lid slightly ajar for airflow. Now you've got yourself a fake fire to smoke your fake meat.

⑤ Adjust the air intake by playing with how large a gap you leave between the lid and the grill for air to flow and stoke the smoke, so it is constantly flowing. Leave the lid slightly ajar, except for when basting ingredients or replenishing the wood so that the temperature stays constant. Lovingly monitor your smoker and stay low and slow so all your hard work doesn't go up in smoke.

SMOKED SALT

MAKES 315 G (1 CUP)

To make the perfect dish finisher or artisanal gift with little extra effort, set up some salt on the side when you've already got a couple of ingredients smoking.

SMOKED SALT	
coarse rock salt (or mix it up, just avoid iodised table salt or fine salt)	315 G (1 CUP)

① If using a barbecue, fill a smoker box half with soaked wood chips and half with dry wood chips. Turn the barbecue grill to high and position the box directly on the grill plate.

② Pour the salt into a foil tray or similar to make a single layer. Fill a spray bottle with water. Lightly spray and mix through to just dampen the salt.

③ Place the tray on the grill away from direct heat or on a wire steamer basket. Every hour replenish the wood chips, spray the salt with more water to dampen very lightly and stir well as only the exposed salt will pick up the smoky flavour. Smoke for 8-16 hours (the longer the smokier!).

COLD SMOKING

The only smoking that's cool. Using a cold smoker or infusion smoker is a rapid way to add smoky flavour to food that is already prepared and doesn't require further cooking.

① Sprinkle fine, dry wood chips loosely into the smoking chamber. To allow air to flow, avoid packing them too tightly. Make sure you are in a well-ventilated space as some smoke may escape as you set everything up.

② Place your ingredients in a covered mixing jug with a spout, under a cloche or in a sealed environment covered in plastic wrap, ensuring the smoke cannot escape.

③ Turn the smoker on so air is flowing, then use a match to light the wood chips until the sealed area is filled with smoke. Remove the nozzle, fully seal the ingredients, then allow to rest for 5 minutes so the smoke settles over the food. If using liquid or something like mayonnaise, swirl or stir the mixture and repeat as desired to increase the smokiness. Try this technique with the Smoked aioli below or the Smoked shallot caviar on page 124.

SMOKED AIOLI

① Place the soy milk, garlic, vinegar, mustard, garlic powder and salt in a large mixing jug. Blend with a stick blender for 20 or so seconds until frothy.

② Mix together the oils, then pour in while blending. Continue to blend for 1-2 minutes until emulsified. Cover in plastic wrap; if it is in large clumps, do not smooth it.

③ Loosely sprinkle wood chips into an infusion smoker, feed the nozzle through the spout on the jug, light and fill with smoke. Allow to settle for 5 minutes, then give the aioli a good stir. Repeat the smoking process twice more. Serve with the Paella on page 160.

SMOKED AIOLI	
soy milk	60 ML (¼ CUP)
minced garlic	2 TSP
apple cider vinegar or white vinegar	¾ TSP
dijon mustard	¾ TSP
garlic powder	½ TSP
salt	¼ TSP
canola oil or other neutral oil	185 ML (¾ CUP)
olive oil	60 ML (¼ CUP)

OTHER TECHNIQUES

Those who have pursued meatless cuisine at home usually have a pretty good handle on baking, steaming, grilling, sautéing and boiling their food. Let's crank up the heat with a few methods that might not feel as familiar, but will produce more intense flavours and crispier crusts if you follow these tips.

PRESSURE COOKING

If you have a pressure cooker, it's a great way to prepare seitan. Because the cooking temperature is higher, the cooking time is reduced, and more flavour is trapped than if you simply steam it. See Lacey Siomos's tips on using this method for the Seitan chicken on page 66. Browning your ingredients before pressure cooking helps increase the flavours trapped inside.

SEARING

Searing creates a crust and adds heaps of flavour to the exterior of your food. You can also achieve a similar effect by placing your ingredients on a wire rack and using a butane torch. Brush fat in the form of oil over the mock meat, so the flame doesn't hit a dry surface, and make multiple passes to sear. Just remember to only use the yellow part of the flame, as the blue part can impart a nasty flavour.

FRYING

To set up your own home deep-frying station, pick an oil with a high smoke point, as you'll be frying at high temperatures. Rapeseed, sunflower, vegetable blends, peanut or canola oil are all great choices. Choose a large heavy-based saucepan for frying – the wider the pan, the more ingredients you can deep-fry concurrently. The idea is that each ingredient has enough room to fry without coming into contact with any others. Pour oil into the pan to no more than halfway and place over medium heat to bring to temperature.

If you've got a kitchen thermometer handy, it's as simple as making sure your oil is above 180°C (350°F) before adding your ingredients. If you don't have a thermometer, less precise methods to check if the oil's reached the right temperature include adding a pinch of salt (which will sizzle) or a wooden skewer (around which the oil will vigorously bubble) to the hot oil. Make sure to reduce the heat when you've reached the right temperature, and increase again when the ingredients are added as they'll reduce the temperature and it's important to keep it between 175–200°C (345–400°F). Temperatures above this will make the oil smoke and the food will brown too quickly for the interior to cook properly.

When frying, keep water and wet utensils well away from hot oil as it will spit, and use a slotted or mesh spoon to fish ingredients out of the oil. Tongs run the risk of piercing your batter and allowing hot oil to rush past the seal into your food. You'll also want a lot of paper towel or a clean tea towel to immediately place the food on, so that excess surface oil is absorbed.

Broken oil (oil that has been fried in at least once) can be reused several times and can even add extra flavour to your food. Allow it to fully cool, then strain out any residue and return it to your pan. Keep covered to bring back to the correct temperature as you need it. For deep-frying on demand, have this ready to party on your stovetop with your thermometer and paper towel nearby. When the oil is unable to be properly filtered or has darkened significantly, pour it back into the original container to dispose of it. Do not pour it down your sink!

A shallow-frying station can be set up on a case-by-case basis as it requires only a thin layer of oil to cover the base of the pan. Depending on what you are shallow-frying, use enough oil to come one-third to halfway up the sides of the ingredients being fried.

NOT

SO

POULTRY

CHICKEN-STYLE STOCK POWDER • BEAN CURD DUCK • PREPARING WASHED FLOUR SEITAN AS POULTRY • SEITAN CHICKEN FROM VWG • GLUTEN-FREE OKARA CHICKEN MINCE • JACKFRUIT POULTRY • SOUTHERN-FRIED CHICKEN • JACKFRUIT NUGGETS • NASHVILLE-FRIED CHICKEN • DINO NUGGS • DUCK & SPRING ONION PANCAKES • PEKING DUCK • GENERAL TSO'S CHICKEN • DUCK FRIED RICE • SCHNITZELS • PUB-STYLE PARMAS • LEMONGRASS DRUMSTICKS • BOURBON CHICKEN • CHICKEN SATAY • CAESAR SALAD • BUFFALO WINGS • TANDOORI DRUMSTICKS • BIRD ROAST • ROAST TURKEY WITH HONEY MUSTARD GLAZE • MAPLE BOURBON FAUXDUCKEN

POULTRY BASES

CAULIFLOWER

EGGPLANT

JACKFRUIT

TVP

MUSHROOMS

SOY CURD

OKARA

TOFU

SEITAN

Poultry as the primary ingredient in dishes has been done to death. Far from being the only ingredient that takes well to marinating, frying, braising or roasting, poultry is one of the easiest meats to substitute. Bland-starting ingredients, such as tofu, TVP, jackfruit and eggplant (aubergine) approximate the texture of cooked chicken and readily absorb flavours. Gluten also works, but needs to be combined with starch, tofu or beans to achieve the right texture. Don't worry, I'll show you how!

Commercial options use chemical flavour compounds to replicate the notes found in cooked poultry, which sets them apart from homemade alternatives. Chicken-style stock powder will help you introduce these flavours into your recipes. Mushrooms and mushroom seasoning are a reliable umami source and varieties, such as chicken of the woods, oyster and saffron milk caps can be thrown into many poultry-inspired recipes with no extra preparation needed.

The star of this chapter is the humble soybean, which, through the process of making soy milk, produces the holy trinity of original meat substitutes: okara, yuba and tofu – all at once! The show-stopping fauxducken (see page 110) at the end of this chapter uses all the soy-based basics for a low-waste and high-drama main event that'll make what everyone else brought for dinner honestly look a bit shit.

FLAVOURS TO USE FOR PLANT-BASED CHICKEN

CELERY SALT • CELERY SEED • GARLIC • MARJORAM • PARSLEY • ROSEMARY
• SAGE • SALT • THYME • WHITE PEPPER • WHITE WINE

BASES:

CAULIFLOWER • EGGPLANT (AUBERGINE) • JACKFRUIT • MUSHROOMS
OKARA • SEITAN • TOFU • TVP • YUBA

CHICKEN-STYLE STOCK POWDER

MAKES ABOUT 150 G (1½ CUPS)

Many store-bought chicken stocks and stock powders are animal-product free. If those aren't available to you, never fear! You can make your own.

INGREDIENTS	
nutritional yeast	60 G (1 CUP)
bay leaves	2
celery salt	1 TBSP
salt	1 TBSP
onion powder	1 TBSP
dried chives	1 TBSP
garlic powder	2 TSP
dried sage	2 TSP
granulated sugar	2 TSP
dried thyme	1½ TSP
dried rosemary	1 TSP
dried marjoram	1 TSP
ground white pepper	¼ TSP
mustard powder	¼ TSP

① Combine the ingredients in a blender and pulse until fine. Store in an airtight jar.

② To use in recipes, mix 1 heaped teaspoon of chicken-style stock powder with 250 ml (1 cup) of boiling water as needed.

BEAN CURD DUCK

MAKES 80 G (2¾ OZ)

Use in the Duck and spring onion pancakes on page 77 or any of the duck-style recipes in this chapter.

INGREDIENTS	
dry yuba skins (dried bean curd sheets)	80 G (2¾ OZ)
DUCK-STYLE STOCK	
chicken-style stock	250 ML (1 CUP)
minced garlic	2 TSP
Maggi seasoning	1 TSP
DUCK SAUCE	
French shallot, thinly sliced	1
hoisin sauce	1½ TBSP
soy sauce or Maggi seasoning	1 TBSP
shaoxing rice wine	1 TBSP
soft brown sugar	2 TSP
minced garlic	1 TSP
peanut oil	2 TSP
Chinese five spice powder	¼ TSP
smoked paprika	¼ TSP
ground white pepper	¼ TSP

① Combine the duck-style stock ingredients in a saucepan and bring to the boil. Remove from the heat.

② Rehydrate the yuba skins in the stock for 5 minutes, then move to a large bowl to cool for 5 minutes. Use kitchen scissors to trim the sheets into long, wide strips.

③ Preheat the oven to 180°C (350°F). Line a baking tray with baking paper.

④ Mix the sauce ingredients in a small saucepan with 2 tablespoons of the leftover duck-style stock. Stir over medium heat for 3 minutes until combined.

⑤ Use a pastry brush to coat the yuba strips with the sauce and place the sheets on the prepared tray, spreading them out so each strip has personal space. Bake for 20 minutes, checking sporadically to turn the strips and make sure they're cooking evenly. Remove from the oven and serve hot in duck pancakes, stir-fries or fried rice.

PREPARING WASHED FLOUR SEITAN AS POULTRY

MAKES ABOUT 400 G (14 OZ)

As this method makes it more difficult to incorporate flavours into the seitan, I prefer to use washed flour for smaller pieces and shreds. If you'd like to make a larger roast, refer to the vital wheat gluten base over the page or use the methods in the preparing seitan as ham recipe (see page 176).

INGREDIENTS

Basic washed seitan, mid-washed (see pages 20 and 24)	1 × QUANTITY (ABOUT 400 G /14 OZ)
olive or neutral oil, for rubbing	2 TSP

FLAVOUR ADDITIONS

white miso paste	2 TBSP
torula yeast or mushroom seasoning	2 TBSP
onion powder	2 TBSP
chicken-style stock powder	2 TSP

① On a clean work surface, knead the flavour additions into the mid-washed seitan until fully dispersed. Alternatively, place in a stand mixer fitted with a dough hook and cut in the ingredients until fully dispersed.

CHICKEN-STYLE SHREDS

① Divide the seitan into four portions. Use your hands to stretch each portion into a long strand. If the seitan is too resistant, allow it rest for 10 minutes before trying again.

② Once stretched, braid or knot each strand as many times as you can to create more gluten folds, which will make shredding easier.

③ Knot the strands into tight balls and wrap securely in foil. Steam for 60 minutes. Transfer to a bowl, cover and cool in the fridge overnight for best texture. Unwrap from the foil and use your hands to pull apart the shreds, then use in any recipe that calls for shredded chicken.

CHICKEN PATTIES, CUTLETS AND SCHNITZELS

① Divide the seitan into four 100 g (3½ oz) portions (for patties) or three 130 g (4½ oz) portions (for cutlets or schnitzels) and use your hands to form them into round patties or longer cutlets.

② Press and roll the portions as thinly as possible, ensuring that the surfaces are flat for even cooking. Develop a crust by rubbing the seitan with oil, then sear in a frying pan over medium-high heat for 5 minutes on each side or bake at 180°C (350°F) for 20 minutes.

Chicken-style shreds

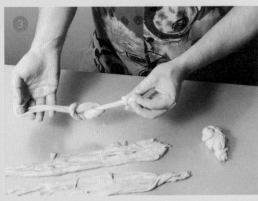

Chicken patties, cutlets and schnitzels

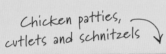

③ Prepare a stock by mixing the flavour additions with 350 ml (12 fl oz) of water. Place in a saucepan and bring to a low simmer. Do not allow the stock to boil or your seitan will become rubbery. Add the seitan and simmer for 60 minutes. Remove from the pan.

④ Set aside to cool, then marinate/grill/prepare in recipes, such as Caesar salad (see page 95), Chicken stinger burger (see page 282) or Pub-style parmas (see page 85).

SEITAN CHICKEN FROM VWG:

SHREDS, PATTIES & CUTLETS

MAKES 475 G (1 LB 1 OZ) SEITAN

Lacey Siomos of Avocados and Ales, originator of the seminal modern method for 'Chickwheat Shreds' chooses chickpeas to form a complete protein with the wheat. To prepare, she kneads her dough with a dough hook for up to 8 minutes and pressure cooks it in a large mass for 2 hours for a texture that shreds like magic when warm from cooking. Try this method, or follow the instructions below to achieve a similar effect by hand. For the uninitiated, cannellini beans or chickpeas are the shipping pallets that come with a tin of aquafaba. Vital wheat gluten–based seitan doesn't require as much kneading as when you form it from flour.

INGREDIENTS	
vital wheat gluten	150 G (1 CUP)
torula yeast or mushroom seasoning	1 TBSP
onion powder	1 TBSP
garlic powder	1 TSP
dried sage	1 TSP
dried thyme	3/4 TSP
dried rosemary	1/2 TSP
ground white pepper	1/4 TSP
tofu OR	150 G (5 1/2 OZ)
drained tinned cannellini beans or chickpeas, aquafaba reserved OR	200 G (7 OZ)
plain (all-purpose) flour	3 TBSP
aquafaba from tofu, cannellini or chickpeas (or water)	175 ML (6 FL OZ)
white miso paste	1 TBSP
canola oil	1 1/2 TBSP
white vinegar	2 TSP

① In a large bowl, stir together the gluten, torula yeast or mushroom seasoning and spices. Place the tofu, legumes or flour, aquafaba or water, miso, oil and vinegar in a food processor and blend to combine.

② Pour the wet mixture into the dry mixture and stir with a spoon to combine. Once the liquid is incorporated, transfer the mixture to a stand mixer fitted with a dough hook and knead for 2 minutes to form the gluten strands. Alternatively, knead by hand for 5 minutes.

③ To make the shreds, patties or cutlets, follow the steps on page 64.

GLUTEN-FREE OKARA CHICKEN MINCE

MAKES 465 G (1 LB)

Dried okara makes for a nifty substitute to breadcrumbs, so this gluten-free version of chicken mince is not only low waste but forms a crispy exterior without any breading steps required: just shape and go!

INGREDIENTS

boiling water	160 ML (5½ FL OZ)
chicken-style stock powder	2 TSP
vegan worcestershire sauce	1 TSP
dijon mustard	2 TSP
TVP mince	50 G (½ CUP)
vegan mayonnaise	1 TBSP

DRY INGREDIENTS

dried okara	140 G (1½ CUPS)
chickpea flour (besan)	55 G (½ CUP)
psyllium husk	2 TBSP
mushroom seasoning	1½ TBSP
onion powder	¾ TSP
garlic powder	¾ TSP
dried thyme	¾ TSP
dried oregano	½ TSP
dried sage	½ TSP
kala namak (Indian black salt) or use sea salt	⅓ TSP

① Combine 125 ml (½ cup) of the boiling water with the stock powder, worcestershire sauce and mustard, then pour over the TVP. Allow to sit and hydrate for 5 minutes until soft.

② Mix all the dry ingredients together in a large bowl.

③ Stir the hydrated TVP into the dry ingredients until well combined to form mince.

④ In a small bowl, mix together the mayonnaise and remaining water, then knead this through the mince. Allow the mixture to rest for at least 20 minutes before using.

JACKFRUIT POULTRY

Jackfruit, the largest tree-borne fruit in the world, is both deliciously sweet and absolutely useless as a meat alternative when ripe. Young, green tinned jackfruit (in brine or water but definitely not syrup!) is available year-round from Asian supermarkets and has little flavour, so it's ready to take direction from a crafty vegan butcher.

Thanh Truong, Fruit Nerd clarifies that 'canned jackfruit has been preserved through either sugar, salt or cooking so it won't have the same look, texture or even aroma as fresh jackfruit', and that's not a bad thing at all when we're putting it in camouflage.

INGREDIENTS

unripe jackfruit in brine (drained)	565 G (1 LB 4 OZ)
chicken-style stock	375 ML (1½ CUPS)

CHICKEN

nutritional yeast	2 TSP
onion powder	1 TSP
liquid smoke	10 DROPS

DUCK

minced garlic	3 TSP
Maggi seasoning or soy sauce	2 TSP

① Stab the tin of jackfruit in the neck with a can opener, then behead it to get at the soft flesh inside.

② Cut away the hard cores from the jackfruit pieces. Squeeze each jackfruit piece so that any seeds pop out and excess liquid is removed.

③ Gently pull the jackfruit pieces to make them stringy, then rinse away the remaining brine under warm running water. Squeeze the jackfruit dry. Finely chop the cores and add them with the rest of the jackfruit to a saucepan.

④ For chicken style, add the stock, nutritional yeast, onion powder and liquid smoke to the pan. For duck style, add the stock, garlic and Maggi seasoning or soy sauce to the pan.

⑤ Bring the mixture to a gentle boil and cook for 20 minutes or until the liquid has evaporated. (If doubling this recipe, double the cooking time.) Allow to cool, then squeeze out any excess liquid, if needed, before using in Duck-fried rice (see page 82), Tandoori drumsticks (see page 98) or Jackfruit nuggets (see page 71).

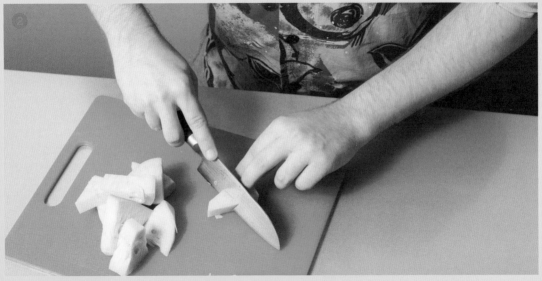

HOT TIPS

1 Stores now sell pouches of jackfruit without the cores. Using the cores in the recipe is at your discretion - if they are chopped and cooked for a decent amount of time, they will be indiscernible.

2 For a quicker recipe, you can leave out the cores to maintain the shredded texture. The seeds should always be removed because they'll be a dead giveaway your recipe is made from fruit.

Southern-fried Chicken

Swap in the stinger-style crumb and marinade (see page 282) for a zesty twist or substitute cauliflower for the mushrooms or tear prepared seitan into chunks and use instead. The world is your oyster: mushroom, king, black pearl and more!

INGREDIENTS	
oyster or black pearl mushrooms	175 G (6 OZ)
canola oil	FOR DEEP-FRYING
sea salt	TO SERVE
BUTTERMILK	
soy milk	125 ML (½ CUP)
white vinegar or freshly squeezed lemon juice	2 TSP
SPICED FLOUR	
plain (all-purpose) flour, plus extra for dusting	110 G (¾ CUP)
soft brown sugar	3 TSP
sea salt	½ TSP
smoked paprika	½ TSP
onion powder	½ TSP
chilli powder	½ TSP
garlic powder	¼ TSP
celery salt	¼ TSP
dried sage	¼ TSP
ground allspice	¼ TSP
dried basil	¼ TSP
dried oregano	PINCH OF
kala namak (Indian black salt) or use sea salt	½ TSP
MSG or torula yeast	1 TSP

Tear the mushrooms into irregular, bite-sized pieces.

Combine the spiced flour ingredients in a large bowl.

To make the buttermilk, whisk together the milk and vinegar or lemon juice in a shallow bowl.

Heat the oil for deep-frying in a large heavy-based saucepan over medium–high heat. Test if the oil is ready by inserting a wooden skewer or the handle of a wooden spoon into the hot oil; if it begins to bubble quickly, then you're ready to go.

Dip each mushroom piece in the buttermilk, then coat in the spiced flour, shaking off any excess. Drizzle extra buttermilk haphazardly over your floured mushrooms and pack on more spiced flour for insane shapes and even more crunch! Move them directly to the oil and fry in two batches for 5–6 minutes, until crispy and golden brown. Drain on paper towel, toss over some salt and serve immediately.

SERVES 2

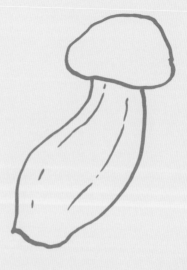

Jackfruit Nuggets

Yuba and rice paper add a skin layer that makes chicken substitutes stand out. They also help hold together loose ingredients, such as jackfruit or mince, when forming into cutlets, bite-sized nuggets (as is the case in this recipe), or many other perfect, neat shapes that don't seem to look a lot like an animal in the first place. Funny that.

INGREDIENTS

Jackfruit chicken (see page 68)	380 G (13½ OZ)
small dry yuba skins (dried bean curd sheets), rehydrated in chicken-style stock for 5 minutes	150 G (5½ OZ)
plain (all-purpose) flour	150 G (1 CUP)
cornflour (cornstarch)	125 G (1 CUP)
onion powder	1 TBSP
garlic powder	1 TBSP
dijon mustard	2 TSP
sea salt	2 TSP
chicken-style stock powder	1 TSP
pepper	1 TSP
MSG	1 TSP
canola oil	FOR DEEP-FRYING

Divide the jackfruit mixture into 15 portions and compress with your hands to hold together in a nugget shape.

Cut the yuba skins into strips. Wrap the yuba around the prepared jackfruit portions and squeeze well to secure everything within the yuba skin. Place the nuggets on baking paper and transfer to the freezer for 4–5 hours to solidify. Make sure they are not touching each other and abide by social distancing regulations to avoid sticking together.

Mix the flour, cornflour, onion powder, garlic powder, mustard, salt, stock powder, pepper and MSG in a large bowl. Toss the frozen jackfruit nuggets in the spiced flour, then remove from the bowl. Mix 500 ml (2 cups) of water into the remaining spiced flour to form a batter. Dunk the nuggets in the batter, coating well, then place back on the baking paper. Return the nuggets to the freezer for 45–60 minutes to firm up. You will have leftover batter.

Heat the oil for deep-frying in a large heavy-based saucepan over medium–high heat. Test if the oil is ready by inserting a wooden skewer or the handle of a wooden spoon into the hot oil; if it begins to bubble quickly, then you're ready to go.

Add a splash of water to the remaining batter, which will have thickened up. Whisk to return it to a thick but runny batter. Remove the nuggets from the freezer. Dip the nuggets in the batter once more and place them directly in the oil. Fry for 6 minutes, making sure to agitate the nuggets so that all surfaces fry evenly. When golden, transfer to paper towel to drain. Grab some sauce, then retire from the kitchen to get snug with your nuggs.

MAKES 15

JACKFRUIT NUGGETS
(SEE PAGE 71)

NASHVILLE-FRIED CHICKEN
(SEE PAGE 74)

DINO NUGGS
(SEE PAGE 75)

SOUTHERN-FRIED
CHICKEN
(SEE PAGE 70)

STINGER CHICKEN
(SEE PAGE 282)

Nashville-fried Chicken

This one bites back! Loads of cayenne, sugar and paprika are whisked into a splash of hot frying oil, then freshly fried chick'n is dunked in while everything is still HOT to trap those fatty flames into every crevice. Why eat whole food when you can eat soul food?

INGREDIENTS

firm tofu, frozen and thawed once (see page 34)	500 G (1 LB 2 OZ)
chicken-style stock powder	1 TSP
hot water	250 ML (1 CUP)
vegetable oil	FOR DEEP-FRYING

BUTTERMILK

soy milk	60 ML (¼ CUP)
white vinegar	1 TSP
hot sauce	DASH

NASHVILLE CRUMB

dry breadcrumbs	25 G (¼ CUP)
plain (all-purpose) flour	35 G (¼ CUP)
kala namak (Indian black salt) or use sea salt	½ TSP
black pepper	¼ TSP

NASHVILLE SPICY OIL

cayenne pepper	1½ TBSP OR TO TASTE
soft brown sugar	2 TSP
smoked paprika	1 TSP
garlic powder	1 TSP
black pepper	PINCH

Press the life force and excess liquid out of the tofu by hand over the kitchen sink or under a heavy weight (like a large saucepan). Combine the stock powder and hot water in a bowl, add the tofu and allow to rest for 20 minutes. Tear into six irregular chunks, then squeeze out excess liquid.

Combine the buttermilk ingredients in a bowl and allow to sit for 5 minutes to thicken. Combine the crumb ingredients, then spread on a plate. In a small heatproof bowl, combine the Nashville spicy oil ingredients.

Dunk each tofu chunk in the buttermilk, then transfer to the plate and coat with the crumb mixture. Use your hands to compact the crumbs around the chunk to create a generous coating. Repeat with the remaining tofu.

To fry the tofu, heat enough vegetable oil for deep-frying in a large saucepan over medium–high heat. Test if the oil is ready by inserting a wooden skewer or the handle of a wooden spoon into the hot oil; if it begins to bubble quickly, then you're ready to go. Add the crumbed tofu chunks in two batches and cook for 6 minutes or until golden brown and crispy. Drain on paper towel.

Carefully ladle 60 ml (¼ cup) of the hot frying oil into the spicy oil mixture and whisk thoroughly. Dunk each fried tofu piece into the Nashville spicy oil to turn it into a world of delicious pain, then return to the paper towel to drain. Serve hot with something creamy.

MAKES 6

Dino Nuggs

It's a scientific fact that dinosaur-shaped nuggets are cooler than other nuggets that tend to be shaped like deep-fried lack of imagination.

INGREDIENTS	
vegetable oil spray	FOR COOKING
Gluten-free okara chicken mince (see page 67)	1 × QUANTITY

Use cooking spray to oil dinosaur-shaped moulds and press the mince into each mould, levelling off the top to make a smooth nugget. You can also use your hands to shape them into less precise dino nuggs. Remember: who can truly say what the exact appearance of each dinosaur was? If you end up with some Jurassic Park–style hybrids, so be it. Place in the freezer for at least 2 hours.

Set your time travel machine (oven) to 180 million years ago (180°C/350°F) and bake for 15–20 minutes (this may vary depending on the size of your dinosaur moulds).

To make quick, regular nuggets, preheat the oven to 180°C (350°F) or time travel machine to 180 million years ago. Divide the mixture into thirteen nuggets and smooth them with your hands into your desired shape. Bake for 20–25 minutes until crisp and heated through. No need to crumb these, they'll come out with a natural crispy coat.

MAKES 13

As the Peking duck on page 78 also uses bean curd sheets as a base, this recipe is a perfect way to employ the leftovers. Use a serrated knife to carve the duck into thin shreds.

Duck & Spring Onion Pancakes

Laminating the pancake dough layers with fat and spring onion greens makes for crispy, yet soft and chewy pancakes with an awesome aroma. Using boiling water in the dough first denatures some of the proteins and gelatinises the starch for a softer pancake. Cold water then means some of the gluten protein becomes stretchy and pliable so it can form a dough.

INGREDIENTS

vegetable oil	FOR BRUSHING AND FRYING
cucumber	90 G (3 OZ)
hoisin sauce	185 ML (3/4 CUP)
Bean curd duck (see page 63)	3 × QUANTITIES
spring onion (scallion) batons	TO SERVE
sliced red chilli (optional)	TO SERVE

PANCAKES

plain (all-purpose) flour	335 G (2¼ CUPS)
sea salt	1 TSP
boiling water	125 ML (½ CUP)
very thinly sliced spring onion (scallion) greens	30 G (1½ CUPS)

OIL PASTE

sesame oil or coconut oil	2 TBSP
plain (all-purpose) flour	2 TBSP
Chinese five spice powder or Sichuan pepper	3/4 TSP

To make the pancakes, mix the flour and salt in a large bowl, pour over the boiling water and stir with chopsticks. Pour over 125 ml (½ cup) of cold water, then knead the mixture for 5 minutes. Allow the dough to sit for 1 hour or cover and refrigerate overnight.

Combine the oil paste ingredients in a bowl.

Divide the pancake dough into six equal portions. Working with one portion at a time and keeping the rest covered, brush a small amount of oil onto your work surface to stop the dough from sticking. As thinly as you can, roll out a portion of dough and brush with some of the oil paste. Sprinkle with one-sixth of the spring onion and gently roll the dough away from you to create a long tube. Roll the tube into a snail shape, then repeat with the remaining dough until you have six little dough 'snails'.

Cruelly flatten each 'snail' with the palm of your hand, then roll between two sheets of baking paper into roughly circular pancakes 23 cm (9 in) in diameter. Cook immediately or freeze between sheets of baking paper and fry directly from frozen as needed.

Fry each pancake in a frying pan over medium–high heat in 2 tablespoons of hot oil for about 2 minutes each side until golden and crisp. Drain on paper towel.

Shred the cucumber and squeeze out the excess liquid with your hands. Add 1–2 tablespoons of hoisin to one half of each pancake and top with the grated cucumber. Roll up the strips of bean curd duck to create loose balls and divide among the pancakes. Scatter with spring onion batons and sliced red chilli (if using), then carefully fold over the pancakes and serve.

MAKES 6

Peking Duck

★ ★

One of the first meat alternatives, 'vegetarian duck' was made by Buddhist monks using the skins formed on top of soy-milk production. If it looks like a duck and tastes like a duck, it just might be well-prepared yuba.

INGREDIENTS

large fresh folded yuba skins (refrigerated soft bean curd sheets)	150 G (5½ OZ)
vegan peking duck sauce	75 ML (2½ FL OZ)

DUCK-STYLE STOCK

chicken-style stock	375 ML (1½ CUPS)
Maggi seasoning	1½ TSP
minced garlic	3 TSP

DUCK FLAVOUR

coconut oil, softened	2 TBSP
shaoxing rice wine	1 TBSP
dried porcini powder	2 TSP
minced garlic	1 TSP
Chinese five spice powder	1 TSP
smoked paprika	1 TSP
salt	1 TSP
ground white pepper	½ TSP

DIPPING SAUCE

tian mian jiang paste	2 TBSP
sesame oil	1 TSP

Preheat the oven to 160°C (320°F). Line a baking tray with baking paper.

Combine the duck-style stock ingredients in a large bowl. Without unfolding, place the yuba skins in the duck-style stock for 5 minutes, massaging in the liquid until it is fully absorbed and you get a little envious of the pampering. Gently squeeze out the excess liquid and lay the yuba on a work surface.

Carefully unfold the yuba until you have a large rectangle of layered sheets. Whisk the duck flavour ingredients in a small bowl until combined. Peel back the first sheet of yuba and use a pastry brush to spread the flavour mix over the one underneath. Then carefully peel back that sheet and repeat the process for all the sheets, folding them into a layered rectangle once done. Brush 3 tablespoons of peking duck sauce over the top sheet.

From one corner, begin to tightly roll the sheets up towards the opposing corner, bunching and folding if you need, to create a dense 'body' with excess hanging out of two sides. The front of your roast will be smoother and the back will be the side where a fold of yuba runs across the roast. Tuck the excess yuba underneath the roast to complete a rounded shape.

Place the duck on the prepared tray, then glaze with the remaining peking duck sauce. Cover with baking paper, then with foil and roast for 1 hour. Remove the foil and baking paper. If the roast has puffed up, use a skewer to stab a few holes to release the steam. Use the skewer to push the roast back into shape and roast for 10–15 minutes, until crisp.

Combine the dipping sauce ingredients in a small saucepan and place over low heat. When hot, whisk in a splash of water to create a thick sauce and pour into a bowl to serve next to the roast. Cut the roast duck into slices and dish it up with the dipping sauce.

SERVES 4

Find peking duck sauce at Asian supermarkets
(and check that it's vegan) or substitute with hoisin,
char siu or a glaze of your choice. Tian mian jiang
paste is a Chinese sweet bean paste with wheat flour
as its primary ingredient. Keep your eye out for it
during your trip to the Asian supermarket.

General Tso's Chicken

Make this flavour-packed General Tso's chicken and you'll realise why they don't call it General Tso-Tso's. The only thing you need to take away is the fact that chicken isn't the part that makes this classic Chinese fast food so delicious.

INGREDIENTS

firm tofu, double frozen and thawed (see page 34)	500 G (1 LB 2 OZ)
broccoli, broken into florets	250 G (9 OZ)
vegetable oil	2½ TBSP
steamed rice	TO SERVE
sesame oil	2 TSP

TSO'S MARINADE

shaoxing rice wine	1 TBSP
sesame oil	1 TSP
liquid smoke	¼ TSP

TSO'S COATING

cornflour (cornstarch)	30 G (¼ CUP)
dried sage	½ TSP
garlic powder	¼ TSP
ground white pepper	¼ TSP
MSG	PINCH

TSO'S SAUCE

spring onions (scallions), sliced, white and green parts separated	2
chilli paste (such as sambal oelek)	1 TBSP
chicken-style stock cubes	2
soft brown sugar	55 G (1¾ OZ)
dark soy sauce	1 TBSP
Maggi seasoning or more dark soy sauce	2 TSP
rice wine vinegar	1 TSP

Wrap the tofu in paper towel and press under a heavy weight (like the crushing disappointment of your ancestors watching you veganise their recipes – or a large saucepan) for 20 minutes.

Combine the marinade ingredients and 2 teaspoons of water in a large bowl. Place the coating ingredients in a small bowl and mix well.

Cut the tofu into 2.5 cm (1 in) cubes and add them to the marinade, tossing until the tofu is coated. Set aside to soak for 5 minutes before tossing in the coating mixture.

Blanch the broccoli in boiling water for 60 seconds to keep the green colour vibrant. Rinse under cool water to stop the cooking process and set aside.

In a large frying pan, heat 2 tablespoons of the vegetable oil until shimmering and add the coated tofu pieces. Fry, tossing occasionally, for 10 minutes until all sides are crispy, then remove to a bowl.

To make the sauce, heat the remaining oil in a large frying pan over medium heat. Add the white spring onion and cook for about 2 minutes, until fragrant, then add the chilli paste, stock cubes, brown sugar, soy sauce, seasoning, vinegar and 125 ml (½ cup) of water. Simmer until the sauce starts to thicken, then quickly toss through the tofu to coat and stir through the broccoli.

Serve on rice, drizzling the sesame oil on top and scattering over the green spring onion to garnish.

SERVES 2

They say two heads are better than one! Get the best head of your life if you replace the tofu with a head of cauliflower, torn into florets for the ultimate herbivorous cruciferous chow down.

Duck Fried Rice

Jackfruit takes to flavour like a duck takes to water and, in this recipe, everyone stays in their elements.

INGREDIENTS

Jackfruit duck (see page 68)	1 × QUANTITY
chicken-style stock or water	SPLASH
mixed frozen diced peas, broccoli, green beans	140 G (5 OZ)
bunch of bok choy (pak choy), white part sliced, leaves roughly chopped	1
vegetable oil	60 ML (¼ CUP)
spring onions (scallions), finely chopped, white and green parts separated	2
garlic cloves, minced	3
cooked rice, cooled	555 G (3 CUPS)
vegan shrimp, sliced	100 G (3½ OZ)
light soy sauce or vegan fish sauce	1 TBSP
Chinese five spice powder	½ TSP
lemon, cut into wedges	1
sesame seeds, toasted	2 TBSP
kala namak (Indian black salt) or use sea salt	½ TSP

SPECIAL SAUCE

French shallots, minced	2
hoisin sauce	60 ML (¼ CUP)
shaoxing rice wine	2 TBSP
soy sauce	2 TBSP
sesame oil	1½ TBSP
soft brown sugar	1 TBSP
minced garlic	2 TSP
Chinese five spice powder	½ TSP
smoked paprika	½ TSP
ground white pepper	¼ TSP

Preheat the oven to 180°C (350°F).

Mix the special sauce ingredients in a saucepan with a splash of water. Stir over medium heat until combined.

Toss the jackfruit duck in the sauce, place on a baking tray and bake for 30 minutes, tossing occasionally to ensure no pieces crisp up too quickly.

Place a wok over medium heat, add a splash of duck-style stock or water. Add the frozen vegetables and bok choy and stir-fry for 2–3 minutes, allowing the liquid to steam the vegetables until softened. Remove the vegetables to a bowl, crank the heat to high and once the liquid has evaporated, add the oil to the wok to heat up.

Add the white spring onion and garlic to the hot oil and fry for a few seconds until fragrant. Quickly add the rice, tossing vigorously through the oil to coat – you want the hot oil to come into contact with as many grains of rice as possible so that the rice actually fries. Cook, tossing frequently, for 3 minutes until the rice begins to crisp.

Add the vegetables plus the shrimp, drizzle over the soy or fish sauce and sprinkle with the Chinese five spice. Mix and add in the baked jackfruit duck. Toss and cook for another minute to combine everything. Serve with the lemon wedges on the side and the sesame seeds, kala namak and green spring onion scattered over the top. Who said you can't have duck fried rice without having to teach a duck how to fry rice?

SERVES 4

The trick to tasty fried rice isn't to add soy sauce until it looks dark enough, but to properly fry the rice to get the colour, then add just enough sauce for flavour. After all, it's not called saucy sautéed rice so don't be shy to fry!

Schnitzels

Look out for free-range, hormone-free eggplants raised and plucked from the ground by loving farmers. If you find an animal farmer who says that they treat their animals like their own children, good news! This means you can purchase their children at a reasonable price per kilogram and use them in your recipes.

INGREDIENTS	
eggplant (aubergine) OR	1
thick slices TVP	10
sea salt and black pepper	TO SEASON
cornflour (cornstarch)	30 G (¼ CUP)
vegetable oil	FOR SHALLOW-FRYING
lemon wedges	TO SERVE
SCHNITZEL STOCK	
chicken-style stock	125 ML (½ CUP)
mushroom seasoning	1 TBSP
nutritional yeast	1 TBSP
SCHNITZEL CRUMB	
dry breadcrumbs	100 G (1 CUP)
nutritional yeast	2 TBSP
black pepper	PINCH
onion powder	2 TSP
garlic powder	1½ TSP
finely chopped flat-leaf parsley	1 TBSP
sea salt	1 TSP
black pepper	½ TSP

TVP schnitzels have more surface area and are much chewier and crunchier!

Whisk the stock ingredients together with 125 ml (½ cup) of water in a mixing jug.

If making eggplant schnitzels, peel the eggplant, cut off the ends and slice lengthways into 2 cm (¾ in) thick slabs. Liberally salt the surface of the eggplant, then wrap in paper towel and rest for 20 minutes to release moisture. Unwrap the eggplant, wipe away the salt and moisture and set aside.

If making TVP schnitzels, place the TVP in a small saucepan, pour in the stock and 250 ml (1 cup) of water and bring to the boil. Keep submerged in the boiling liquid for 5–10 minutes, using a fork to stab and press out any bubbles if the TVP is too thick to fully hydrate. Make sure the slices are fully softened and squeeze out excess liquid before proceeding with the recipe. Set aside the stock.

Preheat the oven to 200°C (400°F). Line a baking tray with baking paper.

Combine the schnitzel crumb ingredients in a large shallow bowl, then place the cornflour in another bowl and season with salt and pepper.

Coat each schnitzel in the seasoned cornflour and place on a plate. Whisk the remaining cornflour into the stock. Dip the schnitzel pieces into the stock, then coat in the crumb mixture, using your hands to firmly press in the crumbs until they hold and create a consistent coating. Double dip by gently lowering the schnitzels back into the stock and covering with a second coating of crumbs.

Heat the oil in a large frying pan over medium heat. Fry the schnitzels in batches for 3–4 minutes until golden and crisp, then drain on paper towel. Layer two TVP schnitzels or place one eggplant schnitzel per serve on a plate and add a lemon wedge. Alternatively, use in schnitty sandwiches or the pub-style parmas opposite.

MAKES 5-6 EGGPLANT SCHNITZELS OR 10 MINI TVP SCHNITZELS

Pub-style Parmas

Originally meat free and made with eggplant, the parmigiana was first adulterated with chicken, then Australian pubs got their hands on it and it went off the rails. The Australian version is now essentially a schnitzel appropriated as a pizza base. Pubs have up to dozens of variants to choose from, all served on a bed of fries. Have someone named Dazza knock half a pint of beer over your lap while it cooks for the full Aussie pub experience. Nobody can decide whether we call it a parma, parmi or parmy. Whichever way you go, the Italians will think it's parmageddon anyway.

INGREDIENTS

freshly cooked eggplant or TVP schnitzels (see opposite)	1 × QUANTITY

TRADITIONAL PARMA

Pizza sauce (see page 202)	¼ × QUANTITY
dairy-free cheese, grated	175 G (6 OZ)
french fries	TO SERVE
salad	TO SERVE

HAWAIIAN-STYLE PARMA

Pizza sauce (see page 202)	¼ × QUANTITY
Smoked ham (see page 210) or store-bought ham	8 SLICES
pineapple rings	4
dairy-free cheese, grated	175 G (6 OZ)
sweet potato fries	TO SERVE
salad	TO SERVE

MEXICAN-STYLE PARMA

salsa	125 G (4½ OZ)
pickled jalapenos, diced	35 G (¼ CUP)
dairy-free cheese, grated	175 G (6 OZ)
avocado, chopped	1
cherry tomatoes, chopped	50 G (1¾ OZ)
drained tinned black beans	100 G (3½ OZ)
coriander (cilantro) sprigs	TO SERVE
corn chips	100 G (3½ OZ)
lime wedges	TO SERVE

Preheat the oven to 200°C (400°F). Line a baking tray with baking paper. Place the schnitzels on the prepared tray.

For traditional parma, spread the pizza sauce over each schnitzel and top with the cheese. Bake for 10 minutes, then serve hot on a bed of freshly cooked fries with a simple side salad.

For Hawaiian-style parma, spread the pizza sauce over each schnitzel. Fold the ham slices in half and lay over the schnitzel, then top with a pineapple ring. Finish with the cheese, then bake for 10 minutes. Serve hot on a bed of freshly cooked sweet potato fries with a simple side salad.

For Mexican-style parma, spread the salsa over each schnitzel, top with the jalapenos, then the cheese. Bake for 10 minutes. While baking, combine the avocado, tomato, black beans and coriander in a bowl.

Divide the parmas among plates and top with the avocado and bean salad. Serve with a handful of corn chips and lime wedges for squeezing on top.

SERVES 4

MEXICAN-STYLE
PARMA

HAWAIIAN-STYLE
PARMA

TRADITIONAL
PARMA

Lemongrass Drumsticks

Move over bird, curd is the word! Using lemongrass as a bone gives a realistic twist to this recipe, while sneaking extra flavour right into the centre of each drumstick. Serve with a spicy salad like the Som tam on page 144.

INGREDIENTS

lemongrass stalks	6
dry yuba skins (dried bean curd sheets)	550 G (1 LB 3 OZ)

DRUMSTICK MARINADE

vegetable oil	3½ TBSP
French shallots, finely chopped	2
minced garlic	2 TSP
minced ginger	1 TSP
vegan oyster sauce	120 ML (4 FL OZ)
golden syrup	100 ML (3½ FL OZ)
lime juice	1 TBSP

DUCK-STYLE STOCK

chicken-style stock	500 ML (2 CUPS)
Maggi seasoning	2 TSP
minced garlic	1 TBSP

TO SERVE

steamed rice	–
sliced spring onion (scallion)	–
sliced red chilli	–

Trim the white part from each lemongrass stalk, then finely chop and place in a bowl. Prepare the rest of the lemongrass by slicing off the dry, smaller end, then use the back of your knife to bruise the other end of the stalk to release flavour and any tension you may be holding in your shoulders.

Preheat the oven to 180°C (350°F). Line a baking tray with baking paper.

To make the marinade, place the oil in a saucepan over medium heat until it shimmers, then add the shallot, garlic and ginger. Cook for 3 minutes, then add the rest of the marinade ingredients and simmer for 10 minutes. Set aside to cool, then pulse with a stick blender or in a blender.

Combine the stock ingredients in a saucepan and warm through. Remove from the heat.

Rehydrate the yuba in the warm stock for 5 minutes until softened. Remove to a large bowl. Lay two sheets, slightly overlapping, on a work surface and use a pastry brush to spread some of the marinade over the top. Lay the bruised end of one of the lemongrass stalks over one edge of the sheet, leaving the unbruised part out to form the visible 'bone'.

Wrap the yuba tightly around the lemongrass, folding and pressing it in to compress the sheet and achieve a rounded shape. As you finish wrapping, tuck the remaining end into one of the folds to secure the drumstick. Repeat with the remaining lemongrass and yuba skins.

Carefully move each drumstick to the prepared tray and glaze the yuba with the remaining marinade. Bake in the oven for 40–45 minutes, rotating every 10 minutes and using tongs to grip the yuba (not the lemongrass stalk). Glaze with the remaining marinade halfway through.

Serve the drumsticks with steamed rice and topped with sliced spring onion and red chilli.

MAKES 6

Yuba skins can be found in the refrigerator, freezer and dry pantry section at most Asian supermarkets. For this recipe, look for dry sheets to rehydrate.

Bourbon Chicken

Cauliflower is right at home as a substitute for chicken and, even better, chickens are more than happy to switch with the cauliflower and take their place chilling in the dirt. Power through this recipe in no time for a quick after-work dinner that can count as a second knock-off drink before you have finished your first.

INGREDIENTS

vegetable oil	1½ TBSP
cauliflower or seitan chicken-style shreds (see page 64)	500 G (1 LB 2 OZ)
garlic cloves, minced	2
minced ginger	2 TSP
sambal oelek or chilli paste	2 TSP
cornflour (cornstarch)	1½ TSP
steamed rice	TO SERVE
spring onion (scallion), green part only, chopped	1

BOURBON SAUCE

bourbon whiskey	60 ML (¼ CUP)
soft brown sugar	45 G (¼ CUP)
chicken-style stock	60 ML (¼ CUP)
reduced-salt soy sauce	60 ML (¼ CUP)
tomato ketchup	3 TBSP
2 teaspoons chinkiang black vinegar	2 TSP

Place the oil in a saucepan and bring to a shimmer over high heat. Add the cauliflower or seitan shreds and fry, tossing occasionally, for 7–8 minutes until crisp.

Mix the bourbon sauce ingredients in a jug.

Add the garlic, ginger and sambal oelek or chilli paste to the pan and toss to coat for 30–60 seconds until fragrant. Pour in the bourbon sauce. Reduce the heat to medium–low and simmer for 12 minutes.

Whisk the cornflour and 2 tsp of water into a paste, then stir into the sauce and simmer for 3 minutes until the sauce is thick.

Spoon out the rice and top with the bourbon chicken and sauce. Garnish with the green spring onion and serve piping hot. Oops, is the bourbon already open? Better pour another.

SERVES 2

Chicken Satay

**Satay refers to food that is skewered and grilled, not the peanut sauce
that it often comes with. That particular peanut sauce is bloody
good though, so that recipe is here too.**

INGREDIENTS

seitan chicken-style shreds (see page 64)	800 G (1 LB 12 OZ)
garlic cloves, minced	5
kecap manis	60 ML (¼ CUP)
vegetable oil	1 TBSP
lettuce leaves	TO SERVE

PEANUT SAUCE

vegetable oil	2 TBSP
bird's eye chillies, minced	2
French shallots, thinly sliced	4
garlic cloves, minced	2
minced lemongrass	1 TSP
kecap manis	2 TBSP
vegan fish sauce (optional)	1½ TBSP
granulated sugar	1 TBSP
full-fat coconut milk	250 ML (1 CUP)
lime juice	1 TBSP
smooth peanut butter	125 G (½ CUP)
crushed peanuts	80 G (½ CUP)

Soak eight bamboo skewers in cold water for 30 minutes
to avoid scorching.

Meanwhile, toss the seitan chicken shreds with the
garlic, kecap manis and oil and set aside to marinate.

To make the peanut sauce, add the oil to a small
saucepan and bring to a shimmer over medium heat.
Add the chilli, shallot, garlic and lemongrass and fry for
3 minutes. Stir in the kecap manis, fish sauce (if using),
sugar and coconut milk. Simmer for 10 minutes before
adding 60 ml (¼ cup) of water, the lime juice and peanut
butter. Use a stick blender to purée the peanut sauce into
a smooth texture. Stir through the crushed peanuts.

Place a chargrill pan over high heat and season with
oil-soaked paper towel. Wrap each seitan chicken shred
into a ball, then thread onto the prepared skewers, aiming
for 100 g (3½ oz) per skewer.

Add the skewers to the pan and if your skewering was
irregular and hasty, press down with a heavy object (such
as another frying pan) so that the skewered seitan chicken
is in full contact with the pan. Cook for 5–10 minutes,
flipping and pressing occasionally until the chicken seitan
is cooked through and beginning to char.

Serve on lettuce leaves for some healthy vibes but
mostly because they'll help catch more of that peanut
sauce when you drizzle it over the satay to finish up. You
really CAN have it all!

MAKES 8

Store-bought vegan chicken,
torn into chunks, can also be
used for this recipe.

Caesar Salad

This dish mightn't have been named after the infamously excessive demise of the Roman dictator, but with cow's cheese, pig's bacon, dried fish and pieces of chicken making up the bulk of the 'salad' they both do share themes of total overkill. The only stabbing pains in your chest that come with this salad, though, are pangs of joy when you try everything together. This salad is heaps healthier and packed with protein, too. You might call it the Brutus salad because this improvement on the original might actually be the salad that slays the Caesar.

INGREDIENTS

stale bread, cubed	2 SLICES
olive oil	2 TBSP
Seitan chicken-style cutlets (see page 64)	2 × 120 G (4½ OZ)
large head cos (romaine) lettuce, leaves separated	1
Coconut bacon (see page 179)	70 G (1 CUP)
Bonito flakes (see page 128)	1 × QUANTITY
vegan parmesan, shaved	70 G (½ CUP)

CAESAR DRESSING

hemp seeds (or soaked cashews)	90 G (3 OZ)
water	125 ML (½ CUP)
garlic cloves, peeled	3
olive oil	2 TBSP
lemon juice	1½ TBSP
white miso paste	2 TSP
capers	2 TSP
dijon mustard	1½ TSP
xanthan gum, to thicken, if needed	¼ TSP

Preheat the oven to 180°C (350°F).

Coat the bread cubes in 1 tablespoon of the olive oil. then place on a baking tray and bake for 10 minutes until golden.

Rub the remaining olive oil over the seitan chicken cutlets, then place on a separate baking tray and bake for 20 minutes until crispy.

Place the caesar dressing ingredients plus 125 ml (½ cup) of water in a blender and blend until smooth.

In a large bowl, combine the lettuce, half the bacon, half the bonito, half the croutons and most of the parmesan and dressing. Mix well, ensuring the dressing coats the lettuce leaves.

Using a serrated knife, slice the seitan chicken cutlets into bite-sized pieces and place atop the salad. Sprinkle over the remaining parmesan, bacon, bonito and croutons and drizzle over the remaining dressing. Divide among smaller bowls or tuck in without sharing if you're a total tyrant.

SERVES 2-4

Buffalo Wings

Now presenting buffalo wings, our primary evidence for the case that not even real meat has any particular rules to what it can and cannot be called. It just so happens that these vegan buffalo wings contain the exact same amount of both buffalo and wing that you'll find in many real ones.

INGREDIENTS

large head cauliflower	1 (ABOUT 900 G/2 LB)
panko breadcrumbs	100 G (1¾ CUPS)
sea salt and black pepper	TO SEASON
vegan ranch sauce	TO SERVE

BUFFALO-WING BATTER

plain (all-purpose) flour	125 G (4½ OZ)
cornflour (cornstarch)	50 G (1¾ OZ)
onion powder	2 TSP
smoked paprika	1 TSP
dried oregano	1 TSP
sea salt	½ TSP
black pepper	¼ TSP
soy milk	250 ML (1 CUP)

BUFFALO SAUCE

hot sauce	125 ML (½ CUP)
dairy-free butter	3 TBSP
white vinegar	1 TBSP
soft brown sugar	1 TBSP
garlic powder	2 TSP
smoked paprika	1 TSP

Preheat the oven to 180°C (350°F). Grease and line a baking tray.

Break the cauliflower into smaller-than-bite-sized florets – about 20 chunks.

In a large bowl, create the batter by stirring together the dry ingredients. Whisk through 200 ml (7 fl oz) of the soy milk and rest for 10 minutes until as thick as someone arguing that plants have feelings, adding more liquid only if needed.

Place the breadcrumbs in a small bowl and season with salt and pepper.

Dunk the florets into the batter, coating generously, then toss them in the breadcrumbs and transfer to the prepared tray. Bake for 20 minutes, flipping halfway through and gathering any batter that may have dripped from the cauliflower – don't let it get away! Scoop it back on top.

While baking, whisk the buffalo sauce ingredients together in a saucepan and heat for 2 minutes until melded together. Using tongs, drown the baked cauliflower one piece at a time in the buffalo sauce, letting it sit for a few seconds to drink up loads of sauce. Revive the cauliflower by returning it to the tray and baking for a further 20–25 minutes, flipping halfway through. Let cool for 10 minutes before serving with the ranch sauce.

SERVES 2

Substitute with the Gluten-free okara chicken mince (see page 67) formed into bite-sized chunks, or combine the two and stuff the cauliflower florets with okara chicken mince. Reserve the cauliflower stem in this recipe to use in Tandoori drumsticks (see page 98).

Tandoori Drumsticks

This method of using cauliflower as a bone to hold jackfruit can be used as a base for the other coatings in this book. Try the stinger coating on page 282, followed by deep-frying for more plant-based drumstick ideas. Use up the leftover florets in recipes like Bourbon chicken (see page 90), or coat in the same spicy yoghurt and bake alongside the drumsticks.

INGREDIENTS	
small heads cauliflower	1½
rice paper sheets or wet yuba skins (refrigerated soft bean curd sheets)	6
Jackfruit chicken (see page 68)	380 G (13½ OZ)
SPICED YOGHURT	
coconut yoghurt or dairy-free yoghurt	160 G (⅔ CUP)
lemon juice	1½ TBSP
minced garlic	2 TSP
garam masala	2 TSP
Kashmiri chilli powder	1 TSP
ground ginger	1 TSP
ground turmeric	½ TSP
smoked paprika	½ TSP
amchur powder (dried mango)	½ TSP
fenugreek (kasuri methi)	½ TSP
ground coriander	¼ TSP
ground cumin	¼ TSP
black pepper	¼ TSP
sea salt	1 TSP
vegan-friendly red food colouring	FEW DROPS

Preheat the oven to 250°C (500°F). Grease and line a baking tray.

To make the spiced yoghurt, combine the yoghurt, lemon juice, garlic, spices and salt in a bowl. Add a few drops of food colouring until you achieve a rich orange–red to get the signature tandoori colour.

To make the 'bone', starting at the base, cut the cauliflower into quarters. You want to keep the stalk attached to the florets as this will be your 'chicken bone' (1).

Use a small knife to carefully remove the leaves. Trim the stalks into a rounded bone shape, then cut off the majority of the florets so you are left with a basic chicken drumstick shape (2). Reserve the florets for another recipe.

Now for the 'skin' and 'flesh'. If using rice paper, use your hands to lightly wet a sheet with water so that it becomes pliable. Place the rice paper sheet or yuba skin on a plate, then use a pastry brush to spread 1 tablespoon of spiced yoghurt mixture over the top (3). Place a tablespoon of the jackfruit chicken in the middle part of the sheet or skin closest to you. Lay a cauliflower drumstick on top of the jackfruit chicken, ensuring the stalk points towards you and sticks out of the skin. Add the remaining jackfruit chicken on top, filling in and loosely covering the florets on the drumstick (4).

CONTINUE ☞

Carefully fold over the skin (5). Pinch, twist and fold the edge of the skin together to enclose and compress the jackfruit (6). Tightly tuck the twisted end of the skin underneath to secure the drumstick. The skin should be tightly wrapped around the jackfruit and florets of the cauliflower, with the stalk bone protruding to create the drumstick effect. Repeat for the remaining drumsticks, placing each one on the prepared tray with space between.

Generously baste the drumsticks with the remaining spiced yoghurt. Bake for 30 minutes, flipping (very carefully rolling the drumsticks over to expose the other side) and basting once halfway through. At this point, remove any spiced yoghurt that has dripped off and may burn. If any tears appear in the skin, fill them with spiced yoghurt.

To finish, slightly blacken the drumsticks by placing them directly under the oven grill (broiler) for 3–4 minutes each side to mimic a tandoor oven. Remember that the cauliflower may give a bone appearance, but it will have softened while cooking, so you will need to carefully transfer the finished drumsticks to keep them intact until they are plated up.

MAKES 6

The spice level of these drumsticks is mild/medium, so increase the Kashmiri chilli powder if you're looking for a spicy bite.

Prepare the drumsticks on a silicone mat so that you can carefully transfer them to the oven and avoid damaging them before they're baked.

Bird Roast

✶ ✶ ✶

Named after Zacchary Bird, esteemed author of this sentence, this bird roast isn't quite meant to be a chicken and it's definitely not a turkey. It's me! A plant-based alternative to roasting your favourite vegan cookbook writer at Sunday lunch. I might taste a bit like chicken, but apparently who doesn't? Tuck into my succulent rump this holiday season, or fight over a piece of my breast. Just be sure to serve me with gravy and a bit of roast veg.

INGREDIENTS

vital wheat gluten	300 G (2 CUPS)
torula yeast or mushroom seasoning	2 TBSP
firm tofu	300 G (10½ OZ)
aquafaba from tofu or tinned cannellini beans or chickpeas (or water)	350 ML (12 FL OZ)
white vinegar	1 TBSP
vegan stuffing mix	200 G (7 OZ)
dairy-free butter	2 TBSP
wet yuba skins (refrigerated soft bean curd sheets)	4 LARGE
vegetable oil	FOR BRUSHING

CHICKEN-STYLE FLAVOUR

white miso paste	2 TBSP
canola oil	2 TBSP
chicken-style stock powder	2 TBSP
soy sauce	1 TBSP
onion powder	2 TSP
garlic powder	1 TSP
dried sage	1 TSP
dried thyme	1 TSP
dried rosemary	1 TSP
ground white pepper	½ TSP

Combine the vital wheat gluten and torula yeast or mushroom seasoning in a bowl. Add your choice of chicken or turkey-style flavourings.

Place the tofu, aquafaba or water and vinegar in a blender and blend until smooth, then transfer to a stand mixer fitted with a dough hook. Add the vital wheat gluten mixture, then knead on medium speed for 3 minutes to bring the dough together and form gluten strands. Remove from the bowl and use your hands to smooth the seitan dough into a 24 cm x 18 cm (9½ in x 7 in) rectangle. If the gluten resists, let the dough rest for 10 minutes to convince it to cooperate. The edges of the rectangle will remain thicker, so tear them off (about one-quarter of the total volume) and mould these into two drumsticks (1).

Fold a piece of foil in half so it is a little wider than the dough and lay the dough on top (do not wrap). Transfer to a steamer and place the drumsticks on top. Cover and steam for 30 minutes, then set aside to cool. Feel free to forget what you were doing until tomorrow or proceed below!

While the dough is steaming, prepare the stuffing mix as per the packet instructions. Incorporate the butter, then form the stuffing into a log and set aside for a few minutes to firm up. Lay the seitan dough over the stuffing log (2).

Use a sheet of plastic wrap to forcefully wrap the seitan around the stuffing, shaping the sides and stretching it as needed. Wrap a second sheet of plastic wrap from top to bottom of the roast and use it to tuck the ends under, making a rounded shape (3). Add a third sheet of plastic wrap, further shaping the roast as desired. Firmly place your hand down on one end of the roast, and allow the other end to balloon out, mimicking the shape of a poultry roast.

TURKEY-STYLE FLAVOUR	
white miso paste	2 TBSP
Maggi seasoning	1½ TBSP
canola oil (knead in last)	4 TBSP
chicken-style stock powder	1½ TBSP
onion powder	2 TSP
liquid smoke	1 TSP
ground allspice	¼ TSP
ground nutmeg	¼ TSP

BIRD GLAZE	
lemons, zested and juiced	3
garlic cloves, minced	6
finely chopped flat-leaf parsley	15 G (½ CUP)
dijon mustard	1½ TBSP
olive oil	2½ TBSP
sea salt	1½ TSP
black pepper	TO SEASON
chilli flakes	PINCH
rice paper sheets	2

Preheat the oven to 180°C (350°F). Grease and line a large roasting tin.

Combine the glaze ingredients in a bowl. Unwrap the moulded roast and carefully place in the prepared tin. Stab the roast vigorously with a skewer for extra glaze access points. Use a pastry brush to baste the roast with one-third of the glaze. Lay one yuba skin squarely over the roast and tuck underneath to seal in the stuffing (4). Spread over more glaze and press the two drumsticks down on the flatter end of the roast (they may shift while cooking – this is OK!).

Lay another yuba skin over the flatter part of the roast to secure the drumsticks, tucking under again. Cut the yuba left hanging off the roast up the middle and twist each piece tightly (5). Tie them together to create a bow – the 'legs' – at the back of the roast. Spread more glaze over everything (6).

Lay another yuba skin over the other half of the roast and tuck under once more. Brush over more glaze. Place the last sheet squarely over the whole roast, tucking underneath and bundling the leftover yuba at either side to make two loose 'wings'. Stop, glaze and glisten. You should have one-third of the glaze left for basting. Use a knife to carve a cloaca into your roast for dramatic effect (you can think of it as a stuffing access point if that helps) and make a small slice in the yuba on the inner side of each drumstick. Tuck the yuba under the drumsticks to define them further. Pour 125 ml (½ cup) of water around the roast, cover with foil and roast for 30 minutes.

Remove from the oven, baste with half the remaining glaze and pour another 125 ml (½ cup) of water around the roast. Recover with the foil and roast for another 30 minutes. Baste again, remove the foil and roast for another 20 minutes. Brush oil over any parts that need to catch up on browning and dab water over any parts that have begun to blacken more quickly than the rest of the roast (i.e., the 'legs') and roast for a further 10 minutes. You may like to cover some of the darker parts with foil so that the skin browns evenly. Remove from the oven, rest for 20 minutes and serve.

SERVES 8 WITH SIDES

GET THE LOOK

Following the instructions in this recipe will make a realistic-looking roast; if this isn't your speed, you can always mould the shape into a large featureless lump. Mmmm, roast featureless lump, just like Mum used to make!

NOT SO POULTRY

Roast Turkey with Honey Mustard Glaze

This roast skips the seitan and hours upon hours of preparation. The longest part involves leaving something to simmer or bake so you can go and have a drink. It's the perfect excuse to make some killer sides to go with this masterpiece of a plant-based centrepiece: think gravy, roasted vegetables, green beans or potatoes. The more fixings, the more likely people will foolishly fill up too quickly and leave you precious leftovers.

INGREDIENTS

VEGAN STUFFING

dairy-free butter	85 G (3 OZ)
large onion, finely diced	1
celery stalk, finely diced	1
fennel seeds	¼ TSP
beer of your choice	60 ML (¼ CUP)
stale bread, processed into breadcrumbs	250 G (9 OZ)
orange, zested and juiced	½
chopped sage leaves	2 TBSP
chopped thyme leaves	2 TSP
dried marjoram	½ TSP
vegan worcestershire sauce	1 TBSP
nutritional yeast	15 G (¼ CUP)
sea salt and black pepper	TO SEASON
chicken-style stock	ABOUT 80 ML (⅓ CUP)

Preheat the oven to 150°C (300°F).

Start on the stuffing. Melt 2 tablespoons of the butter in a small frying pan over medium heat. Add the onion and celery and sauté for 5 minutes. Add the fennel seeds and beer and cook for 5 minutes or until most of the liquid has evaporated.

Meanwhile, spread the breadcrumbs over a baking tray and toast for 5 minutes.

Add the breadcrumbs to the onion and celery mixture, then stir through the orange zest and juice, sage, thyme, marjoram, worcestershire sauce, nutritional yeast and salt and pepper. Mix in the remaining butter and enough stock for the mixture to come together. Lay out a sheet of plastic wrap and heap the stuffing on top – you may not need all of it. (Extra stuffing can be baked for 30 minutes and served alongside the finished roast.) Enclose the stuffing in the plastic wrap and mould into a log. Place in the freezer while you proceed with the rest of the recipe.

Increase the oven temperature to 180°C (350°F).

To prepare the turkey meat, in a large bowl, combine the chicken mix with all the dry ingredients. Mix through the stock, Maggi seasoning and liquid smoke, allow to sit for 10 minutes, then stir through the oil.

Divide the turkey meat into thirds. Lay out a sheet of plastic wrap and place two-thirds of the turkey meat on top. Smooth it out until you have an even layer. Unwrap the stuffing log, then place this on top of the turkey meat. Use the plastic wrap to enclose and completely seal the stuffing in the turkey meat.

TURKEY MEAT	
dry plant-based chicken mix	280 G (10 OZ)
dried sage	1 TSP
onion powder	1 TSP
dried rosemary	3/4 TSP
dried marjoram	1/2 TSP
ground nutmeg	1/4 TSP
ground white pepper	1/4 TSP
chicken-style stock	460 ML (15 1/2 FL OZ)
Maggi seasoning	1 TBSP
liquid smoke	1/4 TSP
vegetable oil	2 TBSP PLUS EXTRA FOR GREASING
TURKEY GLAZE	
vegan honey or rice malt syrup	60 ML (1/4 CUP)
dijon or American mustard	2 TBSP
orange juice	1 TBSP
garlic powder	1 TSP
TURKEY SKIN	
rice paper sheets	2
vegetable oil, for baking	

Using creative licence, shape the body into as realistic a turkey shape as you please – or a simple log will do. For an unrealistic twist, you can invent a creature from the depths of your imagination.

Form the remaining turkey meat into two larger drumsticks and two smaller wings, then position them on your roast. Press them in and reshape as needed so the proportions look right.

Lightly grease a baking tray with oil and place your roast on top. In a small bowl, combine all the turkey glaze ingredients. Use a pastry brush to spread some of the glaze over the roast.

For the turkey skin, briefly wet each rice paper sheet with water and wipe off the excess. When it's pliable, place it over the roast. Use kitchen scissors to trim the excess and cut the rice paper near the various 'folds' of the turkey so that it evenly covers the roast. Tuck in any loose ends and brush more glaze over the skin.

Cover the turkey with foil and roast for 1 hour, lovingly reglazing as needed every 20 or so minutes. Remove the foil and roast for a further 30 minutes until the skin begins to crisp up and turn golden brown. Carve it up, serve it up and when people remark 'Jesus Christ!' you can say 'No, it's supposed to be a turkey.'

SERVES 8 WITH SIDES

GET THE LOOK

This roast takes advantage of newer plant-based dry mixes for meat, which layer TVP, starches and methylcellulose together for you to just add water and fat. The versatility of this base ingredient makes for one of the best ways to control the shape and look of your homemade plant-based meat. Use a reference image or the guide in Bird roast (see page 103) to make this as alarmingly realistic as you please.

Maple Bourbon Fauxducken

The humble soybean and three different ways with a maple bourbon glaze makes for the vegan answer to the turducken – so everybody can feel welcome at your feast: chickens, turkeys, ducks and even gluten-free freegans! For an extra impressive feast, when making tofu and okara, make one large yuba sheet (see page 31) to coat the outside of the roast so everybody at dinner feels very intimidated by how many things you can pull off with just soybeans.

INGREDIENTS

STUFFING

vegan stuffing (see page 106 or use store-bought)	200 G (7 OZ)
dairy-free butter	1 TBSP
apple cider	170–185 ML (2/3–3/4 CUP)

TOFU CHICKEN

smoked tofu, frozen and thawed once (see page 34)	450 G (1 LB)
hot chicken-style stock	750 ML (3 CUPS)
sea salt and black pepper	TO SEASON
olive oil	2 TBSP
garlic cloves, sliced	6
lemon, zested and juiced	1/2

OKARA TURKEY

boiling water	185 ML (3/4 CUP)
chicken-style stock powder	3 TSP
Maggi seasoning	1 1/2 TBSP
white miso paste	1 TBSP
liquid smoke	1 TSP
dijon mustard	1 TBSP
TVP	75 G (3/4 CUP)

Mix the stuffing ingredients in a bowl and allow to rest.

To make the tofu chicken, press the smoked tofu under a heavy weight for 20 minutes, then marinate in the hot stock for 20 minutes. Reserve the stock. Blot the tofu with paper towel and heartily salt and pepper all sides. Pour the oil into a frying pan and sear the tofu over high heat for 20 minutes, turning occasionally to brown all sides.

Place the tofu chicken on a chopping board and score a 2 cm x 2 cm (¾ in x ¾ in) grid on the two large sides. Push the garlic and lemon zest into the crevices and squeeze the lemon over the surface of the tofu.

To make the okara turkey, combine the boiling water, stock powder, Maggi seasoning, miso, liquid smoke and mustard in a jug and pour over the TVP in a bowl. Allow to sit and hydrate for 5 minutes. Combine the remaining turkey ingredients, except the mayo, in a large bowl before stirring into the hydrated TVP to form a mince-like mixture. In a small bowl, mix the mayonnaise with 1 tablespoon of water, then use your hands to knead this into the mince.

Lay out a sheet of plastic wrap. Spoon half the stuffing into the middle of the plastic wrap, press into a 20 cm x 13 cm (8 in x 5 in) rectangle and place the tofu chicken on top. Spoon the remaining stuffing over the top (1). Wrap the plastic wrap around the roast (2), then mould around the tofu chicken to completely enclose (3).

To make the yuba duck, add the Maggi seasoning and garlic to the reserved stock. Carefully unfold the yuba until you have a large rectangle of layered sheets, then soak in the stock for 5 minutes. Lay the stacked sheets on a work surface and reserve the stock.

OKARA TURKEY CONT'D

dried okara	210 G (2¼ CUPS)
chickpea flour (besan)	80 G (¾ CUP)
psyllium husk	3 TBSP
mushroom seasoning	2¼ TBSP
onion powder	1⅛ TSP
garlic powder	1⅛ TSP
allspice	⅓ TSP
ground nutmeg	⅓ TSP
kala namak (Indian black salt) or use sea salt	½ TSP
vegan mayonnaise	1½ TBSP

YUBA DUCK

Maggi seasoning	1 TBSP
minced garlic	1½ TBSP
large fresh yuba skins (refrigerated soft bean curd sheets)	300 G (10½ OZ)
vegan peking duck sauce	120 ML (4 FL OZ)
coconut oil, softened	60 ML (¼ CUP)

Whisk the duck flavour ingredients in a small bowl until combined. Peel back the first sheet of yuba and use a pastry brush to spread the flavour mix over the sheet underneath. Then carefully peel back that sheet and repeat the process for all the sheets, folding them into a layered rectangle once done. Use the brush to spread the peking duck sauce over the top sheet (4). Unwrap the tofu chicken and stuffing and place on top of the yuba sheets, then wrap the yuba around the roast to completely enclose it (5).

Preheat the oven to 180°C (350°F). Line a large roasting tin with baking paper.

Carefully transfer the roast to the prepared tin to continue building. Wet your hands and press three-quarters of the okara turkey over the yuba duck to thinly cover the roast (6). Wet your hands again and smooth the surface into a uniform texture. Gently mould the roast to have one larger end and a flatter end for the drumsticks, using creative licence to approximate the shape. Heap the remaining okara turkey over the sides on the flatter end and mould into two large 'drumsticks' (7). Remould the mince towards the front of the roast to look like two 'wings'.

Combine the glaze ingredients in a bowl and liberally brush some of the glaze over the roast.

Now for the skin, briefly wet each rice paper sheet with water and wipe off the excess. When it's pliable, place it over the roast (8). Start by placing one sheet over each end of the roast, then cut the other sheets in half and use them to cover any gaps. Baste the skin with the glaze (9).

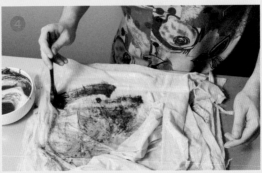

DUCK FLAVOUR	
shaoxing rice wine	2 TBSP
dried porcini powder	1 TBSP
minced garlic	2 TSP
Chinese five spice powder	2 TSP
smoked paprika	2 TSP
sea salt	2 TSP
ground white pepper	3/4 TSP

FAUXDUCKEN GLAZE	
dairy-free butter, melted	2 TBSP
bourbon whiskey	80 ML (1/3 CUP)
soy sauce	1 1/2 TBSP
maple syrup	60 ML (1/4 CUP)
hot sauce	1 TSP
sea salt	3/4 TSP

FAUXDUCKEN SKIN	
rice paper sheets	4

Artfully mould a cloaca into your fauxducken to make sure any non-vegan guests don't accuse you of being inauthentic to their cuisine. Pour 60 ml (¼ cup) of reserved stock around the roast. Cover the roast in baking paper, then in foil. Roast for 1 hour, 20 minutes, basting every 20 minutes and adding another 60 ml (¼ cup) of stock halfway through.

Remove the baking paper and foil, pour over the rest of the glaze and continue to roast the fauxducken for 20 minutes. Baste any parts that have browned too quickly with the remaining stock and roast for a further 10 minutes until golden brown. Serve spectacularly and make sure everyone watches you carving it like the absolute legend you now are.

SERVES 10+

Substitute any of the layers with plant-based dry mix or seitan if you're OK with gluten and want to save a bit of time.

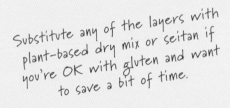

RED
HERRING

AWASE DASHI • FISH SAUCE • PREPARING FRESH BANANA BLOSSOM • FISH FILLETS • SMOKED SHALLOT CAVIAR • KING OYSTER MUSHROOM SCALLOPS • BOQUERONES • BONITO FLAKES • TAKOYAKI • SASHIMI • NIGIRI • EBI FRY ON CABBAGE SALAD • SOM TAM • SQUID INK PASTA • BATTERED FISH WITH LEMON BITTERS MAYO • BAJA FISH TACOS • FISH STICKS • DRAGON ROLL • HEARTY FISH POT PIE • CEVICHE • PAELLA • GRILLED SHRIMP FLAKY BAKED FISH • OYSTERS KILPATRICK

SEAFOOD BASES

KONJAKU

TOFU

WATERMELON

ARTICHOKE

TOMATOES

TEMPEH

EGGPLANT

MUSHROOMS

BANANA BLOSSOMS

SODIUM ALGINATE SPHERIFICATION

DAIKON

PALM HEARTS

Give a man a fish and he'll eat for a day. Teach a man to fish and the oceans could be devoid of sea life by 2050. Thankfully, there's nothing fishy at all about using plants to make meals that are off the hook. Soft, flaky or rubbery textures? Check. Savoury, briny, salty and tangy flavours? Check please, we're taking them to go.

There are five simple ways in this chapter to make fried fish alone, so there's no longer any need to restrict ourselves to just one ingredient. At this point it feels almost uninspired to resort to using real seafood to make seafood. Instead of stealing from the sea, we can steal the techniques honed to perfection over centuries of cooking traditional seafood dishes and apply them to the diverse world of plants. Tomatoes, watermelon, eggplant (aubergine), daikon and artichokes have all been invited for a seaside holiday and they're ready to drink in some local flavour. Your local fruit and veg market will look like a veritable fishmonger once you give your plant-based ingredients new textures through steaming, baking, marinating, battering, pickling, grilling or even microwaving.

Konjaku is a popular ingredient in commercial plant-based seafood for good reason – it's perfect for creating texture and when mixed with pickling lime creates a naturally fishy smell and flavour. You can make a classic Japanese-style konjaku block or mix it with other ingredients for a modern take on shrimp, oysters, octopus or baked fish.

FLAVOURS TO USE FOR FISH:

ASPARAGUS • CAPERS • CITRUS • CORIANDER (CILANTRO) • DILL • GARLIC • MINT • SEAWEED: NORI, KOMBU, DULSE, KELP • WASABI • WHITE WINE

BASES:

ARTICHOKES • BANANA BLOSSOMS • DAIKON • EGGPLANT (AUBERGINE) • KONJAKU • MUSHROOMS PALM HEARTS • SODIUM ALGINATE SPHERIFICATION • TEMPEH • TOFU • TOMATOES • WATERMELON

AWASE DASHI

MAKES 2 LITRES (68 FL OZ)

Dashi is the base broth in many Japanese dishes – most popularly made from kombu and katsuobushi (dried bonito), with kombu or dried shiitake mushroom variants. Awase (combination) dashi uses two bases for maximum umami which is why we're using both kombu AND shiitake for the dashi in this book.

INGREDIENTS

kombu kelp (optional)	20 G (3/4 OZ)
dried shiitake mushrooms	75 G (2³/4 OZ)

① Use kitchen scissors to cut slits/add more surface area to the kombu (if using).

② Combine the shiitake mushrooms, kombu and 2 litres (8 cups) of cold water in a bowl. Cover and soak overnight in the fridge to infuse.

③ Pour the stock into a saucepan and place over low heat. Remove and discard the kombu before the temperature reaches 70°C (160°F) or just as bubbles begin to appear. Remove from the heat.

④ Allow the stock to cool before squeezing the liquid out of the shiitake mushrooms and using the dashi as required. Reserve the rehydrated shiitake mushrooms to use in other recipes, such as Banana peel pulled pork (see page 183), Katsudon (see page 184) or Sweet 'n' sour pork (see page 186).

⑤ The dashi will keep in an airtight container in the fridge for up to 1 week.

HOT TIPS

❶ Using the same collaboration that makes traditional dashi such a powerhouse, mix kombu and shiitake dashi to combine two forms of umami (glutamate and nucleotides) for an amplified umami punch.

❷ To make kombu dashi, Leave out the shiitake and increase the kombu to 40 g (1½ oz).

❸ To make shiitake dashi, leave out the kombu.

FISH SAUCE

MAKES 500 ML (2 CUPS)

Phwoar! This stuff is potent! Once you've bottled up a batch, you just need small amounts to boost the rich umami flavour in recipes. If you don't want to make your own, vegan fish sauce can be found in Asian supermarkets and specialty stores.

INGREDIENTS

Awase dashi (see opposite), shiitake mushrooms reserved	1 × QUANTITY
black garlic cloves OR	6
large garlic cloves, peeled	2
MSG	1 TSP
shoyu (white soy sauce)	80 ML (⅓ CUP)
seaweed flakes	1 TBSP
rice wine vinegar	1 TSP

① Pour the dashi into a mixing jug, add the shiitake and garlic and use a stick blender to combine.

② Strain the stock into a saucepan and simmer over medium heat until reduced to 1 litre (4 cups).

③ Stir in the remaining ingredients and simmer for a further 20 minutes until reduced to 500 ml (2 cups) and stinky, salty and intense.

④ Strain again, bottle up and use as needed in recipes to amplify umami.

⑤ Store your fish sauce in the pantry for up to 3 months.

PREPARING FRESH BANANA BLOSSOM

✷ ✷

MAKES 1 x QUANTITY BANANA BLOSSOM FLORETS AND 2-4 FISH FILLETS

Fresh banana blossom is a vibrant plant with little visual similarity to the tinned prepared versions until you peel back the purple bracts to get at the good stuff inside. Both the florets, once they've had the pistil and calyx plucked out, and the creamy-coloured heart can be used in place of meat in their own unique ways.

INGREDIENTS

lemon, juiced	1/2
sea salt	PINCH
vegetable oil	FOR COATING
fresh banana blossom	1-2

① Fill a large bowl with water and add the lemon juice and salt. Rub the squeezed lemon half over a stainless steel knife. These steps will help stop the banana blossoms oxidising as you prepare them. Lightly coat your hands in oil to avoid being covered in sap.

② To scale the banana blossoms, peel back the tough outer bracts and discard or save to use as serving plates for other recipes.

③ Remove the florets found underneath. You then need to separate the calyx and pluck out the pistil.

④ To do this, use your fingers to carefully prise open the calyx and remove the inside pistil. Discard the pistil and calyx and immediately plunge the florets into the prepared acidulated water.

⑤ Repeat this process with the next layer, until you reach the creamy inner bracts, which can also be used. The smaller florets closer to the heart may be too difficult to remove the pistils and calyxes from. Massage the banana blossoms in the water.

⑥ When you reach the heart of the blossoms, cut off the spine-like core, then cut the heart in half, being careful of the sap. Immediately place in the acidulated water.

⑦ Sit for 2 hours in the water to remove the bitter sap. The hearts can be eaten raw; however, the florets need to be thoroughly cooked to become palatable - trust me, don't try them before cooking! Turn the blossom hearts into Fish fillets (see page 122) and give the florets a go in the Banana blossom floret pulled pork (see page 182).

FISH FILLETS

MAKES 4-6 FILLETS OR 12 FINGERS

A suspiciously fishy fillet can be made from myriad ingredients with just a little bit of prep. Once prepared, finish them in beery batter as Battered fish (see page 149) – just like your local fish and chip shop does – or flick to Flaky baked fish (see page 164) to learn how to make crispy skin out of rice paper!

INGREDIENTS

MARINADE

Awase dashi (see page 118) or water	500 ML (2 CUPS)
lemon juice	60 ML (¼ CUP)
white miso paste	2 TBSP
minced garlic	2 TSP
white wine	125 ML (½ CUP)
spring onions (scallions), finely chopped	2

BANANA BLOSSOM

tins banana blossoms in brine, drained, OR	2 × 510 G (1 LB 2 OZ)
fresh banana blossom heart (see page 120)	1
shredded nori	1 TBSP

HEARTS OF PALM

tins hearts of palm, drained	2 × 400 G (14 OZ)
nori sheets	2

BANANA BLOSSOM

① If using tinned banana blossom, rinse the florets under running water, squeeze out as much brine as possible, then place in a bowl. If using fresh banana blossom heart, follow the instructions on page 120 to prepare, cutting the heart into quarters.

② Combine the marinade ingredients and nori in a separate bowl, then add to the banana blossom and massage through, separating the pieces as you go. Cover with cold water, then cover with plastic wrap and marinate in the fridge for 2-24 hours, tossing occasionally.

③ Scoop out one-quarter of the marinated banana blossom and squeeze. The goal is to wring out the majority of the liquid, but keep just a little moistness. This action should also bring the blossoms together to form a 'fillet' approximately the size of your palm (or, if you have large hands, someone else's palm). Repeat to make four fillets.

HEARTS OF PALM

① Gently rinse the hearts of palm under cold running water and add to a nut-milk bag. Thoroughly squeeze excess moisture from the hearts of palm until they have become a homogenous, mostly dry, lump. Remove from the nut-milk bag and form into 4-6 palm-sized fillets.

② Combine the marinade ingredients in a separate bowl. Trim the nori with kitchen scissors into pieces that match the length of the hearts of palm fillets. Wrap the nori around each fillet and dip briefly into the marinade to add flavour and dampen the nori to secure in place.

TOFISH	
soft–medium tofu, frozen and thawed twice (see page 34)	600 G (1 LB 5 OZ)
nori sheets (optional)	2
TEMPEH	
white tempeh	600 G (1 LB 5 OZ)
LION'S MANE MUSHROOM	
large lion's mane mushroom	1

TOFISH

① Wrap the tofu in paper towel and gently press out the excess moisture. Use a knife to divide the tofu into 4-6 fillets or 12 fingers, then place in a bowl.

② Combine the marinade ingredients in a separate bowl, then pour over the prepared tofu. Cover and marinate in the fridge for 1-12 hours. Remove the tofu from the marinade and gently squeeze out the excess liquid.

③ If making fillets, trim the nori with scissors into pieces that match the length of the tofu fillets. Wrap a nori piece around each tofu fillet, dip your fingers into the marinade and use the moisture to enclose and seal the tofu.

TEMPEH

① Slice the tempeh blocks into 12 fingers.

② Combine the marinade ingredients in a bowl, add the tempeh, then cover and set aside to marinate at room temperature for at least 30 minutes.

③ Remove the tempeh from the marinade and gently shake off the excess.

LION'S MANE MUSHROOM

① Combine the marinade ingredients in a bowl.

② Slice the mushroom into four fillet-shaped slabs and add to the marinade for 30 minutes.

③ Remove the mushroom from the marinade and gently shake off the excess.

SMOKED SHALLOT CAVIAR

✴ ✴

MAKES ABOUT 50 G (1 CUP)

If Willy Wonka went vegan and switched to savoury, this recipe is where he'd start. Using the gelling reaction between calcium and sodium alginate (direct spherification), we can hide an assortment of flavours in caviar-like orbs that pop with liquid centres – that's modern magic! Flavour liquids with calcium (such as many juices), as well as liquids with a pH below 4 will sabotage the process, so use sodium citrate to increase the pH of your liquid. The thicker your flavour liquid, the more it will froth up when blended with sodium alginate, so you'll need to let it sit for longer to settle. Otherwise, you can mix and match loads of flavours to suit different dish requirements.

It's best to serve the caviar fresh, as the spheres will continue to set over time and lose their liquid centres after several hours. You'll need a syringe or eye dropper to create the spheres. There are also spherification devices available to produce dozens of spheres at once if you want to make these regularly and en masse.

INGREDIENTS

sodium citrate	1/2 TSP
sodium alginate	1 1/4 TSP
calcium chloride	2.5 ML (1/8 FL OZ)

FLAVOUR LIQUID

French shallots, peeled and minced	4
olive oil	2 TSP
sea salt	PINCH
sparkling wine or white wine	500 ML (2 CUPS)
vegan-friendly red food colouring	2 DROPS
ume vinegar	2 TSP
sodium alginate	1 1/4 TSP

① To make the flavour liquid, add the shallot and oil to a small saucepan over low heat. Cook, stirring occasionally, for 10 minutes, then add the salt and cook for a further 10 minutes, allowing the shallot to begin to catch in the pan before stirring again. Gently mix together the sparkling wine and food colouring. Turn the heat up to high and deglaze the pan with the sparkling wine mixture. Cook for 5 minutes or until reduced by half, then mix in the ume vinegar. Allow to cool before straining well into a mixing jug, pressing excess liquid out of the shallot. Reserve the liquid.

② Prepare an infusion smoker. Cover the jug with plastic wrap and feed through the nozzle of the smoker and fill the jug with smoke for 1 minute (1). Remove the nozzle and completely seal the jug, leaving it to sit for 5 minutes, swishing the liquid occasionally to incorporate the smoke.

③ Use a high-powered blender to combine the sodium citrate with 250 ml (1 cup) of the strained flavour liquid for 10 seconds, then add the sodium alginate and blend for 1 minute. Set aside for a few hours in the fridge to allow the bubbles to subside.

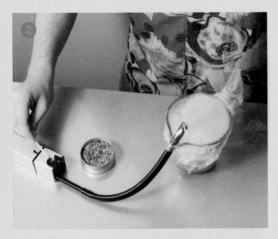

④ To make the setting bath, whisk the calcium chloride into 500 ml (2 cups) of water until dissolved.

⑤ Using an eye dropper or syringe to suck up the prepared flavour liquid, with even pressure and from a height of about 5 cm (2 in), push a constant stream of droplets into the setting bath (2). Experiment with the amount of pressure to make even droplets and to vary the size of your caviar.

⑥ Allow the caviar to bathe in the calcium mixture for 1 minute, then gently rinse the caviar in a bowl of clean water to remove the bitter calcium flavour from the outside of the droplets (3).

⑦ Store in any excess flavour liquid or serve immediately on top of Squid ink pasta (page 146), as tobiko on any sushi recipes in this book or lavishly balanced on a spoon (4).

HOT TIP

Save the shallot to use in pork buns or simply use as a spread on sandwiches!

If the spheres aren't forming from your liquid, thin it out with extra water or adjust the height from which you drop the liquid into the setting bath.

red HERRING

King Oyster Mushroom Scallops

Anyone not convinced of why king oyster mushrooms get royal status needs to start with this recipe. Scoring and searing the stems is all that's required to turn them into freaky good scallops.

INGREDIENTS

king oyster mushrooms	4–5
Kombu dashi (see page 118)	500 ML (2 CUPS)
minced garlic	1 TBSP
miso paste	3 TSP
olive oil	2 TBSP
sea salt and black pepper	TO SEASON

Slice the stem of each mushroom into 2 cm (¾ in) thick rounds. Discard the very end of the stem, and reserve the caps for another recipe.

Use a paring knife to score a diamond pattern lightly into both sides of each scallop round.

Combine the scallops, dashi, garlic and miso in a container small enough to submerge the scallops, massaging the miso with your fingertips to dissolve. Cover and marinate in the fridge for 30 minutes to 12 hours.

Heat the oil in a large frying pan over high heat. Remove the scallops from the marinade and pat dry with paper towel. Sprinkle a small pinch of salt and crack some black pepper over one side of the scallops.

Once the oil is smoking, add the scallops to the pan pepper-side down. Add pepper and salt to the exposed side of the scallops and once the underside begins to char, 2–3 minutes, flip the scallops. Cook for a further 2 minutes until both sides are golden and beginning to blacken. Remove from the pan and serve as is or with the Squid ink pasta on page 146.

MAKES ABOUT 20

Boquerones (OR Bonito Flakes)

Marinating in and serving on olive oil helps to add a fatty mouthfeel to the boquerones, or for a straight-out-of-the-ocean taste you can swap in 200 million gallons of crude BP oil.

Bonito flakes are shaved, dried fish that can be used to make dashi and are often seen scattered on top of Japanese meals where they 'dance' by fluttering in the steam leaving the dish. Here, grated daikon is prepared to have a similar hit of intense, salty flavour, then dried for a creative take on the original flakes. Don't be scared of making a double batch, you'll want to scatter these delicious flakes on EVERYTHING!

INGREDIENTS

large daikon, peeled	1
sea salt	1½ TSP

MARINADE

lemon juice	80 ML (⅓ CUP)
white vinegar	80 ML (⅓ CUP)
olive oil	60 ML (¼ CUP)
bay leaves	2
dried dulse	1 TBSP
knob of ginger, peeled	1.5 CM (½ IN)

TO SERVE (BOQUERONES)

olive oil	2 TBSP
vegan worcestershire sauce	2 TSP, PLUS A SPLASH
capers	1 TSP
garlic cloves, finely chopped	2
finely chopped flat-leaf parsley	1 TBSP
smoked salt	¼ TSP
silver leaf (optional)	A FEW FLAKES

To make the boquerones, use a paring knife and creative licence to carve the daikon into 8 cm (3¼ in) long fish shapes. Round off the head and whittle down the tail to make them look like anchovies. Microwave the daikon anchovies for 1 minute, then toss in the salt and pack into a jar to rest for 1 hour. Once liquid has accumulated at the bottom of the jar, pour it out, keeping the daikon anchovies in the jar.

Blend together the marinade ingredients and pour over the daikon anchovies. Add a splash of water if needed to ensure the liquid covers the contents of the jar. Seal the jar and store for 24–72 hours before using. The longer, the tangier, the better.

To serve, pour the olive oil into a shallow serving bowl and add a few splashes of worcestershire sauce. Remove the marinated daikon anchovies and shake off the excess liquid.

Carefully place the daikon anchovies in the bowl. Squeeze each caper between your fingertips, letting the juice drip over the anchovies, before placing them on top. Follow by scattering over the garlic, parsley and smoked salt. Cover the bowl with plastic wrap and transfer to the fridge for at least 1 hour to allow the flavours to meld. Serve to what can only be thunderous applause if you go for the full silver-leaf option (see opposite).

TO FINISH (BONITO FLAKES)	
vegan worcestershire sauce	SPLASH
cooking oil	SPRAY

To make bonito flakes, use the large holes on a box grater to shred the daikon. Toss the shredded daikon in the salt and pack into a jar to rest for 1 hour.

Once liquid has accumulated at the bottom of the jar, pour it out.

Blend together the marinade ingredients and pour over the shredded daikon. Add a splash of water if needed to ensure the liquid covers the contents of the jar. Seal the jar and store for 24 hours before continuing.

Preheat the oven to 120°C (250°F). Line a baking tray with baking paper.

Remove the shreds from the jar and blot excess liquid with paper towel. Spread the shreds as thinly as possible on the prepared tray, making sure there are no clumps. Splash a small amount of worcestershire sauce over the top. Bake for 1 hour, checking occasionally that no parts are drying more quickly than the rest – agitate if needed, until completely dry.

Spray a light coating of cooking oil over the flakes and bake for a further 10 minutes. Keep a close eye on them and remove from the oven when they have crisped up and begin to blacken. Store in an airtight jar until required and use in recipes such as the Som tam on page 144 or the Caesar salad on page 95.

MAKES 500 G (1 LB 2 OZ) BOQUERONES OR 80 G (1 CUP) BONITO FLAKES

GET THE LOOK

After removing the daikon anchovies from the marinade, place on a chopping board and use tweezers to very carefully manoeuvre edible silver-leaf flakes over one half of each to replicate the silvery two-tone effect anchovies have. Without touching the flake with your fingertips, use the tweezers to press the silver leaf onto the anchovies. Then carefully transfer them to the serving dish.

red HERRING

BONITO FLAKES

BOQUERONES

Takoyaki

To create delicious vegan octopus balls, you can use a specialist takoyaki pan or you can upcycle an impromptu takoyaki pan out of an old cake-pop pan or any old pan with half-sphere moulds.

INGREDIENTS

Basic konjaku (see page 38) OR	125 G (4½ OZ)
king oyster mushrooms	2
cooking oil spray	FOR GREASING
pickled sushi ginger	50 G (1¾ OZ)
spring onion (scallion), white and green parts separated, finely sliced	1
vegan Japanese mayo	TO SERVE
nori flakes	1 TBSP

BATTER

Kombu dashi (see page 118)	500 ML (2 CUPS)
plain (all-purpose) flour	120 G (4½ OZ)
baking powder	1½ TSP
sea salt	PINCH
vegetable oil	1 TBSP
soy sauce	1 TSP

TAKOYAKI SAUCE

tomato ketchup	110 ML (4 FL OZ)
vegan worcestershire sauce	75 ML (2½ FL OZ)
rice wine vinegar	2 TBSP
rice malt syrup	1 TBSP

If using konjaku, bring a small saucepan of water to the boil. Slice the konjaku into 2 cm (¾ in) cubes and boil for 3 minutes, then drain.

If using king oyster mushrooms, slice into 2.5 cm (1 in) cubes and cook with a splash of water in a saucepan over medium heat for 10 minutes. Replenish the water until the mushroom releases its liquid and begins to stick to the pan.

To make the batter, place the kombu dashi in a saucepan over high heat and simmer until reduced by half. Set aside to cool completely, then combine with the remaining batter ingredients.

Meanwhile, place the takoyaki sauce ingredients in a small bowl and whisk to combine.

Lightly grease a takoyaki or an upcycled cake-pop pan with oil spray, then set the pan over medium–low heat. Place the batter, prepared konjaku or mushroom, half the ginger and the white spring onion near the pan.

Three-quarter fill each takoyaki mould with the batter. Divide the ginger and white spring onion among the takoyaki and place a cube of konjaku or mushroom in each mould. Pour the remaining batter over the top, allowing it to run between the takoyaki and cover the entire pan. Cook for 3–4 minutes until the batter begins to set.

Use a toothpick to separate and scrape the batter on top of each takoyaki to enclose the filling, then gently snag the edge of each takoyaki and rotate the ball 180 degrees so that the uncooked batter is flipped to the bottom of each mould. Once the bottom has crisped, use the toothpick to rotate the takoyaki one more time, to ensure all sides are fully cooked. This can take 10–12 minutes in total.

Remove the takoyaki to a serving plate and brush or drizzle the tops with the takoyaki sauce and a good squeeze of Japanese mayo. Scatter the green spring onion, the remaining ginger and the nori flakes over the top and serve immediately with toothpicks or chopsticks.

MAKES 12

Sashimi

Is that a sushi roll in your pocket or are you just happy to sashimi? Here are three ways to turn fruit and veg into a substitute for popular Japanese seafood and raw fish: unagi (eel) made from eggplant; sashimi made from watermelon; and a rich smoked salmon using tomatoes. Serve with the usual suspects (wasabi, shoyu, sushi ginger, pickled seaweed).

INGREDIENTS

EGGPLANT UNAGI

eggplant (aubergine)	500 G (1 LB 2 OZ)
sea salt	1 TBSP

WATERMELON SASHIMI

watermelon, rind removed	400 G (14 OZ)
sea salt	1 TBSP
dried kombu	40 G (1½ OZ)

SASHIMI MARINADE

soy sauce	60 ML (¼ CUP)
mirin	60 ML (¼ CUP)
soft brown sugar	2 TBSP
vegan oyster sauce	1 TBSP

TOMATO LOX

firm, slightly under-ripe tomatoes	6
nori flakes	1 TBSP
soy sauce	125 ML (½ CUP)
ground ginger	1 TBSP
liquid smoke	1 TSP

TO SERVE

shredded daikon	-
shredded carrot	-
shoyu	-
wasabi	-
sushi ginger	-
pickled seaweed	-

EGGPLANT UNAGI

Preheat the oven to 180°C (350°F). Line a baking tray with baking paper.

Peel the eggplant, remove the ends and slice lengthways into 5 mm (¼ in) thick long slabs. Slice the slabs lengthways into halves or thirds, depending on the size of your eggplant. Cover the eggplant in salt and rest on paper towel for 30 minutes to sweat.

Place the sashimi marinade ingredients in a small saucepan and simmer over low heat for 10 minutes.

Wipe the salt and moisture off the eggplant and place on the prepared tray. Baste the slices on both sides with half the marinade and bake, flipping halfway through and basting with the remaining sauce, for 25–30 minutes, until soft and cooked through.

WATERMELON SASHIMI

Cut the watermelon in half and cut out four 10 cm (4 in) rectangles, about 2.5 cm (1 in) thick. Use the knife to carve a rounded end and taper off the opposing end for dramatic effect. Coat all sides of the watermelon in salt.

Sit the kombu in water to soften for 1 minute, then tear off strips and wrap around each piece of watermelon sashimi. Wrap in foil and steam for 25 minutes. When finished, discard the kombu and wrap the watermelon in paper towel. Gently press out the excess liquid.

Place the sashimi marinade ingredients in a small saucepan and simmer over low heat for 10 minutes. Allow to cool a little, then baste the marinade over the watermelon sashimi.

TOMATO LOX

Score a shallow cross in the base of each tomato.

Bring a saucepan of water to the boil over medium-high heat, add the tomatoes and boil for no more than 1 minute. Drain and plunge the tomatoes into a bowl of ice-cold water. This means you can easily remove the skins while keeping the raw tomato texture we want for this dish.

Cut each tomato into eight wedges. Use your fingers to remove and discard the seeds and squeeze out any liquid, leaving only the core and firm flesh. If desired, slice these pieces even more thinly to replicate the thickness of smoked salmon. Pat dry with paper towel.

Place the nori in a small bowl of hot water for 1 minute to hydrate. Drain, then place in a large bowl with the soy sauce, ground ginger, liquid smoke and sliced tomato. Set aside in the fridge to marinate for at least 1 hour or until required.

Serve your chosen sashimi with your favourite sashimi accoutrements, such as shredded daikon and carrot, soy sauce, wasabi, sushi ginger and pickled seaweed.

SERVES 4

GET THE LOOK

Make small diagonal incisions over the top of the watermelon sashimi or tomato lox to replicate the grain in raw salmon.

WATERMELON
SASHIMI

TOMATO LOX

Tezu, or hand vinegar, is like a stronger version of acidulated water and ensures your nigiri or sushi is moist and full of flavour.

Nigiri

Nigiri is hand-moulded rice topped with loads of delicious toppings like unagi (eel), sashimi (raw fish) and kakiage (vegetable tempura). I spent most of my life ordering plates and plates of the latter, but now the modern vegan can access every part of the menu. Try making a variety of toppings to make a platter that'll look as good as it tastes.

INGREDIENTS	
sushi rice	225 G (1 CUP)
nori sheets (optional)	2
rice wine vinegar	1½ TBSP
wasabi paste	TO TASTE
your choice of sashimi (see page 134)	1 × QUANTITY
RICE SEASONING	
sea salt	1 TSP
granulated sugar	1 TBSP
rice wine vinegar	2 TBSP
small piece of kelp	1
TO SERVE	
black sesame seeds (optional)	-
Japanese vegan mayonnaise	-
soy sauce	-
sushi ginger	-
frozen edamame pods, steamed as per packet instructions	-

To prepare the sushi rice, cover the rice with cold water and swish it around to clean the grains. Drain the water and repeat twice more or until the water runs clear. Add the rice to a rice cooker or covered microwave-friendly container with 375 ml (1½ cups) of water. Cook for 13 minutes on High, then allow to sit for 15 minutes.

Meanwhile, bring the rice seasoning ingredients to the boil in a saucepan. Remove the kelp and discard.

Fluff the hot rice with a sushi paddle or spatula, then fold in the seasoning and allow to cool.

Cut the nori with kitchen scissors into 2 cm (¾ in) wide and 13 cm (5 in) long strips.

Prepare a bowl of tezu by combining the rice wine vinegar with 250 ml (1 cup) of water.

To make the nigiri, dampen your hands in the tezu, then scoop up 30 g (1 oz) of cooled rice and compress into an oblong, shrimp-like nigiri shape, dipping your hands in the tezu again if needed.

Smear a very small dollop of wasabi (or none at all if it's not to your taste) onto the nigiri and top with a piece of eggplant unagi, watermelon sashimi or tomato lox. Fold a nori strip over the nigiri (if using) and carefully flip upside down, holding everything together. Dip your free hand back into the tezu and dampen the bottom of the nori to secure it under the nigiri. Use your ugliest piece of sashimi for the first attempt to get the hang of it. You may like to sacrifice this first attempt to the tasting pile to motivate you through the rest. Repeat until you've used up all the rice and unagi, sashimi or lox. Sprinkle with black sesame seeds (if using), and serve with the Japanese mayo, soy sauce, ginger and a heavily salted bowl of prepared edamame.

MAKES ABOUT 20

Ebi Fry on Cabbage Salad

Growing up in a popular Japanese tourist destination and then living as an exchange student by the sea in Minami-cho, Shikoku, ebi fry was by far the most interesting-looking dish I turned down as a young vegetarian. Here's my take on the fried shrimp dish with my favourite accompaniment to Japanese fried food – sweet cabbage salad – for all the flavours that remind me of Japan minus the dish travelling to you on a restaurant conveyor belt. BYO your own train set for a truly authentic home kaitenzushi experience and get on board the vegan sushi train!

INGREDIENTS

tin banana blossom	1 × 510 G (1 LB 2 OZ)
asparagus spears, woody ends trimmed	4
vegetable oil	FOR DEEP-FRYING
sea salt	TO SEASON

SHRIMP MARINADE

Kombu dashi (see page 118)	250 ML (1 CUP)
chicken-style stock cubes	2
minced garlic	1 TSP
lemon, juiced	1

EBI CRUMB

panko breadcrumbs	30 G (½ CUP)
plain (all-purpose) flour	(¼ CUP)
sea salt and black pepper	TO SEASON
vegan egg replacer, prepared as per packet instructions, or buttermilk	80 ML (⅓ CUP)

Rinse the banana blossom under cold running water, then squeeze out as much brine as possible. Place in a bowl.

Combine the shrimp marinade ingredients in a separate bowl, then add to the banana blossom. Cover and marinate in the fridge for 2–24 hours, tossing occasionally.

Remove the marinated banana blossom from the fridge, scoop out one-quarter and squeeze together. The goal is to wring out the majority of the liquid, but keep just a little moistness. Repeat with the remaining banana blossom, then lay the portions on a work surface and divide the mixtures into the larger outer leaves and the spine-like insides. Prepare a square of plastic wrap per ebi – you'll need four in total. Trim the asparagus spears to the approximate length of the blossom spines.

Working with one portion at a time, lay some of the leaves atop one square of plastic wrap to form a base and place an asparagus spear on top, allowing the asparagus tip to peek out the end to replicate a shrimp tail. Lay the blossom spines on top and finish with the remaining leaves to enclose the bodies. Tightly wrap up the ebi to compress the blossom inside the plastic wrap, ensuring the asparagus tip is still peeking out. Repeat for the remaining ebi. Place in the freezer to firm up for 2 hours.

Heat the oil in a large heavy-based saucepan over medium–high heat. Test if the oil is ready by inserting a wooden skewer or the handle of a wooden spoon in the oil; if it begins to bubble quickly then you're ready to go.

Remove the ebi from the freezer and unwrap.

HANA AGE TEMPURA

plain (all-purpose) flour	150 G (1 CUP)
cornflour (cornstarch)	60 G (½ CUP)
sea salt	PINCH
vegan mayonnaise	3 TBSP

JAPANESE TARTARE SAUCE

dill pickles (gherkins), finely chopped	115 G (4 OZ)
finely chopped dill fronds	1 TBSP
Japanese vegan mayo	125 G (½ CUP)
freshly squeezed lemon juice, or to taste	1 TSP
dijon or American mustard, or to taste	½ TSP
caper brine, or to taste	½ TSP

CABBAGE SALAD

granulated sugar	3 TBSP
rice wine vinegar	2 TBSP
light soy sauce	2 TSP
sesame oil	2 TSP
MSG	LARGE PINCH
sea salt	LARGE PINCH
cabbage, shredded, soaked in cold water for 30 minutes	250 G (9 OZ)

Hana age is called flower frying because of the way the batter blossoms in the oil before we attach it to the fried shrimp.

To make the ebi crumb, place the panko in a shallow bowl and the flour in a second bowl. Season both bowls with salt and pepper. Place the egg replacer or buttermilk in another shallow bowl. Set aside for a few minutes.

Coat each ebi in the flour mixture, then dip in the egg replacer. Double dip! Return to the flour mixture, followed by the egg replacer, then coat in the panko. Make sure each ebi is completely coated, using your hands to press the crumbs into the surface and gently shaking off any loose excess.

Fry the ebi in two batches for 2–3 minutes, until completely golden. Transfer to a large plate lined with paper towel to drain and immediately sprinkle with salt.

To make the hana age tempura, combine the flour, cornflour and salt in a bowl. In a separate wide bowl, combine 250 ml (1 cup) of cold water with the mayo (oil-based mayonnaise in the batter fizzles away as it fries, leading to an extra-crispy finish). Gently stir in the flour mixture, just until the flour is loosely mixed in.

As this next step can be tricky, I recommend frying only one ebi at a time. Spoon a tablespoon of the tempura batter directly into the hot oil and allow it to blossom into tempura blobs. Use a slotted spoon or chopsticks to crowd most of the blobs together in the oil to make a bed to lay your ebi fry on.

Working quickly with your free hand, dip the ebi fry into the batter (keeping the asparagus 'tail' batter free) and lay over the clumped blobs in the oil to attach them to the exterior. Use your spoon to gather up any remaining blobs and add them to the top of the ebi fry, pouring extra batter over the top as you want to secure crunchy tempura blobs all over. Cook the ebi fry for a further 3 minutes until fully golden. Transfer to a large plate lined with paper towel to drain and immediately sprinkle with salt. Repeat with the remaining ebi and tempura batter.

To make the Japanese tartare sauce, combine the ingredients in a small bowl.

To make the cabbage salad, place the sugar, vinegar, soy sauce, sesame oil, MSG and salt in a small saucepan over medium heat. Remove from the heat once the sugar has dissolved. Drain the cabbage and divide among four serving plates. Pour over the dressing and spoon a generous amount of tartare sauce to one side. Rest the ebi fry on top of the cabbage to demonstrate its majestic architectural stability and serve straight away.

SERVES 4

Som Tam

This isn't just a salad and it's no mere side dish: it's an experience. Like young green jackfruit, young green papaya is an artist's canvas with loads of texture to splash flavour onto and build a colourful dish. Crushing everything together breaks down the ingredients and allows the chilli, garlic and sauces to soak in. Serve next to the Lemongrass drumsticks (see page 89) for an explosion of flavour.

INGREDIENTS	
bird's eye chillies, roughly chopped (or less if you can't handle spice)	4–6
garlic cloves, peeled	3–4
shredded green papaya	300 G (3 CUPS)
green beans, trimmed	80 G (2¾ OZ)
granulated sugar	2 TSP
tamarind paste	1 TBSP
vegan fish sauce	2 TBSP
limes, juiced	2
Bonito flakes (see page 128)	40 G (½ CUP)
crushed peanuts	3 TBSP
small cherry tomatoes	8–10

Pound the chilli and garlic using a large mortar and pestle. Add the papaya and green beans, then pound and mix until everything is bruised and well combined.

Whisk the sugar, tamarind, fish sauce and lime juice in a jug and pour three-quarters of the dressing over the salad along with three-quarters of the bonito flakes and peanuts. Continue to bruise the salad, deliver some vague threats to make sure it's really beaten down and mix well again.

Add the tomatoes and bruise lightly to press them into the salad. Transfer to a serving bowl and add the remaining dressing if needed. Top with the leftover bonito flakes and peanuts. Serve fresh and cold.

SERVES 2

This fresh salad from Thailand
is magnificently SPICY!

Squid Ink Pasta

✳ ✳ ✳

Texture city! Seared mushroom scallops, slippery cannellini beans, soft tomatoes, chewy pasta and a tangy sauce. This seaside meal will hit you in the face with a bucket of ocean breeze and all the flavours you could wish for in a seafood-inspired dish.

INGREDIENTS

olive oil	2 TBSP
King oyster mushroom scallops (see page 126)	2 × QUANTITIES PLUS 2½ TBSP MARINADE
sea salt and black pepper	TO SEASON
medium–firm tofu	100 G (3½ OZ)
garlic cloves, peeled and crushed	6
capers, chopped	2 TSP
bird's eye chilli, finely chopped (optional)	1
plain (all-purpose) flour	1½ TBSP
white wine	100 ML (3½ FL OZ)
lemon, zested and juiced	1
cherry tomatoes, halved	100 G (3½ OZ)
tinned drained cannellini beans (aquafaba reserved)	150 G (5½ OZ)
chopped flat-leaf parsley	2 TBSP
Smoked shallot caviar (see page 124; optional)	1 × QUANTITY
smoked salt	TO SERVE

PASTA

fine semolina, plus extra for dusting	280 G (10 OZ)
plain (all-purpose) flour	1 TBSP
activated charcoal powder	3 G (¼ OZ)
aquafaba (from the tinned cannellini beans)	95 ML (3¼ FL OZ)
caper brine	60 ML (¼ CUP)
aonori seaweed flakes	1 TBSP
dark soy sauce	1 TSP

To make the pasta, combine the semolina, flour and charcoal in a mixing bowl and form a well in the centre. Mix together the remaining pasta ingredients and pour into the well, then fold into the flour. Knead the dough for about 10 minutes, until soft, then cover and rest for 1 hour.

Dust a work surface with semolina, then roll out the dough into a thin, long oval, guiding it into a neat shape as you go. Fold the ends into the middle, then repeat. Fold over in the opposite direction, then once more in the first direction to make a laminated dough parcel. Roll out one last time as thinly as possible, flipping and dusting in semolina, until the dough is almost translucent and completely even. If you are struggling to roll it out, let the dough rest for 5 minutes between flips.

Dust both sides of the dough with more semolina to stop the pasta sticking. Halve the dough, then fold each half in half lengthways, then fold twice in the other direction. Trim the edges, then cut the dough into thin even strips. Unfold the dough and shake the ribbons loose, then transfer to a bowl and toss through a little more semolina. When ready to serve, cook for 1½–2½ minutes in salted boiling water until cooked through. Drain.

Grease a large frying pan with oil and place over high heat. Pat the scallops dry with paper towel and generously season with salt and pepper. Sear for 2–3 minutes each side until browned and charred. Remove from the pan.

Blend the tofu and the reserved scallop marinade.

Add the olive oil to the pan, then fry the garlic, capers and chilli for 1 minute. Sprinkle in the flour and cook for 1 minute, then deglaze with the wine and pour in the tofu mixture. Cook until reduced by half, then add the lemon zest and juice. Add the tomato and cook for 30 seconds, then stir through the freshly cooked pasta, beans and parsley. Scatter over the scallops and caviar, then crack some pepper and smoked salt on top before serving hot.

SERVES 2-3

Fresh pasta takes less time to cook. You can substitute the handmade pasta with your favourite pasta and prepare as per packet instructions, then skip the caviar step for a meal that will take 30 minutes or less.

Serve with HOT CHIPS!

Battered Fish with Lemon Bitters Mayo

✳ ✳

Plant-based fish encased in a light and crispy beer batter! Alcohol-based batters cook in a short time so the soft ingredients that work well as vegan fish (tofu, hearts of palm, fresh or tinned banana blossom, or mushrooms) won't overcook. Better cook up some hot chips while you've got the oil heated, as the delightfully tangy lemon bitters mayo on the side needs to hitch a ride to your tastebuds.

INGREDIENTS

self-raising flour	150 G (1 CUP)
sea salt and black pepper	TO SEASON
beer or soda water (club soda)	250 ML (1 CUP)
ToFish, Hearts of palm, Lion's mane or Banana blossom fish fillets (see pages 122–123)	1 × QUANTITY
canola oil	FOR DEEP-FRYING
lemon wedges	TO SERVE
hot chips	TO SERVE

LEMON BITTERS MAYONNAISE

vegan mayonnaise	125 G (½ CUP)
olive oil	1 TBSP
freshly squeezed lemon juice	1 TBSP
angostura bitters	½ TSP
small garlic clove, peeled	1
sea salt	PINCH

Place the lemon bitters mayonnaise ingredients in a mixing jug and combine with a stick blender. Transfer to a dipping bowl and set aside until ready to use. This mayo pairs well with most dishes in this chapter.

Season the flour with salt and pepper, then transfer a few tablespoons to a bowl and set aside. Place the remaining seasoned flour and the beer or soda water in the freezer for 1 hour to get super cold ahead of frying.

Lightly coat the prepared fillets in the reserved seasoned flour to create a dry exterior.

Heat the oil in a large heavy-based saucepan over medium–high heat to 180°C (350°F). Test if the oil is ready by inserting a wooden skewer or the handle of a wooden spoon into the oil; if the oil begins to bubble quickly, then you're ready to go.

Now it's time to prepare your batter. Slowly pour and mix the cold beer or soda water into the seasoned flour, stopping intermittently to fully incorporate the liquid before adding more, until the batter just comes together. Use immediately while cold and still bubbly.

Dip each fillet in the batter, making sure it is completely coated. Slide two battered fillets into the hot oil in a fluid motion and cook for 3–4 minutes until golden and crisp. The less fluid your motion, the more misshapen blobs you'll get in your batter. They're just extra deliciousness, so don't be upset if this happens to you. Drain on a plate lined with paper towel and repeat with the remaining fillets. Salt, then serve with lemon wedges, hot chips and the lemon bitters mayonnaise.

SERVES 4

Baja Fish Tacos

In Mexican slang, *taco de ojo* translates to 'taco of the eye' (like savoury eye candy) and I think that's beautiful. These Baja-style fish tacos will surely be the *tacos de ojo* you'll want to take home at the end of the night, especially once you notice they're wearing that tequila batter (yes, TEQUILA BATTER) they know you like.

INGREDIENTS

canola oil	FOR DEEP-FRYING
ToFish, Hearts of palm, Lion's mane or Banana blossom fish fillets (see pages 122–123)	1 × QUANTITY
small corn tortillas	6
lime wedges	TO SERVE

TEQUILA BATTER

self-raising flour	110 G (¾ CUP)
baking powder	¼ TSP
sea salt and black pepper	TO SEASON
tequila	60 ML (¼ CUP)

RED CABBAGE SLAW

red cabbage, finely shredded	⅛ HEAD
red onion, thinly sliced	⅛
tinned drained sweetcorn kernels	40 G (1½ OZ)
lime, juiced	1

CHIPOTLE MAYONNAISE

vegan mayonnaise	185 G (¾ CUP)
chipotles in adobo sauce, finely chopped	2
adobo sauce	1 TBSP
freshly squeezed lime juice	1 TSP
garlic powder	½ TSP

To make the tequila batter, season the flour and baking powder with salt and pepper, mix well, then transfer a few tablespoons to a bowl and set aside. Place the remaining seasoned flour, 125 ml (½ cup) of water and the tequila in the freezer to get super cold ahead of frying.

Lightly coat the prepared fillets in the reserved seasoned flour to create a dry exterior.

To make the red cabbage slaw, combine the ingredients in a bowl and set aside.

To make the chipotle mayonnaise, combine the ingredients in a separate bowl and set aside.

Heat the oil in a large heavy-based saucepan over medium–high heat to 180°C (350°F). Test if the oil is ready by inserting a wooden skewer or the handle of a wooden spoon into the oil; if the oil begins to bubble quickly, then you're ready to go.

Meanwhile, let's finish the batter. Slowly pour the chilled water and tequila into the cold seasoned flour, stopping intermittently to fully incorporate the liquid before adding more, until the batter just comes together. Use immediately while cold for best results.

Dip each fillet into the batter, making sure it is completely coated. Slide two battered fillets into the hot oil in a fluid motion and cook for 3–4 minutes, until golden and crisp. Drain on a plate lined with paper towel and repeat with the remaining fillets. Salt immediately.

Unless you are a heathen, you'll want to warm the tortillas with a brief pan-fry or blast in the microwave, covered in a damp paper towel, for 30 seconds.

Heap ¼ cup of the slaw on top of each warm tortilla before smothering in the chipotle mayonnaise. Place a freshly fried fish-style fillet on top of each taco and serve while warm with lime wedges on the side.

MAKES 6

Fish Sticks

Simple fish sticks without any extra fuss, although the avocado wasabi sauce has just enough kick and creaminess to make the whole combo feel pretty darn gourmet anyway. Nobody will complain of vegans shaping their food like meat with this recipe shaped like more traditional vegan fare: sticks.

INGREDIENTS	
canola oil	FOR DEEP-FRYING
Tempeh fish fillets or ToFish fillets (see page 123), prepared as 2.5 cm x 10 cm (1 in x 4 in) sticks	300 G (10½ OZ)
sea salt	TO SEASON
AVOCADO WASABI SAUCE	
avocado	1
vegan aioli	2 TBSP
lemon juice	2 TSP
wasabi paste	1 TSP
FISH STICK CRUMB	
panko breadcrumbs	60 G (1 CUP)
nutritional yeast	2 TBSP
sea salt and black pepper	TO SEASON
SEASONED FLOUR	
plain (all-purpose) flour	75 G (½ CUP)
smoked paprika	1 TBSP
sea salt and black pepper	TO SEASON
BUTTERMILK	
soy milk	250 ML (1 CUP)
white vinegar or freshly squeezed lemon juice	1 TBSP

Preheat the oven to 180°C (350°F).

Mash the avocado wasabi sauce ingredients together in a bowl until smooth.

To make the crumb, spread the panko breadcrumbs over a baking tray and toast for 5 minutes or until they start to turn golden. Combine with the nutritional yeast in a wide bowl and season with salt and pepper.

To make the seasoned flour, place the flour and smoked paprika in a bowl. Season with salt and pepper.

Make a basic buttermilk by combining the soy milk, half the seasoned flour and the vinegar or lemon juice in a large bowl. Set aside for a few minutes to thicken.

Heat the oil in a large heavy-based saucepan over medium–high heat. Test if the oil is ready by inserting a wooden skewer or the handle of a wooden spoon into the oil; if the oil begins to bubble quickly, then you're ready to go.

Place the marinated tempeh or ToFish sticks in the seasoned flour and toss to coat. Dip in the buttermilk, then roll in the crumb mixture. Make sure each stick is completely coated by using your hands to press the crumbs into the surface and gently shaking off any loose excess. Be especially careful to not break the fingers during this process or else you'll be serving fish fingertips.

Fry the fingers in small batches in the hot oil for 2–3 minutes until completely golden. Transfer to a large plate lined with paper towel to drain. Immediately sprinkle with salt, then serve with the avocado wasabi sauce on the side for dipping.

MAKES 6

Pre-baking the breadcrumbs ensures the outside becomes crispy before the inside overcooks!

Dragon Roll

★ ★ ★

Dragon meat, thanks to the overhunting of real, live dragons, is these days scarce to find. Nobody quite agrees on what dragons used to taste like, so tough luck disputing my claim that they actually tasted a lot like banana blossom ebi fry, which happens to be on page 140. What a coincidence!

INGREDIENTS	
nori sheet, halved lengthways	1
cucumber, sliced into batons	50 G (1¾ OZ)
spring onions (scallions), green part only, sliced	2
ebi tempura (see page 141)	1 × QUANTITY
avocado, thinly sliced	1
SUSHI RICE	
sushi rice	450 G (2 CUPS)
medium-sized piece of kelp	1
sea salt	2 TSP
granulated sugar	2 TBSP
rice wine vinegar	60 ML (¼ CUP)
SPICY MAYO	
vegan Japanese mayo	3 TBSP
hot sauce	TO TASTE
TO SERVE	
vegan Japanese mayo	–
thick dark soy sauce	–
Smoked shallot caviar (see page 124; optional)	–
black and white sesame seeds	–
thin carrot ribbons	–

To prepare the sushi rice, cover the rice with cold water and swish it around to clean the grains. Drain the water and repeat twice more or until the water runs clear. Add the rice to a rice cooker or covered microwave-friendly container with 375 ml (1½ cups) of water. Place the kelp on top and cook for 13 minutes on High, then allow to sit for 15 minutes. Remove and discard the kelp.

Meanwhile, place the salt, sugar and vinegar in a saucepan and bring to the boil. Fluff the rice with a spatula, then fold in the seasoning while the rice is hot.

Make a tezu (see page 139). Cover a bamboo sushi rolling mat with plastic wrap. Lay half a nori sheet on the plastic wrap, shiny side down. Dip your hands in the tezu and evenly spread half the sushi rice across the sheet. Flip the nori over and lay half the cucumber, spring onion and ebi tempura along the side closest to you. You may need to squash the ebi tempura down to make the filling fit.

Using the bamboo mat, roll away from you, firmly pushing the mat over until the end comes into contact with the rest of the roll, securing the fillings inside. Rotate the sushi and use the mat to finish rolling the sushi into a smooth, complete roll then place on a chopping board. Gently press half the avocado slices, overlapping, along the length of the sushi roll. Cover in plastic wrap and roll again to smooth the avocado around the roll. Dip a knife into water and slice the roll into six pieces. Unwrap the rolls, then repeat with the remaining ingredients.

Mix the spicy mayo ingredients together in a bowl. Use the Japanese mayo, thick soy sauce and a little of the spicy mayo to draw dragon-like spikes or swirls on a serving dish that capture the spirit of a dragon. Position the sushi next to the swirls, then drizzle on some spicy mayo, spoon over the caviar (if using) and sprinkle with the sesame seeds. Add caviar eyes and carrot tendrils, then serve and enjoy.

SERVES 2-4

red HERRING

Hearty Fish Pot Pie

Hearty in every way, artichoke hearts and hearts of palm will fill your heart and belly with joy, as will the filling in this pie.

INGREDIENTS

dairy-free butter or olive oil	2 TBSP
large onion, finely diced	1
jar artichoke hearts in oil, drained and chopped	275 G (9½ OZ)
plain (all-purpose) flour	3 TBSP
soy milk, plus extra for brushing	185 ML (¾ CUP)
vegetable stock	250 ML (1 CUP)
dill pickles (gherkins), finely diced	80 G (2¾ OZ)
lemon, zested and juiced	1
shredded nori	3 TSP
dried dill	1½ TSP
dijon or American mustard	1 TSP
tins hearts of palm, drained and chopped	2 × 400 G (14 OZ)
sea salt and black pepper	TO SEASON
frozen dairy-free puff pastry sheets, just thawed	2–3

Preheat the oven to 200°C (400°F).

Heat the butter or olive oil in a frying pan over medium heat, add the onion and cook, stirring occasionally, for 10 minutes until soft and translucent. Add the artichoke hearts and cook for a further 5 minutes. Sprinkle in the flour and cook, stirring, for a further 2 minutes. Slowly stir in the soy milk, then stir in the vegetable stock to create a thick sauce. Add the pickles, lemon zest and juice, nori, dill and mustard. Remove from the heat and stir in the chopped hearts of palm. Season with salt and pepper as needed.

Spread a sheet of puff pastry over the base of a 25 cm (10 in) pie dish or similar, then trim the excess so the pastry snugly fits. Bake for 15 minutes or until the pastry is starting to puff up. Remove from the oven and press the pastry down, then pour in the prepared filling and use a spatula to spread it out evenly.

Trim another sheet of puff pastry to match the size of the dish and place over the top to create an upper crust. Brush the pastry with plant-based milk before placing in the oven to bake for up to 1 hour or until golden brown all over. Check occasionally and move the pie around in the oven, if needed, to crisp up evenly. Eat your heart out.

SERVES 4-6

GET THE LOOK

Using a 2 cm (¾ in) cookie cutter, cut out circles from the upper pie crust and gently overlap them on top of the filling to give the effect of fish scales. Genius!

Alternatively, use extra pastry to carve small fish or hearts to decorate the top of the pie.

Ceviche

Usually, the star ingredient in ceviche is freshly dead fish 'cooked' in an acid with onion and chilli. Wait, *real fish*? They're so old hat. What a relief to know that talented understudy hearts of palm are ready to go on instead. The supporting cast of passionfruit, lime, avocado, radish, cucumber, tomato and red onion will make sure this show-stopping salad gets rave reviews from all audiences.

INGREDIENTS	
red onion, thinly sliced	½
tin hearts of palm	1 × 400 G (14 OZ)
radishes	6
large lime, juiced	1
dulse flakes (optional)	2 TSP
olive oil	2 TSP
sea salt and black pepper	TO SEASON
garlic clove, finely chopped	1
small fresh jalapeno, thinly sliced	1
chopped coriander (cilantro) leaves	2 TBSP
small avocado, cut into large dice	1
tomato, diced	1
small cucumber, deseeded and diced	½
strained passionfruit pulp (from 2 passionfruit) or freshly squeezed lime juice	1 TBSP

Soak the red onion in a bowl of cold water for 10 minutes. Drain and set aside.

Scale the palm hearts by removing them from the tin. Mandoline or thinly slice the palm spears and radishes.

Combine the lime juice, dulse flakes (if using), olive oil, salt and pepper in a large bowl and toss in the palm spears and radishes. Set aside for 20 minutes.

Add the remaining ingredients, including the onion, to the bowl and toss well, sprinkling more salt generously over the top. Allow to sit in the fridge for 20 minutes, then serve not too long after so that liquid doesn't collect at the bottom of the ceviche.

SERVES 6

Paella

Paella is all about that saffron tinge to the rice, a little sofrito, meat or seafood and the star attraction: socarrat – the delicious crust that forms on the base of the pan – you *definitely* want this. The saffron milk cap mushrooms are meaty enough, but if they're out of season, use store-bought frozen konjaku shrimp instead.

INGREDIENTS

saffron milk cap mushrooms	200 G (7 OZ)
olive oil	1 TBSP
dry white wine	100 ML (3½ FL OZ)
green beans, trimmed	150 G (5½ OZ)
short-grain rice (preferably bomba)	300 G (10½ OZ)
sea salt	TO SEASON
flat-leaf parsley leaves	TO SERVE
lemon wedges	TO SERVE
Smoked aioli (see page 55)	TO SERVE

PAELLA STOCK

crushed fennel seeds	½ TSP
dried thyme	½ TSP
bay leaf	1
smoked paprika	2 TSP
vegan fish sauce	2 TBSP
saffron threads	¼ TSP
chicken-style stock	850 ML (28½ FL OZ)

SOFRITO

olive oil	75 ML (2½ FL OZ)
onion, finely chopped	1
dried chile de arbol	2
minced garlic	2 TSP
tomato paste (concentrated purée)	2 TBSP
granulated sugar	PINCH
roma (plum) tomatoes, roughly chopped	250 G (9 OZ)

Combine the stock ingredients in a mixing jug. Set aside.

Use a paring knife to carve the mushroom caps into half-circle strips in the shape of shrimp. Roughly chop the stems and remaining mushroom. Heat the oil in a heavy-based frying pan over medium–high heat, add the mushroom half circles and sauté for about 10 minutes, until crisp. Remove from the pan and set aside.

Place the sofrito ingredients in a food processor and process until chunky, then pour into a 35 cm (14 in) paella pan or large frying pan and cook over medium heat, stirring occasionally, for 15 minutes or until the liquid evaporates. Add 600 ml (20½ fl oz) of the stock, the white wine, green beans and chopped mushroom, then bring to the boil. Stir in the rice and cook for 2 minutes, then reduce the heat to low. Arrange the green beans so they are not clumped together and make sure the rice isn't concentrated in the centre. Avoid agitating the rice at all from this point. Cook for 10 minutes, rotating the pan over the flame to ensure everything cooks evenly.

Pour over an extra 250 ml (1 cup) of hot stock, then cook for a further 10–15 minutes, watching the rice carefully as time will be of the essence towards the end. Once there is very little steam leaving the rice, increase the heat for 2–3 minutes to develop a socarrat on the base of the paella. Pay close attention to avoid burning!

Remove from the heat, arrange the mushroom half circles over the paella, then cover with foil and allow to rest for 10 minutes. Scatter over a little salt and parsley, then eat straight out of the pan with the lemon wedges and more smoked aioli on the side than you think you're going to want (so double the batch, duh).

SERVES 4

Grilled Shrimp

Konjaku is great for folding in extra ingredients to achieve different textures. You can also fold in parts of a marinade (such as fresh herbs and garlic) so that the flavour is interspersed from the inside out.

INGREDIENTS	
cooked basmati rice	120 G (4 OZ)
roughly chopped flat-leaf parsley	3 TBSP
garlic cloves, finely chopped	4
sweet paprika	1 TBSP
unset Konjaku (page 38)	1 × QUANTITY
lemon wedges	TO SERVE
small loaf crusty bread, warmed	TO SERVE
SMOKY, SPICY MARINADE	
olive oil or melted dairy-free butter, plus extra for greasing	60 ML (¼ CUP)
long red chilli, finely chopped	1
smoked paprika	2 TSP
lemon, zested and juiced	1
smoked salt and black pepper	TO SEASON

Soak six bamboo skewers in cold water for 30 minutes.

Mash the cooked rice with the parsley, garlic and paprika. Fold into the unset konjaku, making sure the rice mixture is well dispersed, then set aside for 15 minutes.

Using lightly dampened hands, grab 25 g (1 oz) of the mixture at a time and shape into rough shrimp shapes. (Forming a replica digestive tract is only necessary if you're going for absolute authenticity.)

Lay the shrimp on a plate lined with baking paper and microwave on High for 1 minute. Alternatively, for a softer texture with a more defined shape, place the shrimp in boiling water for 15 minutes.

Using a mortar and pestle, mash together the marinade ingredients. Place the prepared shrimp in a bowl and pour over the marinade. Allow to sit for 1 hour, then thread the shrimp onto the prepared skewers.

Heat a barbecue grill or chargrill pan to medium and season with oil or melted butter. Add the shrimp skewers and grill, turning occasionally, for 5–6 minutes. Brush some extra fresh marinade over the shrimp and serve with lemon wedges and warm crusty bread.

SERVES 3-4

Once set, these shrimp can be used in other recipes, such as the paella on page 160 or fried with your favourite spices and served with a dipping sauce.

GET THE LOOK

Fill shrimp-shaped moulds with the prepared mixture and freeze overnight. Pop the shrimp out of the moulds and microwave on High for 1 minute (or up to 2 minutes for smaller, denser shrimp) to defrost and achieve no-fuss realistic-looking results.

Flaky Baked Fish

Konjaku for structure, tofu for softness and rice paper for skin – this simple combination of ingredients makes an incredible substitute for baked fish. Quickly prepared accordion-style potatoes (hasselback potatoes gone wild!) take the same amount of time to bake as the fish and the prep for everything can be done in less than 10 minutes if you've already got a batch of fresh konjaku on the go.

INGREDIENTS

firm tofu	180 G (6½ OZ)
vegan XO sauce	60 ML (¼ CUP)
Unset konjaku (see page 38)	½ × QUANTITY
lemon, juiced, plus lemon wedges	1
rice paper sheets	4
sea salt and black pepper	TO SEASON
large potatoes	2
olive oil	FOR BASTING
tartare sauce (see page 284)	TO SERVE

Pulse the tofu and half the XO sauce in a food processor until finely crumbled. Stir through the unset konjaku. Form into four fish-shaped fillets and transfer to a sheet of baking paper. Microwave on High for 1½–2 minutes, flipping halfway, until firm. Allow to cool.

Preheat the oven to 225°C (435°F). Line a baking tray with baking paper. Soak four bamboo skewers in water for 20 minutes.

Spread half the remaining XO sauce over the fillets. Squeeze a little of the lemon juice over the rice paper sheets and use your hands to smear it over the sheets to soften. Place a fish fillet towards one end of the sheet and fold over to enclose. Trim the excess rice paper at one end and fold the other end into a tail. Repeat with the remaining fillets and rice paper sheets.

Squeeze over the remaining lemon juice, brush with the remaining XO sauce and season. Place on the prepared tray.

To make the accordion potatoes, slice off the sides of each potato to make a squared-off rectangle. Cut the rectangles in half lengthways, then place two chopsticks underneath each end of one potato and use a knife to slice through the potato until it hits the chopstick. Flip the potato over and make another series of cuts, but this time diagonally. Thread the potato onto one of the skewers (this can be difficult and will need force). Use your fingertips to gently spread the potato out on the skewer. Baste with some olive oil and crack over some salt and pepper, then repeat with the remaining potato.

Add the potatoes to the baking tray and bake everything for 35 minutes, flipping halfway through. Serve while it's all nice and hot with tartare sauce and lemon wedges on the side.

SERVES 4

Oysters Kilpatrick

Anything can be made vegan, even the things that nobody ever asked for, so here are slimy and chewy oysters. I'm told oysters taste a bit like gelatinous seawater, but purists will be disappointed as I've chosen to make this variant taste delicious instead.

INGREDIENTS

king oyster mushroom caps or fresh shiitake mushrooms	8
granulated sugar	1 TBSP
dairy-free butter	160 G (5½ OZ)
ume vinegar	1 TBSP
black pepper	TO SEASON
fresh Basic konjaku (see page 38), not boiled or microwaved	½ × QUANTITY
vegan bacon, diced	100 G (3½ OZ)
vegan worcestershire sauce	1 TBSP
dry white wine	2 TBSP
baby cos (little gem/ romaine) lettuce hearts (optional)	4

TO SERVE

hot sauce	–
lemon wedges	–
crusty bread	–

Place the mushrooms in a small saucepan with a splash of water. Bring the water to a simmer and cook, replenishing the water when it runs dry, for 10 minutes or until the liquid from the mushrooms has evaporated. Squish down with a cup to compress the mushrooms.

Mix together the sugar, 2 tbsp of the butter, the vinegar and pepper, then pour the mixture over the mushrooms and cook for 5 more minutes until brown and fragrant. Allow to cool.

Bring a saucepan of water to the boil. Use wet hands to grab a handful of unset konjaku and mould around a mushroom to fully enclose. Remove any excess konjaku so that only a thin layer coats the entire mushroom without making it too large. Repeat with the remaining mushroom and konjaku to make eight oysters. If you don't recoil at how disgusting they look, you've done it wrong. Lower them into the boiling water and cook for 20 minutes to set. Carefully fish out the oysters with a slotted spoon and drain in a colander.

Place the vegan bacon, worcestershire sauce and remaining butter in a small saucepan over low heat and allow to bubble away for 5 minutes. Deglaze with the white wine, then remove from the heat.

Preheat the oven grill (broiler) to high.

If using the lettuce, halve the baby cos lengthways and tear out the centre to create a cavity for each oyster. Place the lettuce shells in serving bowls. Alternatively, for truly authentic presentation, fill a shallow bowl with rock salt.

Place the oysters in a shallow dish and pour over the bacon mixture. Grill (broil) for 5 minutes.

Spoon an oyster into each lettuce shell or carefully place on the rock salt, then spoon over the bacon mixture. Serve with hot sauce, lemon wedges and crusty bread.

MAKES 8

SAVING

SOMEONE'S

BACON

PORK-STYLE STOCK • WATERMELON ROAST • WATERMELON STEAKS • PREPARING SEITAN AS HAM • BACON • PULLED PORK • KATSUDON • SWEET 'N' SOUR PORK • BACON-COATED BRUSSELS SPROUTS • TAQUITOS • KOREAN BARBECUE RIBS • BANANA PEEL CHAR SIU BAO • SWEET 'N' SPICY CORN RIBS • QUICHE LORRAINE • CARBONARA • SHIITAKE PEPPERONI PIZZA • CHICARRONES • PORK BELLY • SMOKED WATERMELON ROAST • SMOKED HAM ROAST

PORK BASES

ZUCCHINI

CARROTS

WATERMELON

EGGPLANT

SWEETCORN

MUSHROOMS

BANANA PEEL

TEMPEH

JACKFRUIT

SEITAN

COCONUT

Get that pork off your fork because culinary talent is what's for dinner. Let's go the whole hog and take the time to brine, smoke and sear our way to pink plant-based perfection.

The flavour of plant-based pork lies somewhere between beef and chicken, with more sweetness and a little smoke. Bacon, though, is a whole other story. Intensely rich, salty, umami, fatty and a little sourness are going to improve just about anything, so why not baconify absolutely *everything* (see page 178)?

Gently bathe a ball of dough like a newborn baby, then rear it yourself into a full-grown seitanic pig. You'll shed a proud tear of joy when your seitan has its own offspring because spawn of seitan is your key to the fattiness of ham. The range of recipes in this chapter is positively macabre: there's fat, bones, skin and flesh. I'm not telling porkies when I say 'vegan butcher'.

There are so many ways to smoke your own vegan meats, as explored on page 50. Investing in a smoker (or even a cheap roll of foil and some wood chips) is your excuse to sit outside for a whole carefree afternoon. It's this chapter's gift to your mental health, and that smoke and time will turn your ingredients into the most convincing fake meat of your life. They're the smoke and mirrors that take an outrageous starting point, such as a whole damn watermelon, to a proper centrepiece that'll read more as ham and less as a total sham.

FLAVOURS TO USE FOR PORK OR BACON:

APPLES: JUICE AND FRUIT • BROWN SUGAR • CORIANDER SEEDS • FENNEL SEEDS • GARLIC • GINGER: FRESH AND GROUND • LIQUID SMOKE • ONION • RED MISO PASTE • SAGE • STAR ANISE • TORULA YEAST

BASES:

BANANA PEEL • CARROTS • COCONUT • EGGPLANT (AUBERGINE) • JACKFRUIT • KING OYSTER MUSHROOMS • RICE PAPER • SEITAN • SPAWN OF SEITAN • TEMPEH • TOFU • TVP WATERMELON • ZUCCHINI (COURGETTE)

PORK-STYLE STOCK

MAKES 1.5 LITRES (51 FL OZ)

Commercial pork- and ham-style stocks are slowly becoming more available, and they are my top recommendation to use due to the commercial flavours they can add to a dish. If they aren't available near you, try this as a base for simmering seitan or simply simmer for an hour and strain to use as the flavouring liquid in recipes. You may also choose to add reserved zero-waste ingredients for this stock from other recipes.

INGREDIENTS	
beef-style stock	1 LITRE (34 FL OZ)
chicken-style stock	500 ML (2 CUPS)
roughly chopped mushrooms, such as brown, cup or rehydrated dried shiitake	100 G (3½ OZ)
large onion, halved	1
garlic bulb, halved horizontally	½
red miso paste	2 TBSP
soy sauce	60 ML (¼ CUP)
smoked paprika	1 TBSP
liquid smoke	2 TSP

① Combine the stocks, mushroom, onion and garlic in a stockpot and simmer over low heat for 2 hours. Alternatively, cook in a slow cooker for 4 hours.

② Strain into a saucepan or container, pressing out as much liquid solids as you can (discard the pulp). Stir in the miso, soy sauce, paprika and liquid smoke and use in recipes or store in the fridge until needed.

WATERMELON ROAST

★ ★ ★

MAKES I SMALL ROAST

This is not a prank! Watermelon can be transformed into a variety of textures depending on the preparation method. Steaming watermelon (as in Watermelon sashimi on page 134) leads to a soft, fish-like bite; whereas brining, then grilling (broiling), smoking or baking creates a lovely chew that is not reminiscent of a piece of fruit. There can be a residual sweetness to the meat, but adding loads of complementary flavours transforms the watermelon into a stellar competitor to animal analogues.

INGREDIENTS	
melonball or small seedless watermelon	ABOUT 1.5 KG (3 LB 5 OZ)
WATERMELON BRINE	
sea salt	65 G (½ CUP)
pickling spice	35 G (¼ CUP)
chopped rosemary leaves	2 TBSP
garlic bulb, halved horizontally	1
liquid smoke	2 TSP
mushroom soy sauce	2 TBSP

① Cut the rind from the melonball or watermelon, leaving as much flesh intact as possible.

② Have a tall, sealable container that can hold the watermelon at the ready - i.e., a bucket. Add all the brine ingredients and 1.5-2 litres (51-68 fl oz) of water. If you have a marinade injector (recommended), fill with brine and inject into multiple parts of the watermelon until it is seeping with brine. Add the watermelon to the container and make sure the watermelon is covered in liquid.

③ Leave for 2-5 days at the back of your fridge before proceeding to add more flavour, and then roast or smoke as per the Smoked watermelon roast on page 208.

WATERMELON STEAKS

MAKES ABOUT 4 STEAKS

Start here to make the Katsudon on page 184, or for a lovely summer salad toss together dairy-free feta, rocket (arugula), red onion, balsamic vinegar and crushed walnuts, then slice the grilled watermelon steaks and serve on top.

INGREDIENTS

seedless watermelon	450 G (1 LB)
vegetable oil	FOR RUBBING

WATERMELON MARINADE

pork-style stock	250 ML (1 CUP)
liquid aminos	2 TBSP
torula yeast	1 TBSP
red miso paste	2 TSP
onion powder	1 TSP
smoked paprika	½ TSP
liquid smoke	¼ TSP

① Brutally slaughter the watermelon with a knife, remove the rind and cut the flesh into large steak-shaped slabs about 2.5 cm (1 in) thick and 10 cm (4 in) wide. Use paper towel to soak up the surface liquid, or sit in a colander to wick away extra moisture, then, using a toothpick, stab all over the watermelon steaks.

② Combine all the marinade ingredients in a bowl and mix well. Transfer to a large container, add the watermelon steaks, cover and marinate in the fridge for 1–12 hours.

③ Preheat the oven to 180°C (350°F). Line a baking tray with baking paper.

④ Remove the watermelon steaks from the marinade. Reserve the marinade. Rub 2 teaspoons of oil over each steak and place on the prepared tray. Roast for 45 minutes, flipping occasionally and blotting away the excess liquid with paper towel.

⑤ Remove and rest on paper towel until cool to the touch. Grill or crumb to cook further before serving. The steaks are now ready to be used in Katsudon (see page 184).

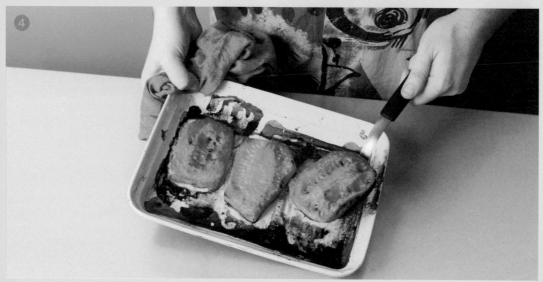

PREPARING SEITAN AS HAM

✦ ✦ ✦

SERVES 6-8

Turn your fatty washed seitan into a sham roast! In this method, we layer the separate strands of washed, prepared gluten with spawn of seitan to create a freaky meat-like texture inside. Vegan pork-style stock powder is becoming more available in shops and online, but if you can't find any, simply subsititute 1½ tablespoons beef-style stock plus 1 tablespoon chicken-style stock.

INGREDIENTS	
garlic powder	1 TBSP
onion powder	1 TBSP
smoked paprika	2 TBSP
pork-style stock powder	2 TBSP
Fatty washed seitan (see page 22)	1 × QUANTITY
FAT	
dairy-free butter	2 TBSP
red miso paste	1 TBSP
Spawn of seitan (see page 26)	60 ML (¼ CUP)
soft brown sugar	1 TBSP
ground white pepper	½ TSP
xanthan gum	¼ TSP

① Mix together the garlic powder, onion powder, paprika and stock powder in a bowl. Place the seitan and spice mixture in a stand mixer fitted with a dough hook and mix on medium spped until the ingredients are completely dispersed. Alternatively, thoroughly knead the spice mixture into the seitan by hand.

② Separate the seitan into at least ten pieces. Stretch out each piece, suspend a wooden spoon over a stockpot and hang the threads over the spoon handle. (This allows the gluten to rest and the threads to droop further.)

③ Combine the fat ingredients in a bowl. Select another large bowl that will approximately match the volume of the seitan. Tie each of the seitan strands together to make one long piece of gluten, then brush the entire surface with the fat mixture.

④ Coil and knot everything together into one large lump inside the bowl.

⑤ Microwave the roast on High in three 1-minute bursts, then remove and wrap in several layers of foil once cooled.

⑥ Place a steaming rack in a pressure cooker, add the 'ham' and cook at high pressure for 1 hour.

⑦ Remove the ham and allow to cool on a wire rack for 30 minutes. Unwrap, transfer to a container and place in the fridge, exposed, for an hour, to form a skin. Flip over, pour out the liquid that has gathered and allow the exposed part to form a skin. The ham is now ready to be used to make the Smoked ham roast on page 210.

BACON

Danish couple Karina and Kasper (the veganer.nu blog) originated the insane rice-paper bacon concept as an accessible DIY bacon alternative in response to the high volumes of bacon produced in Denmark. To get perfect strips and to avoid breaking the paper when cutting, they recommend you 'leave your bags of rice paper open in the fridge 24 hours. Alternatively, quickly soak and place the rice paper on a wooden cutting board then cut them with a pizza cutter when they are soft enough.' Bacon seems to be the go-to reason people just can't possibly be vegan, so here's how to make it out of rice paper and just about anything else but pigs.

INGREDIENTS

BACON MARINADE

nutritional yeast	3 TBSP
mushroom soy sauce or dark soy sauce	2 TBSP
vegetable oil	1 TBSP
vegan worcestershire sauce	1 TBSP
maple syrup	1 TBSP
liquid smoke	1 TSP
smoked or hot paprika	½ TSP
onion powder	½ TSP
garlic powder	½ TSP
vegan-friendly red food colouring for drama (optional)	A FEW DROPS

Combine the bacon marinade ingredients in a bowl and set aside.

CARROT BACON (CRUNCHY)

Peel carrots, then square them off with a knife to make a rectangle. Quarter lengthways to make bacon strips and microwave on High for 1½ minutes. Place in a container, pour over marinade, then cover and marinate in the fridge overnight. Bake at 150°C (300°F) for 45–60 minutes.

ZUCCHINI BACON (CHEWY)

Slice the top, bottom and skin off one side of a zucchini (courgette), then run a vegetable peeler down the exposed side to create thick strips. Brush the marinade (about 60 ml/¼ cup per zucchini) over both sides of each strip. Bake at 160°C (320°F) for 30 minutes or until desired chewyness.

EGGPLANT BACON (CHEWY)

Slice an eggplant (aubergine) into slabs no thicker than 1.5 cm (½ in), then into 4 cm (1½ in) wide strips. Brush the marinade over both sides of each strip. Bake at 130°C (250°F) for 45 minutes.

DAIKON BACON (CRISPY)

Slice off the top and bottom of a
daikon, then peel. Run a vegetable
peeler down one side to create thick
strips. Salt the daikon strips
and sit for 30 minutes. Wipe away
the moisture and salt with paper
towel. Brush the marinade (about
60 ml/¼ cup per daikon) over both
sides of each strip. Bake at 160°C
(320°F) for 30 minutes or until
desired crispiness.

RICE PAPER BACON (CRISPY)

Wet a sheet of rice paper under
running water, then wipe away the
excess water with your hand. Spread
some marinade over a plate, lay the
dampened rice paper on top and coat
the exposed side with more marinade.
Cut into 4-5 strips with scissors
and deep-fry in hot canola oil for
1-2 minutes per side until crisp.

RICE PAPER BACON (CHEWY)

Follow the crispy rice-paper
instructions using 2-3 sheets of rice
paper wet together before marinating
and frying.

YUBA BACON (CRISPY)

Use fresh yuba for this recipe.
Cut one sheet into 4-5 strips,
brush with the marinade and deep-fry
in hot canola oil for 3-4 minutes
until crisp.

TEMPEH BACON (CHEWY)

Slice tempeh into thin strips
and marinate in the bacon marinade
for 1 hour. Bake at 200°C (400°F)
for 20 minutes or deep-fry for
10 minutes in hot canola oil.

SEITAN BACON (CHEWY)

Prepare mostly washed seitan dough
(see page 24) and tear into chunks.
Allow the gluten to rest, then roll
out into flat strips. Microwave on
High for 1 minute to create a bubbled
fat texture, then cover and marinate
in the fridge overnight. Deep-fry
for 5 minutes in hot canola oil.

KING OYSTER MUSHROOM BACON (CHEWY)

Slice off the cap and end of the
mushroom, then run a vegetable peeler
or a knife down the mushroom stalk to
make six strips. Prepare the marinade
without the vegetable oil, then add
the strips and marinate for 1 hour.
Bake at 160°C (320°F) for 40 minutes
or deep-fry for 5-7 minutes in hot
canola oil.

COCONUT BACON (CRISPY)

Stir 60 ml (¼ cup) of the marinade
into 55 g (1 cup) of coconut flakes.
Spread out on a lined baking tray
and bake at 170°C (340°F) for
10 minutes. Use as crispy bacon
to top salads, such as the Caesar
salad on page 95, baked potatoes
or eat as a ready-made snack.

SPAWN OF SEITAN BACON (CRISPY)

Use the marinade here and follow the
instructions on page 227 to achieve
perfectly marbled streaky bacon.

Use up the last of your veg to make a bacon degustation for breakfast and you'll be set for life, or at least till lunch.

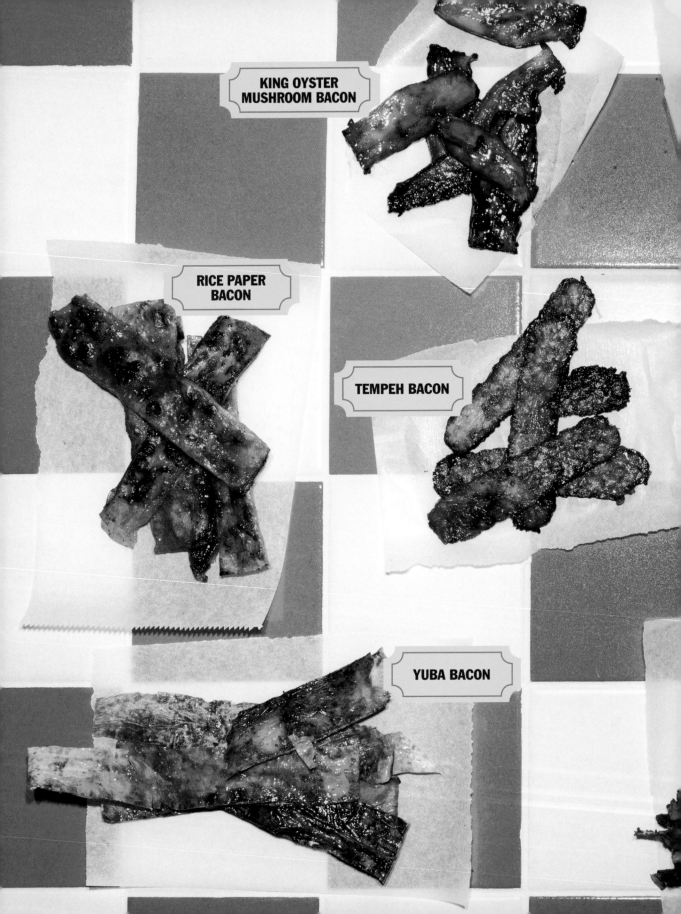

KING OYSTER
MUSHROOM BACON

RICE PAPER
BACON

TEMPEH BACON

YUBA BACON

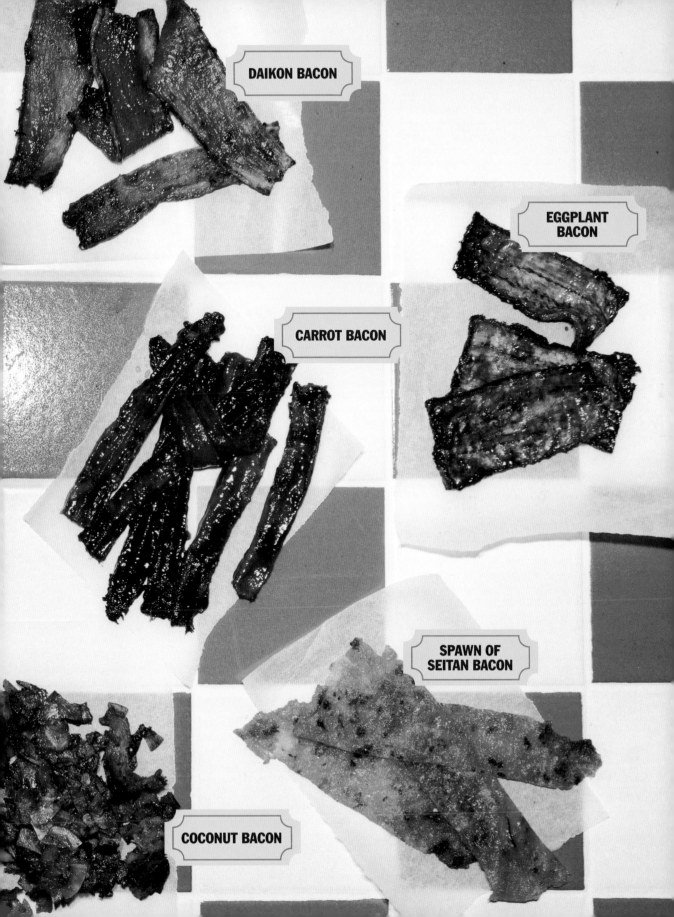

DAIKON BACON

EGGPLANT
BACON

CARROT BACON

SPAWN OF
SEITAN BACON

COCONUT BACON

PULLED PORK

MAKES I x QUANTITY

From the florets leftover after preparing a baby banana blossom, to the discarded peels of a fully grown banana, at all stages of life, banana scraps can be turned into shredded barbecue meat. Either way you choose, this shit is BANANAS!

INGREDIENTS

BANANA BLOSSOM

banana blossom florets, prepared (see page 120)	180 G (6½ OZ)
smoked paprika	2 TSP
ground cumin	1 TSP
onion powder	½ TSP
garlic powder	½ TSP
black pepper	TO SEASON
vegetable oil	1 TBSP
smoky barbecue sauce	90 ML (3 FL OZ)

BANANA PEEL

banana peels from barely ripe, large bananas	190 G (6½ OZ)
sesame oil	1 TBSP
minced garlic	2 TSP
king oyster mushrooms	190 G (6½ OZ)
vegetable oil	1 TBSP
onion, sliced	1

CHAR SIU SAUCE

hoisin sauce	60 ML (¼ CUP)
cornflour (cornstarch)	2 TBSP
rice malt syrup	2 TBSP
soy sauce	2 TBSP
shaoxing rice wine	1 TBSP
rice wine vinegar	1 TBSP
grated ginger	1 TSP
Chinese five spice powder	¾ TSP
vegan-friendly red food colouring	¼ TSP
ground white pepper	SMALL PINCH

BANANA BLOSSOM FLORET PULLED PORK

① Remove the banana blossom florets from the acidulated water and lay on paper towel to blot moisture.

② In a large bowl, sprinkle the spices over the florets.

③ Heat the oil in a frying pan over medium heat, then add the florets. Fry for 10 minutes, allowing the blossoms to sizzle and crisp up. Pour over the barbecue sauce, reduce the heat to low and mix. Cook for 2 minutes, stirring to coat the blossoms and thicken the sauce.

④ Remove from the heat and use in Pulled-pork burgers (see page 288).

Char siu sauce can be used as a glaze for other recipes in this pork chapter — try it on Sweet 'n' spicy corn ribs (see page 197)!

BANANA PEEL PULLED PORK

① Peel the bananas and reserve the banana flesh for another recipe. Slice off the banana skin ends, then use a spoon to scrape out the remaining flesh.

② Thoroughly wash the banana skins and pat dry with paper towel. Place the skins on a chopping board and use a fork to shred the skin.

③ Place in a bowl, drizzle with the sesame oil and massage in the garlic.

④ Slice off the king oyster mushrooms caps and shred the stalks. Save the caps for another recipe.

⑤ Combine the char siu sauce ingredients in a bowl, microwave for 30 seconds, then whisk to combine. Alternatively, whisk in a small saucepan over low heat until thickened.

⑥ Heat the vegetable oil in a wok over medium heat. Add the onion and shredded mushroom and toss for 5 minutes to brown. Mix through the banana peel mixture. Cook for 5 minutes.

⑦ Pour in the char siu sauce. Allow to thicken for another 5 minutes, tossing frequently until the banana peel changes appearance. Remove from the heat and allow to cool, then use in Banana peel char siu bao (see page 194) or on Pulled-pork burgers (see page 288).

SAVING *someone's* BACON

Katsudon

Katsudon (from tonkatsu 'pork cutlet' and donburi 'rice bowl') is not just a pork schnitzel served on rice. It usually comes with a rich stock to which egg is added to pack in extra flavour. This recipe doesn't compromise on recreating all of these elements out of plants. In the end, the vibrant colour of watermelon might be the only thing to give it away when hidden in this abundance of umami, and if you do pick up any sweetness it ends up tasting right at home.

INGREDIENTS

plain (all-purpose) flour	50 G (1/3 CUP)
black pepper	1 TSP
panko breadcrumbs	120 G (1 CUP)
Watermelon steaks, plus watermelon marinade (see page 174)	1 × QUANTITY PLUS 125 ML (1/2 CUP)
vegetable oil	2–3 TBSP
onion, thinly sliced	1
rehydrated dried shiitake mushrooms, sliced	50 G (1¾ OZ)
soy sauce	1 TBSP
mirin	1 TBSP
Awase dashi (see page 118)	250 ML (1 CUP)
chickpea flour (besan)	55 G (1/2 CUP)
nutritional yeast	2 TBSP
steamed rice	370 G (2 CUPS)
kala namak (Indian black salt) or use sea salt	1 TSP
spring onion (scallion), finely chopped	1

KATSU SAUCE

tomato ketchup	170 ML (2/3 CUP)
vegan worcestershire sauce	90 ML (3 FL OZ)
malt vinegar	2 TBSP
granulated sugar	2 TSP
mustard powder	2 TSP
garlic powder	1 TSP
onion powder	1 TSP

Combine the katsu sauce ingredients in a small bowl.

Place the plain flour and pepper in a shallow bowl and the breadcrumbs in another shallow bowl. Coat the watermelon steaks in the seasoned flour, then place on a plate. Whisk the watermelon marinade into the flour to make a batter, then dip in the steaks. Press the steaks into the breadcrumbs, using your fingers to firmly adhere the crumbs. Gently shake off any excess.

Heat a splash of the vegetable oil in a large heavy-based frying pan over medium heat. Add the steaks to the hot oil, increase the heat to high and fry for about 3 minutes each side until cooked through. Replenish the oil as you flip so that the crumbs turn golden on each side (this is not the moment to attempt an oil-free lifestyle). Transfer the steaks to paper towel and slice into thick strips.

Add the onion and shiitake to the pan and sauté for 3 minutes. Stir in the soy sauce, mirin and 125 ml (½ cup) of the dashi and allow to bubble away for a further 5 minutes.

Blend the rest of the dashi with the chickpea flour and nutritional yeast. Whisk the dashi mixture through the onion and shiitake, then reduce the heat to low. Place the watermelon katsu strips on top, cover the pan and cook for 5 minutes.

Scoop the steamed rice into serving bowls. Use a spatula to halve the katsu mixture in the pan and slide each portion into the bowls. Drizzle over the katsu sauce, sprinkle over the kala namak and spring onion, say 'itadakimasu!' and get to eating.

SERVES 2

Sweet 'n' Sour Pork

Full of variety, it's great to reserve half of this dish for packed lunches you can be sure your loved ones – when they realise they're having last night's leftovers – won't toss straight into the bin, again.

INGREDIENTS

pork-style stock	750 ML (3 CUPS)
TVP slices	200 G (7 OZ)
vegetable oil	FOR FRYING
cornflour (cornstarch)	140 G (5 OZ)
salt and black pepper	TO SEASON
mixed capsicums (bell peppers)	250 G (9 OZ)
sesame oil	2 TSP
tin pineapple pieces in juice, undrained	400 G (14 OZ)

SWEET 'N' SOUR SAUCE

apricot jam	105 G (⅓ CUP)
Chinese rice vinegar	60 ML (¼ CUP)
tomato ketchup	3 TBSP
soft brown sugar	115 G (½ CUP FIRMLY PACKED)
soy sauce	1 TBSP
minced garlic	1 TSP
Chinese five spice powder	½ TSP
vegan-friendly red food colouring (optional)	2-3 DROPS

LO MEIN

dried noodles	250 G (9 OZ)
sesame oil	2 TSP
baby bok choy (pak choy), sliced	190 G (6 ½ OZ)
snow peas (mange tout)	100 G (3½ OZ)
spring onions (scallions), finely sliced	2
vegan oyster sauce	60 ML (¼ CUP)
vegan fish sauce	1 TBSP
coriander (cilantro) leaves	TO SERVE

Bring the pork stock to a rapid boil in a saucepan over high heat. Add the TVP slices and boil for 10 minutes or until the pieces are soft and bend to your bidding. Allow to cool.

Heat 1 cm (½ in) of vegetable oil in a large heavy-based saucepan over medium heat.

Meanwhile, place 125 g (1 cup) of the cornflour in a zip-lock bag and season with salt and pepper. Fish the TVP slices out of the stock and halve into bite-sized pieces. Reserve 60 ml (¼ cup) of stock. Place the TVP in the bag, seal, then toss in the seasoned cornflour.

Test if the oil is ready by inserting a wooden skewer or the handle of a wooden spoon into the hot oil; if it begins to bubble quickly, then you're ready to go. Add the coated TVP and fry for 10 minutes or until golden brown. Remove from the pan.

Meanwhile, mix the sweet and sour sauce ingredients in a jug and set aside.

Roughly chop the capsicums, then heat the sesame oil in a wok over medium–high heat, add the capsicum and cook for 2 minutes. Move the capsicum to one side, tip in the sauce and cook for another minute, stirring until it comes to the boil. Add in the pineapple (with juice!) and TVP and cook, stirring, for another 2 minutes. Whisk the remaining cornflour with the reserved cooled stock and stir into the wok. Remove from the heat – the sauce will thicken further as it cools.

To make the lo mein, cook the noodles as per the packet instructions or via the intuition you gain from years of eating nothing but cheap packet ramen. Drain. Heat the sesame oil in another wok and add the bok choy and snow peas and cook for 2 minutes. Add the spring onion, oyster sauce and fish sauce, cook for 30 seconds, then toss through the noodles.

Divide the lo mein among bowls and scatter with a few coriander leaves. Serve with loads of sweet and sour pork.

SERVES 4-6

Taquitos

Picture this: it's just you alone with a hot and creamy jalapeno, corn and cheese dip. Oh, what's this? Crunchy carnitas taquitos just pulled up outside. They're both pretty hot. What if? Haha just kidding . . . unless? Easy to make, this recipe has two components that come out of the oven at the same time for a single moment in time where everything is perfect. It's super hot and nobody has to get hurt.

INGREDIENTS	
corn tortillas	18 SMALL
tin refried beans	1 × 400 G (14 OZ)
JALAPENO CHEESE DIP	
fresh jalapenos	2
cashews, soaked in hot water for 1 hour	155 G (1 CUP)
soy milk	125 ML (½ CUP)
olive oil	1 TBSP
plain (all-purpose) flour	1 TBSP
grated dairy-free cheese	100 G (1 CUP)
hot sauce (optional)	DASH
sweetcorn kernels	100 G (½ CUP)
spring onion (scallion), finely chopped	1
JACKFRUIT CARNITAS	
tins jackfruit, prepared (see steps 1–3 on page 68)	2 × 565 G (1 LB 4 OZ)
chipotle powder	1 TSP
ground cumin	1 TSP
dried oregano	1 TSP
smoked paprika	½ TSP
minced garlic	2 TSP
vegetable oil	1½ TBSP
red onion, thinly sliced	1
fresh jalapeno, thinly sliced	1
Maggi seasoning	2 TBSP
soft brown sugar	2 TSP
beer	125 ML (½ CUP)
lime juice	2 TBSP

To make the jalapeno cheese dip, preheat an oven grill (broiler) to high. Place the jalapenos under the grill for 5 minutes, turning regularly, until beginning to char.

Drain the cashews, then place in a blender with the soy milk and jalapenos and blend until creamy.

Heat the oil in a saucepan over medium heat, whisk in the flour and cook for 1–2 minutes. Pour in the blended cashew cream, then stir in the cheese and switch off the heat. Taste, stir through the hot sauce if needed, then add the corn and spring onion. Transfer to a baking dish.

Preheat the oven to 200°C (400°F). Line a baking tray with baking paper.

To make the jackfruit carnitas, coat the jackfruit in the spices and garlic and set aside. Place the oil in a large saucepan over medium–high heat. Add the onion and jalapeno and fry for 5–10 minutes, until beginning to brown. Add the jackfruit and cook for 3–5 minutes, allowing it to smoke and slightly char. Combine the Maggi seasoning, sugar and beer in a jug, then add to the pan and stir to deglaze. Cook for 3 minutes or until the jackfruit begins to stick to the pan, then remove from the heat and stir through the lime juice. If you'd like to add the carnitas to tacos, cook for another few minutes until the jackfruit is crisp.

Microwave the tortillas under a damp cloth in 30-second bursts until warmed through.

Smear 1 teaspoon of refried beans along one side of a tortilla, then heap on 1 tablespoon of carnitas. Roll up the tortilla and place on the prepared tray, seam-side down. Repeat for the others and line them up snugly on the tray. Spray with cooking oil and place the taquitos and jalapeno cheese dip in the oven. Bake for 20 minutes of raw sexual tension, until the taquitos are crisp and the dip is bubbly. Serve together and unite these lovers at last.

SERVES 2-4

Perfect to serve with Sweet 'n' spicy corn ribs (see page 197) on the side!

Bacon-coated Brussels Sprouts

Brussels sprouts get a bad rap from people who haven't let them blossom from little green caterpillars into delicious butterflies by cooking them right. Give brussels sprouts a good wrap by covering them in plant-based bacon and dousing them with maple syrup. People will start inviting you to parties solely on the merit of your hors d'oeuvres game.

INGREDIENTS

brussels sprouts	24
dairy-free butter, melted	1 TBSP
sea salt and black pepper	TO SEASON
smoked maple syrup or maple syrup	2 TBSP
store-bought vegan bacon (or make the Rice paper bacon on page 179)	12 PIECES

Preheat the oven to 170°C (340°F). Line a baking tray with baking paper.

Cut the hard end off each brussels sprout, then make a slice from the top to almost halve the sprout, leaving the base intact. Transfer to a plate and microwave for 1 minute on High.

Place the butter in a mixing jug and whisk in the salt, pepper and maple syrup. Gently prise open the sprouts and use a pastry brush to drizzle in the maple syrup mixture, then treat the sprouts by brushing the outsides with even more.

Halve the bacon pieces lengthways. Prise open a sprout again and feed one end of a bacon piece into it as though the sprout is Pac-Man. Gently rotate the sprout along the bacon strip to wrap it up, then secure with a toothpick. Glaze with a little more maple mixture and place on the prepared tray. Repeat with the remaining sprouts and bacon.

Bake for 45 minutes, flipping halfway through, until the outside is crispy. Remove from the oven and drizzle over the remaining maple syrup while the sprouts are still hot. Serve with other delicious finger food as a decadent dinner party starter.

MAKES 24

Korean Barbecue Ribs

Ribs took a few billion years of evolution to nut out and then another few million to make tasty, and yet here we are intelligently designing similar results out of jackfruit and gluten in an hour.

INGREDIENTS	
tin unripe jackfruit in brine, drained	565 G (1 LB 4 OZ)
dark beer (stout or Guinness)	250 ML (1 CUP)
soy sauce	60 ML (¼ CUP)
tahini	2 TBSP
red miso paste	1 TBSP
tomato paste (concentrated purée)	1 TBSP
liquid smoke	1½ TSP
vital wheat gluten	330 G (2 CUPS)
torula yeast or mushroom seasoning	1 TBSP
onion powder	1 TBSP
smoked paprika	1 TBSP
garlic powder	1½ TSP
pork-style stock powder	1 TSP
black pepper	PINCH
sesame oil	1 TBSP
RIB GLAZE	
apple or pear (Asian pear is best), grated	⅓
soy sauce	60 ML (¼ CUP)
water or tomato juice	125 ML (½ CUP)
gochujang paste	3 TBSP
soft brown sugar	2 TBSP
mirin	1½ TBSP
minced garlic	1 TBSP
minced ginger	1 TSP
liquid smoke	1 TSP

Cut away and reserve the hard cores from the jackfruit pieces, then squeeze the fruit so that any seeds pop out and any excess liquid is removed. Gently pull the jackfruit pieces to make them stringy, then rinse away the remaining brine under warm running water. Squeeze the jackfruit dry.

Place the jackfruit cores, beer, soy sauce, tahini, miso, tomato paste and liquid smoke in a blender and blend to combine well.

In a large bowl, combine the vital wheat gluten, torula yeast or mushroom seasoning, onion powder, paprika, garlic powder, stock powder and pepper. Pour in the blended ingredients and combine with a fork to form a dough. Add the shredded jackfruit and knead for 1 minute to form a cohesive ball.

Rest the dough for 10 minutes, then use your hands to knot and shape it into a long rectangular slab.

Preheat the oven to 180°C (350°F) and line a baking tray with baking paper. Alternatively, prepare a charcoal barbecue and wait until the coals are covered in a thin layer of ash.

Coat the dough in the sesame oil. Heat a frying pan over medium heat, add the dough slab and sear on each side for 3 minutes to form a crust.

Whisk the glaze ingredients with 2 tablespoons of water and microwave on High for 1 minute to thicken.

Carefully transfer the ribs to the prepared tray or the barbecue grill. Cook for 10 minutes, then brush both sides of the ribs with half the glaze. Cook for another 25–30 minutes, basting once more. Allow to cool for 20 minutes before attempting to divvy up. You can also smoke the ribs instead or use an infusion smoker after baking to add that real barbecue flavour that truly says 'my species has mastered fire'.

SERVES 2

GET THE LOOK

Cut a bunch of enoki mushrooms into quarters lengthways to make
four 'bones'. You may need to trim the lengths to get a realistic look.
Insert the bones halfway through once the seitan slab is formed, with
even spacing between each. These are just for aesthetic and point-
 proving purposes.

Banana Peel Char Siu Bao

It's hard to laugh at someone slipping on a banana peel once you discover they make a great shredded meat substitute. Now it just seems wasteful. Make this recipe alongside the Smoked shallot caviar (see page 124) as the leftover shallots are perfect to mix in with the bao filling for a low-waste combo.

INGREDIENTS

Banana peel pulled pork (see page 183) or other plant-based pulled pork	380 G (13½ OZ)
finely chopped spring onion (scallions)	TO SERVE
chinkiang black vinegar or soy sauce	TO SERVE

BAO

active dried yeast	1 TSP
warm water	60 ML (¼ CUP)
cake flour, plus extra for dusting	235 G (8½ OZ)
baking powder	¼ TSP
caster (superfine) sugar	1 TBSP
sea salt	¼ TSP
neutral-flavoured oil	1 TBSP PLUS EXTRA
soy milk	60 ML (¼ CUP)

If using store-bought plant-based pork, fry with the Char siu sauce on page 182 and use as the filling in this dish.

To make the bao, combine the yeast and warm water in a jug. Set aside for a few minutes, then add a pinch of the flour. Once the yeast froths up, it's ready to go.

Combine the remaining flour, baking powder, sugar and salt in a large bowl and make a well in the centre. Whisk 1 tablespoon of the oil and all the soy milk into the yeast mixture, then pour into the well. Gently stir to combine until the yeast mixture is completely incorporated, then form into a loose dough.

Transfer the dough to a floured work surface and knead for 5 minutes or until the dough is smooth and elastic. It's ready when you press down on the dough and it springs back. Place in a lightly oiled bowl, cover with a tea towel and leave for 1½ hours or until doubled in size.

Give the risen dough a quick knead and divide into 12 balls. Lay a large sheet of baking paper on your work surface. Roll each dough ball into a round, flat disc and divide the pork mixture in the centre of each. Place a dough disc in one hand and use your other hand to fold and pinch the edge of the dough over the filling, moving around the entire circumference until you can pinch the folds together at the top to seal the bun in a neat spiral. Repeat to make 12 bao. Cover the buns with a tea towel and rest on individual squares of baking paper for 30 minutes.

Prepare a large steamer.

Steam the char siu bao on their baking paper squares in two batches for 12 minutes. Allow to cool for 20 minutes before attempting to dig in. These are best eaten fresh, scattered with spring onion and served with chinkiang vinegar or soy sauce for dipping.

MAKES 12

Sweet 'n' Spicy Corn Ribs

You'll need your sharpest knife, strongest arm and, worst case, most disposable loved one to execute the hardest part of this recipe.

INGREDIENTS	
sweetcorn cobs, husks and silks removed	2–3
vegetable oil	2 TBSP
SWEET 'N' SPICY SAUCE	
rice malt syrup or vegan honey	2 TBSP
tomato ketchup	1 TBSP
hot sauce	1 TSP
garlic powder	1 TSP
hot mustard	3/4 TSP
malt vinegar	1/2 TSP
onion powder	1/2 TSP
liquid smoke	1/2 TSP

Use a sharp knife to humanely split the sweetcorn cobs in half lengthways through the 'bone'. Be careful! You may need to use a rocking motion or a fair bit of force to split the core. Cutting through the corn side (not the core side) to avoid squashing the kernels, halve lengthways again to make long quarters. Depending on the size of your corn, you may need to keep cutting to get long individual corn ribs about four kernels wide.

Combine the sweet 'n' spicy sauce ingredients in a small saucepan and cook over low heat for 5 minutes.

Preheat the oven to 180°C (350°F).

Coat the corn ribs in the oil, then transfer to a baking tray and bake for 10–15 minutes, until they curl. Glaze with the sauce and bake for a further 3–5 minutes, keeping your eye on them so that the kernels are still juicy by the time they're done. Serve hot with napkins readily available or throw caution to the wind and don a bib to put away these ribs.

MAKES 8-12

You could skip the sauce and serve these elote-inspired ribs covered in vegan mayo, paprika, tajin and lime juice.

SAVING someone's BACON

Quiche Lorraine

Kala namak (Indian black salt) loses its flavour with heat, so cooking it in this recipe won't do much good. Sprinkle on generously right before serving, however, and you'll achieve a maximum eggy kick. I recommend store-bought vegan bacon for this recipe, as the flavour and colour tend to stand out in a mixture like this, as opposed to vegetable-based bacons, which tend to read as vegetables once again after being baked in a quiche.

INGREDIENTS

vegetable oil	1 TBSP
store-bought vegan bacon, roughly chopped	200 G (7 OZ)
French shallots, sliced	2
garlic cloves, minced	2
frozen dairy-free puff pastry sheets, just thawed	2
grated dairy-free cheese	100 G (1 CUP)
cooking oil	SPRAY
kala namak (Indian black salt) or use sea salt	2 TSP

EGG FILLING

chickpea flour (besan)	165 G (1½ CUPS)
medium–firm tofu, pressed	150 G (5½ OZ)
nutritional yeast	30 G (⅓ CUP)
water	500 ML (2 CUPS)
olive oil	60 ML (¼ CUP)
black pepper	TO SEASON
dried sage	¼ TSP

Preheat the oven to 200°C (400°F).

Heat the oil in a frying pan over medium heat. Add the bacon, shallot and garlic and sauté for 10 minutes to coax out the flavours. Set aside to cool.

Slightly overlap the puff pastry in a 22.5 cm (9 in) pie tin to cover the base and side. Trim off any excess if required and use it to fill any gaps. Work out your feelings by stabbing a fork into the pastry 20 times, then line with a sheet of baking paper, add baking beads and bake for 15 minutes.

Blend together the egg filling ingredients. Transfer to a bowl and stir in three-quarters of the grated cheese.

Remove the pastry from the oven and lift out the baking paper and baking beads. If the pastry has still found a way to inflate, use the base of a small saucepan to compress the baked pastry shell into the tin. Fill the crust with the cooked bacon mixture, then pour over the egg filling and scatter on the remaining cheese. Bake for 50–60 minutes, until the egg filling has completely set.

Leave to cool slightly, then spray the top with cooking oil spray and sprinkle over the kala namak. Divvy up whatever sized portions your heart draws you to and serve with a salad of your choice.

SERVES 6

Carbonara

Switch in store-bought vegan bacon, pre-cooked mushrooms, sliced sundried tomatoes or a mix, depending on what you need to use up in your fridge.

INGREDIENTS

dried spaghetti	250 G (9 OZ)
Eggplant bacon (see page 178), cooked for 5–10 minutes longer until extra crisp	150 G (5½ OZ)
King oyster mushroom bacon (see page 179), cooked for 5–10 minutes longer until extra crisp	150 G (5½ OZ)
minced garlic	2 TSP
dairy-free butter	2 TBSP
grated vegan parmesan or nutritional yeast	30 G (⅓ CUP)
kala namak (Indian black salt) or use sea salt	½ TSP
black pepper	TO SERVE
chopped parsley	3 TBSP

CARBONARA SAUCE

dairy-free butter	1 TBSP
vegan heavy cream OR	250 ML (1 CUP)
silken tofu	300 G (10½ OZ)
tapioca flour (starch)	1 TSP
freshly squeezed lemon juice	1 TBSP

Cook the spaghetti in salted boiling water for 8 minutes, or until just less than al dente. Drain and reserve 80 ml (⅓ cup) of the cooking water.

Place the reserved cooking water and the carbonara sauce ingredients in a blender and blend until smooth.

Slice the bacon into 5 cm (2 in) pieces. You're already halfway done!

In a large saucepan over medium–low heat, sauté the garlic in the butter for 2 minutes. Pour in the carbonara sauce and cook, stirring, for 2 minutes. Toss in the cooked spaghetti, followed by the parmesan or nutritional yeast and bacon pieces.

Remove from the heat and plate up. Sprinkle the black salt, pepper and parsley over the top of each dish. Serve in a safe location in case you find you can't move once you've put away a whole plate.

SERVES 2-3

If you can find egg-free fresh spaghetti or you make it yourself, use 500 g (1 lb 2 oz) of fresh pasta in place of the dried spaghetti and cook for around 2 minutes.

Shiitake Pepperoni Pizza

The pizza dough and sauce in this recipe make enough for two pizzas. Use the remaining pizza base to go wild with any of the plant-based meat in this book to make the ultimate meat loather's pizza! Use barbecue sauce as the base, pick your proteins and top with the smoked aioli on page 55.

INGREDIENTS

grated dairy-free cheese	25 G (¼ CUP)
Shiitake pepperoni slices (see page 225)	1 × QUANTITY

PIZZA DOUGH

active dried yeast	¾ TSP
warm water	80 ML (⅓ CUP)
Italian 00 flour, plus extra for dusting	150 G (1 CUP)
sea salt	1 TSP
olive oil	2 TSP, PLUS EXTRA

PIZZA SAUCE

tinned plum or roma tomatoes	200 G (7 OZ)
tomato paste (concentrated purée)	45 G (1½ OZ)
small garlic cloves	2
fennel seeds	½ TSP
dried thyme	½ TSP
dried oregano	½ TSP
celery salt	½ TSP
onion powder	¼ TSP
dried basil	¼ TSP
chilli powder	⅛ TSP
granulated sugar	¼ TSP
black pepper	¼ TSP

To make the pizza dough, combine the yeast and warm water in a jug. Set aside for a few minutes, then add a pinch of the flour. Once the yeast froths up, it's ready to go.

Tip the flour into a large bowl and sprinkle in the salt. Make a well in the centre and pour in the yeast mixture. Fold the flour into the liquid with a spatula until you have a loose dough, then use your hands to knead in the olive oil. Knead for several minutes until the dough is smooth and elastic. Place the dough in a lightly oiled bowl, then cover with a tea towel and leave to prove for at least 1 hour.

Meanwhile, to make the pizza sauce, place all the ingredients in a blender and process to a smooth sauce.

Preheat the oven to 250°C (500°F) or the highest temperature it will go and place a large baking tray or pizza tray in the oven to heat up.

Back to the dough. Lightly dust a work surface and a rolling pin with flour. Cut the dough in half, then roll out to form a 26 cm (10¼ in) pizza base, dusting with flour and rotating the dough as you go. Carefully drag the pizza base onto a large square of baking paper. Wrap the remaining dough in plastic wrap and store in the fridge to make another pizza later in the week.

Cover the pizza base with almost half the pizza sauce, leaving a border around the edge for the crust. Sprinkle most of the cheese over the sauce, then press in the shiitake pepperoni. Finish with the remaining cheese and a few extra blobs of pizza sauce for good luck. (Save the leftover sauce for another pizza.)

Remove the hot tray from the oven and very carefully transfer the pizza and baking paper to the tray. Place on the top shelf of the oven and bake for 12–15 minutes, until the cheese is bubbling and the crust is cooked.

Remove the pizza from the oven, cut into six or eight slices and serve immediately.

MAKES 1 LARGE PIZZA

Chicharrones

Crunchy, fatty, salty crackle. Skin and rind recipes in this book sometimes call for rice paper and sometimes call for spawn of seitan. The whole squad is getting together to create a vegan take on the ultimate deep-fried meaty indulgence of fried pork rinds (or, for those on a keto diet, a casual, healthy snack).

INGREDIENTS

vegetable oil	FOR DEEP-FRYING
very thick Spawn of seitan (see page 26)	125 ML (½ CUP)
tapioca flour	2 TBSP
soy sauce	1 TBSP
liquid smoke	3 TSP
pork-style stock cubes	2
rice paper sheets	6
sea salt	TO SEASON

Heat the vegetable oil in a large heavy-based saucepan over medium heat.

Scoop the spawn into a bowl and mix in the tapioca flour, soy sauce, liquid smoke and stock cubes to form a thick sludge.

Lightly dampen a rice paper sheet with water and use a pastry brush to smear the sludge over one side. Fold in half and coat in sludge again, then fold in half one more time like a piece of slimy origami. Add a little of the sludge to the outside, then use kitchen scissors to fashion the sheet into a rectangle. Excess pieces can be fried alongside the chicharrones. Make three to four small incisions halfway through the sheet to recreate ribs. Alternatively, use scissors to cut the rice paper into even shreds to make these rind style. Repeat with the remaining sludge and rice paper sheets.

Test if the oil is ready by inserting a wooden skewer or the handle of a wooden spoon into the hot oil; if it begins to bubble quickly, then you're ready to go.

Drop the chicharrones into the hot oil and fry for 2–3 minutes, agitating so they fry evenly. If making rind strips, you may like to use tongs to hold them under the oil in a curved shape for a few seconds so that they curl up. They should puff up a little, mostly in pride at how far you've come as a cook. Transfer to paper towel to drain and lightly sprinkle salt over the top. They'll stay super crispy for an hour. They'll be a little more chewy the next day but will still be good.

SERVES 2-4

Like a traditional ham roast, the leftovers (fat or, in this case, spawn) can be used to make pork crackling.

Pork Belly

Deep-frying the pork belly adds fat to this dish, which is after all what we are trying to recreate – so don't skip this part!

INGREDIENTS

hard smoked tofu, frozen and thawed once (see page 34)	400–500 G (14 OZ–1 LB 2 OZ)
soft brown sugar	2 TSP
fresh folded yuba skins (refrigerated soft bean curd sheets)	50 G (1¾ OZ)
vegetable oil	FOR DEEP-FRYING
hoisin sauce	2 TBSP
sea salt	TO SEASON
dipping sauce (optional)	TO SERVE

PORK BELLY STOCK

pork-style stock	250 ML (1 CUP)
liquid aminos	2 TBSP
torula yeast	1 TBSP
red miso paste	2 TSP
onion powder	1 TSP
smoked paprika	1 TSP
liquid smoke	¼ TSP

PORK BELLY FAT

wheat starch	180 G (1½ CUPS)
glutinous rice flour	25 G (¼ CUP)
mushroom seasoning	2 TSP
smoked paprika	1 TSP
ground white pepper	½ TSP
garlic powder	½ TSP

Combine the pork belly stock ingredients in a saucepan and bring to the boil. Remove from the heat.

Slice the tofu into four thick strips and plunge into the boiling hot stock. Soak for 1 hour, then drain, pat dry and rub the brown sugar into the exterior.

Line a small baking dish that will snugly fit the tofu in a single layer with foil, then baking paper, allowing extra foil and paper to hang over the edges. Add the tofu to the dish. Cut the yuba in half, then fold both halves into two long strips that match the height of the dish. Place the strips between the tofu and the edges of the dish.

Combine the pork belly fat ingredients in a bowl, then add the stock and mix well. Pour over the tofu to fill the dish, the fold over the baking paper and foil to secure.

Prepare a large steamer, then steam the pork belly in the dish for 30 minutes. Allow to cool.

Heat the oil in a large heavy-based saucepan over medium–high heat. Test if the oil is ready by inserting a wooden skewer or the handle of a wooden spoon into the hot oil; if it begins to bubble quickly, then you're ready to go.

Slice the pork belly into twelve slabs and deep-fry in two batches for 5 minutes, agitating occasionally so all sides crisp up. Drain on paper towel to drain, then brush the hoisin sauce over the yuba parts of the belly slices and sprinkle with salt. Serve warm with your choice of dipping sauce if desired.

SERVES 6

Smoked Watermelon Roast

It's no savoury felony to taste watermelony when paired with grilled asparagus or a simple salad of vegan feta, rocket (arugula) and balsamic vinegar. To best disguise the watermelon, the longer you brine it the better you'll find your kinda swine.

INGREDIENTS	
prepared and brined watermelon roast (see page 173)	1 × QUANTITY
canola oil	1 TBSP
grilled asparagus or your choice of salad	TO SERVE

BARBECUE SPICE RUB	
smoked paprika	1 TBSP
porcini powder	1 TBSP
onion powder	2 TSP
sea salt	1 TSP
black pepper	¼ TSP

Remove the watermelon and 3–4 garlic cloves from the brine. Finely mince the garlic, then set aside. Gently compress the watermelon with your hands over a sink to press out the excess moisture for a few minutes. Place the watermelon on a wire rack over a plate to continue to drip liquid while you prepare a smoker as per the instructions on page 52. Once the box begins smoking, place a pan under the grill but away from the heat, to catch the liquid from the melon, then place the melon on top of the grill. Close the smoker, leaving a gap for airflow, and smoke and cook the melon for 2 hours. Transfer the melon directly to the heated grill and cook, turning, for 5 minutes to begin the formation of a crust. Remove the melon to a tray and cover the smoker in the meantime.

Combine the barbecue spice rub ingredients in a bowl. Mix together the minced garlic and canola oil, then spread the mixture all over the melon, avoiding eye contact as you pour it inside any crevices and massage it into the interior. Coat the melon in the spice rub to form a crust, then return to the barbecue and smoke for another 4 hours, rotating occasionally and replenishing the wood chips as needed. It's important to keep moving the melon; otherwise, it may brown too quickly on one side. By the end it will have formed a skin on the outside and feel soft and jiggly under the surface with a firm interior.

Remove to a chopping board and cool for 20 minutes before slicing. Allow the roast to sit for a further 10 minutes, letting the juices seep out. Serve up the watermelon and drizzle the juices like gravy over the pink flesh to boost the umami. Served with grilled asparagus or your favourite salad. If there are any leftovers, use the slices and juice to make Watermelon jerky (see page 239).

SERVES 4-6

Smoked Ham Roast

✱ ✱ ✱

That's a nice ham you've got there. It'd be a shame if someone were to put an 's' in front of it and an 'e' on the end. My family's Boxing Day breakfast tradition is cold day-old slices of ham served with a big blob of Gran's mango chutney. This here's a sham of a ham, forged for vegans in the dark, smoky pits of hell through the work of seitan and its spawn. It, too, is great with mango chutney.

INGREDIENTS

apple or pineapple juice	250 ML (1 CUP)
seitan prepared as ham (see page 176)	1 × QUANTITY
Spawn of seitan (see page 26)	185 ML (3/4 CUP)
rice paper sheets	8
vital wheat gluten	2 TBSP
pineapple rings and glace cherries (optional)	TO DECORATE

HAM GLAZE

pineapple juice	80 ML (1/3 CUP)
soft brown sugar	95 G (1/3 CUP)
whiskey	60 ML (1/4 CUP)
soy sauce	2 TBSP
dijon mustard	1 TBSP
ground ginger	1/2 TSP

Soak a few handfuls of wood chips in the apple or pineapple juice. Set aside. Prepare a smoking box on a barbecue or smoker as per the instructions on page 52, ensuring that the smoking box is above the heat souce. Place a baking tray under the grill but away from the heat.

To prepare the roast, baste the seitan ham with 2 tablespoons of spawn, then place on top of the grill above the baking tray. Close the barbecue or smoker, leaving a gap for airflow, and smoke for 2 hours, turning occasionally and basting with another 2 tablespoons of spawn halfway through. Replenish the wood chips as needed.

Combine the ham glaze ingredients in a saucepan, place over medium heat and simmer, whisking occasionally, for 5 minutes until beginning to thicken. Baste the roast with the glaze and smoke for another 1 hour before removing from the smoker. Cover the smoker to retain heat and smoke for when the roast returns!

One at a time, lightly dampen the rice paper sheets and if there are irregular parts of your roast, bunch up 3–4 sheets and place them into the crevices to look like marbled fat. Mix the remaining spawn with 60 ml (¼ cup) of the glaze and brush over the roast. Sprinkle the vital wheat gluten evenly over the top. Use the remaining damp rice paper sheets to cover the entire outside of the roast in a skin. Glaze the exterior and return to the smoker for 2 hours, lovingly returning to baste it every 20–30 minutes.

Optionally, finish the roast by covering it in a single, even layer of pineapple rings. Place a glace cherry in the centre of each ring and spear a toothpick through the heart of each cherry to hold everything in place. Bake at 175°C (345°F) for 30 minutes or smoke for another 1 hour until everything has crisped up. Allow the roast to cool, then slice thinly and plate up!

SERVES 6-8

CHAR-
CUT-
ERIE

STUFFING SAUSAGES • SAUSAGES WITH SPRAY-ON ALGINATE CASING • MEXICAN BEAN SAUSAGES • FAUX GRAS
SEITAN PEPPERONI • SHIITAKE PEPPERONI SLICES • MORTADELLA • PROSCIUTTO • SEITAN SALAMI

CHARCUTERIE BASES

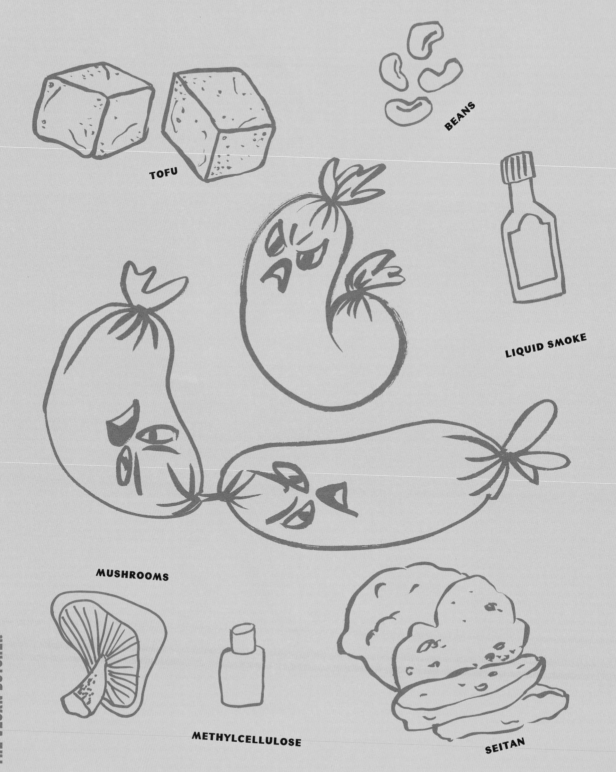

TOFU

BEANS

LIQUID SMOKE

MUSHROOMS

METHYLCELLULOSE

SEITAN

Traditional vegan-friendly antipasto options are plentiful: think olives, dolmades, sundried tomatoes, roasted capsicum (bell pepper), hummus, guacamole, pickles, dairy-free cheeses and so on. This means the real challenge when bringing a vegan antipasto platter to a party is not having time to socialise because you're too busy monitoring the food table to make sure nobody does anything insane like try to dip ham into your baba ghanoush. The solution? Make the meat vegan, too.

Accusing a vegan of being a grass grazer is a testament to culinary creativity and a welcome compliment! We harvest that very grass, turn its wheat grain into vital wheat gluten, use that to transform it into beautiful vegan charcuterie meats and then graze on them instead. Sausages, sliced meats, smoked meats, cured meats and even foie gras all have a plant-based take in this chapter, so you can make an entire kinder kinda charcuterie board to place next to your antipasto and show off that choosing vegan doesn't mean you have to miss out.

FLAVOUR BASES:

SHALLOTS • SOY SAUCE • LIQUID SMOKE • LIQUID AMINOS • VEGAN FISH SAUCE • MSG MUSHROOM SEASONING • NUTRITIONAL YEAST • RED MISO PASTE • TOMATO PASTE (CONCENTRATED PURÉE) • WALNUTS • DRIED MUSHROOMS • PORK/BEEF-STYLE STOCK • BRINES • BOOZE

BASES:

BEANS • MUSHROOMS • SEITAN OR VITAL WHEAT GLUTEN • SPAWN OF SEITAN COUSCOUS • QUINOA • ALGINATE • AGAR AGAR

STUFFING SAUSAGES

✦ ✦

An unmistakably non-vegan technique, stuffing a plant-based sausage feels naughty in every way and not just because it's a lot like filling a condom. You can even make your own sausage skins by following the alginate guide on page 218. Alternatively, plant-based sausage skins can be ordered online or found in specialty stores. They are made from polysaccharides, such as carrageenan, and they give you the full experience of hand-filling each sausage and twisting them into links, which is part of the fun of reclaiming every technique that vegans just aren't *supposed* to do.

For small batches, I find a cheap hand-crank sausage machine the least fiddly to work with. Some stand mixers have a sausage stuffing attachment, which will grind the ingredients and then eject them through a tube, but vegan sausage mixes generally don't require a grinding step, so this isn't necessary.

Vegan sausages can be fried in oil, grilled, baked or even microwaved. Make sure they are well spaced when cooking as, if touching, the casings will break and peel from the sausages. Never boil or simmer them in water or stock as contact with liquid also breaks the casings. Unlike traditional skins, they do not need to be pre-soaked before stuffing.

TO GET STUFFED

① Wind the crank all the way out of the tube so that it is clear. Unscrew one end and load your sausage mixture into the tube. Fit the appropriate-sized nozzle for your casings to the machine and tightly screw closed both ends.

② Being very careful not to pierce the casing, feed one end of a sausage casing onto the nozzle and thread it on until the length of the nozzle is loaded with casing. Cut off the casing, leaving 5 cm (2 in) free at the end. Turn the crank to compress the sausage mixture, and hold the free casing with your other hand until a small amount of the mixture is pushed out of the nozzle into the casing - this is to avoid air bubbles.

③ Twist the opposite end of the casing closed and steadily turn the crank, guiding the filled sausage with your free hand away from the machine. Continue until either the casing is used up or the filling runs out, then twist the other end of the casing closed. Reload the machine or nozzle and continue as required.

④ Twist the casing at even points to create links, then cook the sausages following the recipe instructions.

SAUSAGES WITH SPRAY-ON ALGINATE CASING

Spherification uses the reaction between sodium alginate and calcium chloride to create a soft gel membrane around a flavoured liquid, as demonstrated on page 124. This exact same reaction and membrane can be used to form sausage skins – right around pre-formed sausages. Dip the sausages into the sodium alginate solution so they are fully coated, then spray calcium chloride over the top and, hey presto!, the membrane sets so you've got a sausage skin that'll grill like magic. Sneaking liquid smoke into the alginate solution means even if you can't barbecue these up over charcoal, you'll get all the flavour anyway.

INGREDIENTS

Basic methylcellulose mince (see page 280)	1 × QUANTITY
sodium alginate	10 G (¼ OZ)
liquid smoke	1 TSP
distilled water	750 ML (3 CUPS)
calcium chloride	5 G (⅛ OZ)
vegetable oil	FOR COOKING

① Lay a 20 cm (8 in) square of plastic wrap on a work surface, then spoon 60 g (2 oz) of the mince mixture into the centre. Fold over to enclose, smooth the mince mixture into a sausage shape and wrap up tightly. Repeat until you've used up all the mince. Move the sausages to the freezer for at least 1½ hours until very firm.

② To prepare the sausage casing solution, combine the sodium alginate, liquid smoke and 500 ml (2 cups) of the distilled water in a blender and blend for 1 minute to combine. Pour into a tall glass, cover and move to the fridge for an hour so it's ready to go when the sausages are.

③ Whisk the calcium chloride into the remaining 250 ml (1 cup) of distilled water and pour into a spray bottle. Set up a washing station: fill a deep container with cold water to serve as a washing bath (for cleansing the bitter calcium from the casing) and place some paper towel on a tray.

④ Unwrap the sausages. Insert a skewer lengthways into each sausage so that you can dip them into the casing solution. Without touching the glass, dip each sausage into the casing solution until it is fully coated, then pull it out and allow the excess solution to drip off while holding the sausage over the sink.

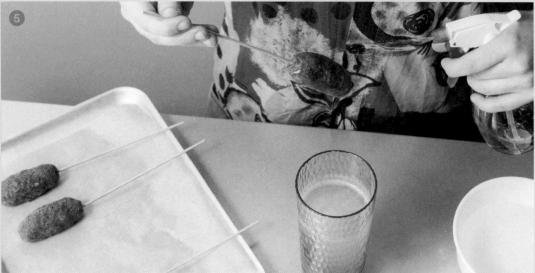

⑤ Spray all over the sausage with the calcium solution to form the casing - you'll notice it's instantaneous!

⑥ Dunk the sausage into the prepared washing bath, then carefully remove the skewer and place the sausage on the paper towel to drain. (There may be a sacrificial snag on your first attempt as you try to get the hang of keeping the sausage intact on the skewer until it enters the water bath.) Repeat this process until all the sausages have a casing.

⑦ Heat a thin layer of vegetable oil in a large frying pan over medium heat. Place the sausages on a microwavable plate covered in a layer of baking paper. Microwave for 1 minute on High to set the shape of the sausages. Add the sausages to the hot pan and cook on all sides for 8-10 minutes until piping hot throughout with lovely charring all over. For the best, firmest texture, serve hot or reheat in the microwave right before eating.

Mexican Bean Sausages

It's time for boring old bean sausages to get a reboot. Crank up the flavour and crank the handle on a sausage-stuffing machine for a totally levelled-up sausage in every way. These sausages retain their firm texture even when served cold, unlike sausages stuffed with methylcellulose-based fillings, so they'll go great on a cold-meat platter once they've been fully cooked.

INGREDIENTS

vegetable oil	FOR FRYING
French shallots, finely diced	2
minced garlic	1 TSP
dried chile de arbol, chopped	1–2
soy sauce	3 TBSP
liquid smoke	1 TSP
vegan fish sauce	1 TBSP
TVP mince	100 G (1 CUP)
red yeast rice powder	1 TSP
cornflour (cornstarch)	2 TBSP
potato starch	4 TSP
carrageenan	2 TSP
rice paper sheets (optional)	6

BEAN MIX

flaxseed (linseed) meal	2 TBSP
drained tinned four bean mix	250 G (9 OZ)
chipotles in adobo sauce	3 TBSP
mushroom seasoning or nutritional yeast	1 TBSP
smoked paprika	1 TBSP
dried oregano	1 TBSP
red miso paste	1 TSP
ground cumin	1 TSP
chilli flakes	½ TSP

Heat 1 tablespoon of vegetable oil in a saucepan over low heat, add the shallot and cook, stirring occasionally, for 15 minutes until browned. Add the garlic and chile de arbol and cook for 30 seconds, then tip in the soy sauce, liquid smoke, fish sauce and 60 ml (¼ cup) of water. Bring to a simmer, then stir through the TVP and switch off the heat. Allow to hydrate while you continue with the recipe.

To make the bean mix, combine the flaxseed meal with 60 ml (¼ cup) of water to form a gel-like egg. Add it and the remaining bean mix ingredients to a food processor and process until smooth. Transfer to a large bowl and stir through the hydrated TVP.

Mix the yeast, cornflour, potato starch and carrageenan together in a bowl, then fold into the TVP and bean mixture.

Follow the sausage-stuffing guide on page 216 to complete the preparation. Alternatively, crack out your can-do attitude for a DIY casing: using moist hands, shape the TVP and bean mixture into six sausages, then dampen the rice paper sheets with water and encase a sausage in each one.

Heat a barbecue grill to medium or heat a small amount of oil in a frying pan over medium heat. Cook the sausages for 8–10 minutes, until cooked through. They may be slightly soft as they leave the pan, but will firm up after a rest. Just enough time to invite ya mates around for a good old sausage fest.

MAKES 6

Faux Gras

It's no secret that force-feeding geese and ducks is fauxed up. This creamy, buttery and savoury mousse clone is the good twin of foie gras, politely turning down the use of torture in its method and instead doing a bang-up job with plants and a food processor. Hold the liver, please. Serve with charcuterie accoutrements and either crackers, toasted bread or vegetables cut into batons to dip with.

INGREDIENTS	
firm or hard tofu	160 G (5½ OZ)
mixed mushrooms	300 G (10½ OZ)
cooking oil	SPRAY
walnuts	140 G (¾ CUP)
sundried tomato oil	2 TBSP
small French shallots, finely chopped	4
small carrot, finely diced	½
sundried tomatoes, chopped	3 TBSP
garlic cloves, minced	2
cognac or sherry	2 TBSP
shoyu or soy sauce	1 TBSP
nutritional yeast	2 TBSP
tahini	1 TBSP
beetroot (beet) powder	2 TSP
dairy-free butter	2 TBSP
chopped sage leaves	2 TSP
smoked salt and black pepper	TO SEASON

Wrap the tofu in paper towel and press under a heavy weight for 20 minutes.

Prepare a steamer basket. Steam the whole mushrooms for 3 minutes. Pulse the mushrooms in a food processor into rubble, then tip into a large bowl.

Lightly spray a frying pan with cooking oil and crumble in the walnuts. Toast over medium heat for 2 minutes, then transfer to the food processor and process until fine. Add to the mushroom rubble.

Add the sundried tomato oil to the pan, then add the shallot and carrot and cook, stirring occasionally, for 15 minutes until starting to brown. Add the sundried tomato, garlic, booze and shoyu or soy sauce, then remove from the heat. Transfer the mixture to the food processor, add the nutritional yeast and pulse until a chunky paste forms. Add to the mushroom mixture and give everything a good stir.

Unwrap the tofu and place in the food processor. Add the tahini, beetroot powder, butter and sage and process on high until you have fine pink crumbles. Return the mushroom mixture to the food processor and add loads of smoked salt and black pepper. Process on low until just well mixed. Don't overprocess! Scoop into a small shallow bowl, up-end onto a serving plate and mould into a homogenous shape. Cover and refrigerate until needed and serve as cold as the heart of anyone who would pick real foie gras over this version that leaves the geese and ducks to be.

SERVES 2-4

MORTADELLA
(SEE PAGE 226)

PROSCIUTTO
(SEE PAGE 227)

WASHED SEITAN
STEAK
(SEE PAGE 235)

MEXICAN BEAN
SAUSAGES
(SEE PAGE 220)

FAUX GRAS
(SEE PAGE 221)

SEITAN PEPPERONI
(SEE PAGE 224)

SHIITAKE
PEPPERONI
(SEE PAGE 225)

Seitan Pepperoni

You've found the cure . . . to bland plant-based antipasto platters: cured-style meat, made at home and without the potential hazards to health of poorly cured meat. Only the vegan versions can boast that. We've even got the speckled fat (pearl couscous!) and all the rich flavour to make incredible shiitake pepperoni pizzas (see page 202), or eye-catching slices nestled among other nibbles.

INGREDIENTS

red wine	200 ML (7 FL OZ)
tomato paste (concentrated purée)	2 TBSP
liquid aminos or soy sauce	2 TBSP
liquid smoke	2 TSP
red miso paste	2 TSP
vital wheat gluten	150 G (1 CUP)
torula yeast or mushroom seasoning	1 TBSP
smoked paprika	2 TSP
garlic powder	1 TSP
ground fennel	1 TSP
chilli flakes	1 TSP
agar agar powder	1 TSP
granulated sugar	1 TSP
cayenne powder	½ TSP
ground aniseed	½ TSP
dried basil	½ TSP
ground allspice	¼ TSP
dried thyme	¼ TSP
grated vegan shortening	2 TBSP

FAT SPECKLES

pork or beef-style stock	125 ML (½ CUP)
liquid smoke	½ TSP
pearl couscous	60 G (2 OZ)
sundried tomato oil	3 TBSP PLUS EXTRA TO COAT

To prepare the fat speckles, bring the stock and liquid smoke to a rapid boil in a wide saucepan over high heat. Add the couscous, reduce to the heat to low, then cover and simmer for 6–7 minutes, until the stock is absorbed. Stir to avoid sticking, then pour the sundried tomato oil over the top and allow to cool.

Pour the red wine into a saucepan, bring to the boil over medium–high heat and bubble away until reduced by half. Allow to cool. Combine the reduced red wine with the tomato paste, liquid aminos or soy sauce, liquid smoke and miso paste and set aside.

In a large bowl, stir together the remaining ingredients, except the shortening, then mix in the red wine mixture until just combined. Tip in the shortening and prepared couscous, then knead with your hands to bring the dough together for about 1 minute, making sure the couscous is dispersed throughout the mixture.

Lay a 30 cm (12 in) square of plastic wrap on a work surface, then spoon the mixture into the centre. Fold over to enclose, then shape the mixture into a smooth, long log and wrap up tightly. Press down slightly to flatten.

Place the pepperoni on a plate and microwave on High for 90 seconds to set. Remove the plastic wrap, then tightly wrap in foil, this time making the pepperoni rounded as you will be locking it into its final form.

Preheat the oven to 170°C (340°F). Place the pepperoni on a baking tray and bake for 30 minutes. Alternatively, follow the smoking guide on page 50 and smoke for 2 hours for even more cheeky flavours. Allow to cool fully, still wrapped in foil, then rest overnight in the fridge. For additional flavour and fatty mouthfeel, store the pepperoni coated in a slick of extra sundried tomato oil.

MAKES I LARGE PEPPERONI

Shiitake Pepperoni Slices

Squashing a fresh shiitake mushroom as it cooks produces a perfectly round slice of pepperoni without even having to unsheathe your knife. The mushroom's flavour and texture get condensed, then we marinate it in more flavour . . . then we rub in a little more. Oh, and then you should definitely put it on a pizza with the awesome pizza sauce on page 202. Who knew mushrooms had so mush room for improvement?

INGREDIENTS	
fresh shiitake mushrooms	10
cooking oil	SPRAY
PEPPERONI MARINADE	
red wine	3 TBSP
soy sauce	1 TBSP
liquid smoke	¼ TSP
PEPPERONI SPICE RUB	
fennel seeds	¼ TSP
garlic powder	½ TSP
onion powder	½ TSP
star anise	½ TSP
chilli flakes	SMALL PINCH
smoked paprika	¼ TSP
soft brown sugar	¾ TSP

Combine the pepperoni marinade ingredients in a large bowl and add the whole mushrooms. Soak for at least 1 hour. Remove from the marinade, then shake off the excess liquid.

Place a large frying pan over medium heat. Add the shiitake mushrooms and use a smaller frying pan to compress them into flat discs as they cook for 3 minutes. Flip the mushroom pepperoni slices and cook for another 3 minutes, pressing down occasionally. Set aside to cool.

Crush the spice rub ingredients using a mortar and pestle, then rub over the mushroom pepperoni slices. Either coat in cooking oil spray and bake at 180°C (350°F) for 10–15 minutes or use on pizza and in other recipes, where they will be cooked further and paired with something nice and fatty.

MAKES 10 PEPPERONI SLICES

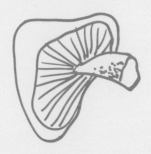

Mortadella

A tin of beans provides the ways and means to a gluten-free and animal-free version of mortadella! Be sure to keep some slices aside to use in the ultimate deli beast: the Muffuletta on page 290.

INGREDIENTS

Ingredient	Amount
quinoa, rinsed well	65 G (⅓ CUP)
minced garlic	1 TBSP
drained tinned cannellini beans	200 G (1 CUP)
psyllium husk	2 TBSP
vegan shortening	2 TBSP
tomato paste (concentrated purée)	2 TBSP
soft brown sugar	2 TSP
onion powder	2 TSP
liquid smoke	1½ TSP
salt	1 TSP
MSG	1 TSP
beetroot (beet) powder	½ TSP
smoked paprika	½ TSP
ground coriander	½ TSP
ground mace	¼ TSP

AGAR AGAR MIX

agar agar powder	2 TBSP
red wine	125 ML (½ CUP)
olive brine	60 ML (¼ CUP)

FILLING

pitted green olives or pimento	3 TBSP
unsalted shelled pistachios	1½ TBSP
mixed whole peppercorns	1 TSP
cornflour (cornstarch)	30 G (¼ CUP)

Combine the quinoa, garlic and 170 ml (⅔ cup) of water in a small saucepan. Bring to the boil, cover and reduce the heat to low. Simmer for 10 minutes, then switch the heat off and keep covered for another 10 minutes. Fluff the quinoa, then transfer to a food processor with the remaining ingredients. Pulse until the texture is smooth and homogenous.

Place the agar agar mix ingredients in a saucepan and heat until simmering. Pour into the food processor and pulse to incorporate with the mortadella mixture. Transfer to a large bowl.

Stir together the filling ingredients, then fold through the mortadella mixture.

Prepare a large steamer basket. Lay out a 30 cm (12 in) square of foil and heap the mortadella mixture on top. Mould into a thick log and smooth with moist hands. Wrap securely in the foil and finesse the shape before transferring to the steamer. Steam for 20 minutes, then chill overnight in the fridge to complete the transformation. What was once beans isn't now just fake meat, it's a full-on drag bean. Unwrap and slice up for charcuterie.

MAKES I LARGE SAUSAGE

Prosciutto

Papery prosciutto is a breeze to make and uses up wastage from the seitan washing process (see page 20). For a crisper, bacon-like finish, substitute the flavour ingredients here with the bacon marinade on page 178. Marble the two-coloured mixtures in an oiled frying pan and fry over medium heat for 8–10 minutes until set. Break into strips, then allow to brown and crisp up further in the hot pan until you've got beautiful, streaky bacon.

INGREDIENTS	
Spawn of seitan (see page 26)	1 × QUANTITY
olive brine	2 TSP
red miso paste	1 TSP
garlic powder	1 TSP
torula yeast	1 TSP
sweet paprika	½ TSP
shoyu	1 TSP
ground white pepper	¼ TSP
granulated sugar	¼ TSP
agar agar powder	½ TSP
vegan-friendly red food colouring	FEW DROPS
vegetable oil	FOR RUBBING
sea salt	TO SEASON

Reserve the first two washes of liquid after washing seitan (see page 20) and place in a tall jug. Allow the sludge to settle to the bottom over several hours. Pour off the clear water at the top and the remainder is ready to go: you need 125 ml (½ cup) of spawn. As the viscosity can vary, if needed, you can always thin out the spawn with water so it cooperates in this recipe.

Mix the spawn with the olive brine, miso paste, garlic powder, torula yeast, paprika, shoyu, pepper, sugar, agar agar and 1 teaspoon of water in a mixing bowl. Divide into thirds and add drops of food colouring to two-thirds of the mixture to achieve a convincing prosciutto pink! Leave the remaining portion white for the marbling effect.

Cover a microwave-friendly side plate with baking paper. Drizzle over a thin layer of the pink mixture to cover most of the plate. Follow with the white mixture, drizzling between the gaps in the pink mixture to create the streaky fat effect. Microwave on High in 30-second bursts, checking each time until the liquid has fully set (it won't take long!). The longer you blast it the firmer and chewier the texture will be: going for too long won't get you papery prosciutto but can create other textures to mimic more deli meat varieties. Remove, then carefully peel the prosciutto from the paper and allow to cool. Repeat this process with the remaining pink and white mixtures.

Use your fingertips to rub a small amount of vegetable oil onto the surface of each slice, then rub on a little salt. The texture of the prosciutto will improve over the next few days, so cover it and allow it to age in the fridge before adding to a charcuterie platter.

MAKES 3 LARGE PROSCIUTTO SLICES

CHARCUTERIE

Seitan Salami

This salami is milder than pepperoni and is just begging to sit next to it on a charcuterie board. Why choose, though? You've got every excuse to make both pepperoni and salami at the same time because neither version takes months of waiting before it's ready to eat. Another win for vegan cured-style meats!

INGREDIENTS

red wine	200 ML (7 FL OZ)
tomato paste (concentrated purée)	2 TBSP
liquid aminos or soy sauce	2 TBSP
red miso paste	2 TSP
balsamic vinegar	1 TSP
vital wheat gluten	150 G (1 CUP)
torula yeast or mushroom seasoning	2 TBSP
onion powder	2 TSP
garlic powder	2 TSP
smoked paprika	2 TSP
agar agar powder	1 TSP
granulated sugar	1 TSP
ground allspice	½ TSP
black pepper	½ TSP
dried basil	½ TSP
dried thyme	½ TSP
ground mace	¼ TSP
grated vegan shortening	2 TBSP

FAT CHUNKS

pork or beef-style stock	125 ML (½ CUP)
liquid smoke	½ TSP
pearl couscous	60 G (2 OZ)
sundried tomato oil, plus extra	3 TBSP PLUS EXTRA TO COAT

To prepare the fat chunks, bring the stock and liquid smoke to a rapid boil in a wide saucepan. Add the couscous, reduce to the lowest heat, then cover and simmer for 6–7 minutes until the stock is absorbed. Stir to avoid sticking, then pour over the sundried tomato oil and allow to cool.

Pour the red wine into a saucepan, bring to the boil over medium–high heat and bubble away until reduced by half. Allow to cool. Combine the reduced red wine with the tomato paste, liquid aminos or soy sauce, liquid smoke and miso paste and set aside.

In a large bowl, stir together the remaining ingredients except the shortening, then mix in the red wine mixture until just combined. Tip in the shortening and prepared couscous, then knead with your hands to bring the dough together for about 1 minute, making sure the couscous is dispersed throughout the mixture.

Lay a 30 cm (12 in) square of plastic wrap on a work surface, then spoon the mixture into the centre. Fold over to enclose, then shape the mixture into a smooth, long log and wrap up tightly. Press down slightly to flatten.

Place the salami on a plate and microwave on High for 90 seconds to set. Remove the plastic wrap, then tightly wrap in foil, this time making the salami rounded as you will be locking it into its final form.

Preheat the oven to 175°C (345°F). Place the salami on a baking tray and bake for 30 minutes. Alternatively, follow the smoking guide on page 50 and smoke for 2 hours for even more cheeky flavours. Allow to cool fully, still wrapped in foil, then rest overnight in the fridge. For additional flavour and fatty mouthfeel, store the salami coated in a slick of extra sundried tomato oil.

MAKES 1 LARGE SALAMI

WHERE'S THE BEEF (... AND LAMB)?

BEEF-STYLE STOCK POWDER • WASHED SEITAN STEAK • PREPARING WASHED SEITAN AS BEEF MINCE • SEITAN BEEF FROM VWG JERKY • STEAK 'N' SHROOMY SAUCE • SPAGHETTI BOLOGNESE • GUINNESS PIE • MAAFÉ • BARBECUE BEER BRISKET BEET TARTARE • LAMB SHISH KEBAB • GOZLEME • CHIMICHURRI STEAK TACOS • MEATBALLS IN SAUCE • MUSHROOM STEAK FRITES • ROGAN JOSH • GIANT SPAGHETTI-STUFFED MEATBALL • BEET WELLINGTON • HERB-CRUSTED LAMB CHOPS

BEEF AND LAMB BASES

TOFU

MUSHROOMS

TVP

TEMPEH

LENTILS

METHYLCELLULOSE

SEITAN

BEETROOT

Zero per cent of actual beef is needed to create the umami, salty and a little sour and sweet flavours usually found in cow-based dishes; you really don't need to have a cow, man. Searing, slow cooking, smoking, roasting and other methods of coaxing umami out of your ingredients are vital tools for making food taste like meat because they're why meat tastes like meat!

Due to this array of techniques, beef- and lamb-inspired textures range from soft to chewy. This is why seitan shines in this chapter, shapeshifting into them all, then culminating in a multi-textured hours-long smoked barbecue beer brisket that just screams 'the vegans have gone too far this time!' – and then goes a little further.

Modern plant-based meat technology employs the best of science to really get into the business of mimicking animal products – and now at home you can, too. In the advanced recipes, make your own store-grade beef mince alternative and put it to work to make realistic lamb chops or steaks.

Mushrooms can perform double duty as soldiers of the umami army as well as provide chewy texture. Explore how mushroom varieties can become substitutes for different animal products: try oyster mushrooms for lamb-like shish kebabs, lion's mane for beef steaks or shiitakes for a guinness pie that's not short on flavour.

FLAVOURS TO USE FOR BEEF AND LAMB:

DRY: UNSWEETENED COCOA POWDER • COFFEE • DRIED PORCINI • DRIED SHIITAKE MUSHROOMS • GARLIC • MINT • ONION • PAPRIKA • PARSLEY • PEPPER • ROSEMARY • SUMAC • THYME
WET: GUINNESS • LIQUID SMOKE • MOLASSES • SOY SAUCE • STOUT BEER • TOMATO JUICE • VEGAN WORCESTERSHIRE SAUCE • VEGEMITE/MARMITE

BASES:

BEETROOT (BEETS) • LENTILS • MUSHROOMS • QUINOA • SEITAN • TEMPEH • TVP

BEEF-STYLE STOCK POWDER

✦

MAKES 180 G (6½ OZ)

The stocks in this book have less sodium than store-bought ones, so you can be more heavy-handed with smoked salt and other finishing salts.

INGREDIENTS	
porcini powder and shiitake powder mix	130 G (1 CUP)
bay leaves	4
soft brown sugar	1 TBSP
celery salt	1 TBSP
onion powder	1 TBSP
tomato powder	1 TBSP
dried parsley	1 TBSP
coarse smoked salt	1 TBSP
garlic powder	2 TSP
sumac	2 TSP
dried thyme	1½ TSP
dried rosemary	1 TSP
cacao powder	1 TSP
dried sage	1 TSP
dried marjoram	1 TSP
ground white pepper	½ TSP
coriander seeds	½ TSP
FOR LIQUID STOCK	
vegemite or marmite	¼ TSP
boiling water	250 ML (1 CUP)

① Combine the ingredients in a blender and pulse until fine. Store in an airtight jar for up to 6 months.

② To make liquid stock, mix 1 heaped teaspoon of beef-style stock powder with the vegemite or marmite and boiling water and use as needed.

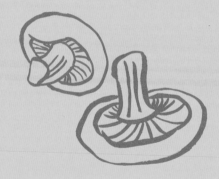

WASHED SEITAN STEAK

MAKES 2

This is not a missed steak! Vegans, like unpopular emperors, have a long history of being suspicious of what's in our meal. You'll make this whole recipe out of plants from start to finish, bite in and still do a double take. So, refer back to this sentence when you need to remind yourself that it's all 100% vegan.

INGREDIENTS

Basic washed seitan, mostly washed (see pages 20 and 24)	1 × QUANTITY
olive oil	2 TBSP

STEAK SPICE MIX

onion powder	1 TSP
torula yeast	1 TSP
porcini powder	1 TSP
garlic powder	1 TSP
red rice yeast powder	½ TSP
ground pepper	¼ TSP
sea salt	¼ TSP

STEAK GLAZE

red wine	175 ML (6 FL OZ)
soy sauce	3 TBSP
prepared horseradish	2 TSP
vegemite or marmite	½ TSP
liquid smoke	¼ TSP

Alternative serving choices include using the cooked steaks in place of beef patties for a mean steak burger or, once seared, slicing thinly and serving on a charcuterie board.

① To make the steak spice mix, combine the ingredients in a bowl.

② On a clean work surface and using your hands, thoroughly knead the steak spice mix ingredients into the seitan dough until fully dispersed. Alternatively, place the dough in a stand mixer fitted with a dough hook, add the spice mix and cut in until fully dispersed.

③ Stretch out the dough into a long strand, then tie several loose knots into the strand. Knot together the entire piece of dough into a rough ball shape, then divide the dough into two portions. Stretch each portion out and press into thin steak shapes using your palms.

④ Heat half the olive oil in a heavy-based frying pan over high heat. Add the steaks and sear, flipping occasionally and using a spatula to press them down and coerce them to stay in shape, for 10-12 minutes, until a crust forms on both sides.

⑤ Mix together the steak glaze ingredients and pour over the steaks. Reduce the heat to medium-low and simmer, flipping the steaks occasionally, for 20-25 minutes. Increase the heat to medium-high during the last few minutes, so the liquid thickens into a sauce that the steaks will eagerly drink up.

⑥ When the pan is mostly dry, remove the steaks from the heat and allow to fully cool in the pan. Scrape up any extra sauce and use to glaze the steaks. Treat them to another stay in the fridge for a few hours and DO NOT taste the glaze or else the temptation to not wait long enough will be too great.

⑦ When ready to serve, heat the remaining oil in a frying pan over high heat. Season the steaks with salt and pepper, then sear for 2-3 minutes each side. NOW you can dig in.

PREPARING WASHED SEITAN AS BEEF MINCE

MAKES ABOUT 400 G (14 OZ)

The cheapest beef on the market. Just wash a bag of flour into fatty washed seitan, knead in some flavour then crumble in a food processor. Use as mince and build in familiar flavours (ideas galore in this chapter!) for chewy, beefy meals.

INGREDIENTS

Fatty washed seitan (see page 22)	½ × QUANTITY

BEEF SPICE MIX

onion powder	1 TSP
torula yeast	1 TSP
porcini powder	1 TSP
garlic powder	1 TSP
red rice yeast powder	½ TSP
black pepper	¼ TSP
sea salt	¼ TSP

① Combine the beef spice mix ingredients in a bowl. On a clean work surface, knead the beef spice mix into the mid-washed seitan until fully dispersed. Alternatively, place in a stand mixer fitted with a dough hook and cut in the ingredients until fully dispersed.

② Divide the fatty washed seitan into four portions. Use your hands to stretch each portion into a long strand. If the seitan is too resistant, allow it rest for 10 minutes before trying again.

③ Once stretched, braid or knot each strand as many times as you can to create more gluten folds for textural variety.

④ Knot the strands into tight balls and wrap securely in foil. Steam for 60 minutes. Transfer to a bowl, cover and cool in the fridge overnight for best texture.

⑤ Unwrap from the foil and transfer the seitan to a food processor. Blitz until finely chopped and the seitan resembles mince. Use in any recipe that calls for beef mince, such as the Spaghetti bolognese on page 242 or Guinness pie on page 244.

SEITAN BEEF FROM VWG:

SHREDS, CHUNKS, PATTIES & CUTLETS

MAKES 400 G (14 OZ)

Seitan made from vital wheat gluten is much easier to incorporate flavours into the interior so we're loading up! Prepare a double batch of steps one and two and you're already well on your way to making a the Barbecue beer brisket on page 248.

INGREDIENTS

DRY INGREDIENTS

vital wheat gluten	150 G (1 CUP)
psyllium husk	1½ TBSP
porcini powder	1 TBSP
smoked paprika	1 TSP
ground cumin	¾ TSP
garlic powder	2 TSP
onion powder	2 TSP
soft brown sugar	2 TSP
MSG	½ TSP
agar agar powder	½ TSP
black pepper	½ TSP
red yeast rice powder (optional, for colour)	¼ TSP

WET INGREDIENTS

red wine	100 ML (3½ FL OZ)
tomato paste (concentrated purée)	2 TBSP
soy sauce	2 TBSP
liquid smoke	¾ TSP
grated vegan shortening	1 TBSP

① Combine the dry ingredients in a large bowl and create a well in the centre.

② Mix together the wet ingredients in another bowl. Pour the wet ingredients into the well and stir until completely combined. Transfer the mixture to a stand mixer fitted with a dough hook and knead for 1-2 minutes, to form the gluten strands.

BEEF-STYLE SHREDS AND CHUNKS

① To make beef-style shreds, follow steps 2-4 opposite to prepare the seitan. Once steamed, unwrap from the foil and use your hands to pull the seitan into shreds. Use in recipes wherever shredded beef is called for or replace the mushrooms in the Lamb shish kebab on page 252.

② To make larger chunks, tear each ball into two to four pieces, following the knotted grains within the seitan to create wonderfully irregular hunks of beefy seitan meat. Use in the Maafé on page 246 or in stews and braises.

BEEF-STYLE PATTIES AND CUTLETS

① To make beef-style patties and cutlets, divide the dough into four 100 g (3½ oz) portions (for patties) or three 130 g (4½ oz) (for cutlets) and use your hands to press each out into round patties or longer cutlets.

② Press and roll the patties or cutlets as thinly as possible, then wrap securely in foil, keeping them flat as they may rise slightly while cooking. Steam for 60 minutes.

③ Set aside to cool, then unwrap and grill for about 5 minutes each side.

WHERE'S the BEEF (... and LAMB)?

A cheap dehydrator makes
these jerkies quick and easy;
however, you can approximate
the results by setting your
oven to its lowest temperature,
placing the prepared jerkies
in and leisurely monitoring until
you've achieved jerky perfection
(a few hours give and take from
the dehydrator directions).

Jerky

We know that shiitake mushrooms get an umami punch from the dehydrating process, so let's try it at home. Switch in lion's mane, portobello, king oyster or whatever's on hand for a variety of meat-free jerkies that take the being a jerk out of making some jerk. Alternatively, redeem any failed seitan attempts or use up your offcuts to make seitan jerky, or try slices of the Smoked watermelon roast on page 208, plus the juices, to make smoky watermelon jerky.

INGREDIENTS	
MUSHROOM JERKY	
large fresh shiitake mushrooms, thinly sliced	800 G (1 LB 12 OZ)
soy sauce	240 ML (8 FL OZ)
mirin	120 ML (4 FL OZ)
soft brown sugar	100 G (3½ OZ)
minced ginger	1 TBSP
sesame oil	1 TBSP
minced garlic	1 TBSP
black pepper	1 TSP
liquid smoke	1 TSP
smoked salt (optional)	1½–2 TSP
WATERMELON JERKY	
Smoked watermelon roast, with juices (see page 208)	1 × QUANTITY
SEITAN JERKY	
offcuts of already cooked seitan	400 G (14 OZ)
soy sauce	200 ML (7 FL OZ)
vegan fish sauce	100 ML (3½ FL OZ)
granulated sugar	150 G (5½ OZ)
maple syrup	3 TBSP
vegan worcestershire sauce	2 TSP
liquid hickory smoke	2 TSP
black pepper	½ TSP
cayenne pepper	½ TSP

To make the mushroom jerky, place the mushroom in a large bowl. Whisk the remaining mushroom jerky ingredients, except the smoked salt, in a separate bowl, then pour over the mushroom and massage in the marinade. Cover and place in the fridge for 1–12 hours to marinate (the longer you leave it the better the flavour).

Transfer to a dehydrator lined with baking paper and baste the mushroom with the remaining marinade in the bowl. Dehydrate on medium–low for 12 hours, then taste and (if desired!) rub in some smoked salt – the jerky'll taste better a day later so be patient. Store in an airtight glass jar for up to 3 months.

To make the watermelon jerky, slice the watermelon and position it on a dehydrator tray. Use a pastry brush to baste the juices from smoking over the pink flesh of the watermelon. Dehydrate on high for 18–24 hours until dry and chewy. Store in an airtight glass jar for up to 3 months.

To make the seitan jerky, thinly slice the seitan into even-sized pieces, then transfer to a bowl.

Whisk together the remaining ingredients and pour over the sliced seitan. Toss to coat and allow to marinate for at least 1 hour. Dehydrate on medium–low for 8–12 hours, until chewy and intensely delicious. Store in an airtight glass jar for up to 3 months.

Steak 'n' Shroomy Sauce

✷ ✷

This is one of my favourite recipes in this book and I recommend you don't skip it on your to-cook list! This dense, savoury seared steak with the most lip-smacking glaze you'll ever put together with your own two hands is the ultimate triumph for plant-based meats and a real flex for what can be achieved by washing a ball of dough. Extra shroomy sauce on top for a double savoury smackdown, because vegans didn't go so long lacking in umami-rich options for us to skimp on it now.

INGREDIENTS	
cooked Washed seitan steaks (see page 235)	1 × QUANTITY
SHROOMY SAUCE	
dairy-free butter	1 TBSP
French shallot, minced	1
mixed mushroom medley, chopped	500 G (1 LB 2 OZ)
sea salt and black pepper	TO SEASON
thyme sprigs	4
dry white wine	125 ML (½ CUP)
soy milk or oat cream	200 ML (7 FL OZ)
mustard powder	2 TSP
chopped dill fronds	2–3 TBSP
vegan worcestershire sauce	2 TSP

To make the shroomy sauce, melt the butter in a saucepan over medium–low heat, add the shallot and cook for 5–7 minutes, until soft and fragrant. Stir in the mushroom and a pinch of salt and cook for 15 minutes until the mushrooms are browned. Add the thyme and cook for 1 minute. Pour in the wine and stir (or for fancy folk: deglaze), then add the remaining ingredients. Simmer, stirring occasionally, for 10–15 minutes, until reduced to a thick sauce. Crack in lots of pepper, to taste.

Transfer the just-cooked seitan steaks to two plates, pour over the shroomy sauce and dig in.

SERVES 2

Spaghetti Bolognese

Experts say a well-planned vegan diet can be suitable for humans at every stage of life. For the rest of us, a poorly organised, almost entirely impulsive vegan diet seems to work just fine. Whichever lane you fall in, nearly everybody's got the time and ingredients to throw together a classic bowl of spag bol.

INGREDIENTS	
dried spaghetti	200 G (7 OZ)
TOMATO SAUCE	
olive oil	1½ TBSP
onion, diced	1
carrot, diced	½
celery stalk, diced	½
tomato paste (concentrated purée)	1½ TBSP
garlic cloves	4
passata (puréed tomatoes)	750 ML (3 CUPS)
beef-style stock powder	1 TBSP
dried oregano	1 TSP
unsweetened cocoa powder	½ TSP
ground nutmeg	¼ TSP
bay leaf	1
balsamic vinegar	2 TSP
soy or oat milk	125 ML (½ CUP)
red wine	125 ML (½ CUP)
sea salt and black pepper	TO SEASON
SEITAN MINCE	
seitan beef mince (see page 236)	300 G (2 CUPS)
liquid smoke	½ TSP
OR WALNUT LENTIL MINCE	
walnuts	150 G (1½ CUPS)
cooked brown lentils	150 G (¾ CUP)
sundried tomatoes	50 G (⅓ CUP)
olive oil	1 TBSP
liquid smoke	¼ TSP

To get started on the tomato sauce, heat the oil in a saucepan over medium–low heat. Add the onion, carrot and celery and gently cook, stirring frequently, for 30 minutes or until completely soft. Stir in the tomato paste and cook for 2 minutes. Process the garlic and passata in a blender, then add to the pan along with the stock powder, oregano, cocoa, nutmeg, bay leaf, vinegar, milk and wine. Simmer, stirring occasionally, for 1 hour. Add the salt and pepper to taste and fish out the bay leaf.

To make the seitan mince, add the seitan beef crumbles, the liquid smoke and 60 ml (¼ cup) of water to the sauce during the last 20 minutes of cooking.

Alternatively, to make the walnut lentil mince, use a food processor to crumble the walnuts, lentils and tomatoes into a mince. Heat the olive oil in a saucepan over medium heat, then toast the mince for 5 minutes. Add the mince, liquid smoke and 60 ml (¼ cup) of water to the sauce during the last 10 minutes of cooking.

Cook the pasta in plenty of salted boiling water as per the packet instructions, then drain. Aim to cook your pasta about 10 minutes before the sauce is ready, so all the dish elements are punctual and fresh at your appointed serving time (about 1½ hours after you start).

Stir the pasta through your chosen sauce and serve.

SERVES 2-3

WHERE'S _the_ BEEF (... _and_ LAMB)?

Guinness Pie

In this pie, the usual chewy, gravy-laden meat goo gets spiked with a good swig of stout, which is then encased in flaky pastry like an edible flask. Use stock made from mushroom stock powder, rehydrated shiitakes or a mix of fresh mushrooms, or even the steaming water from Faux gras (see page 221). Select a medley of different mushrooms to make up the 200 g (7 oz) for more complex flavour.

INGREDIENTS	
frozen dairy-free puff pastry sheets, thawed	2
olive oil	2 TSP
soy milk	1 TSP
steamed green peas	TO SERVE
mint leaves	TO SERVE

PIE FILLING	
mushroom stock	240 ML (8 FL OZ)
TVP mince	100 G (3½ OZ)
dairy-free butter	2 TBSP
French shallots, finely diced	2
mixed mushroom medley, roughly chopped	200 G (7 OZ)
carrot, finely diced	1
celery stalk, finely diced	1
plain (all-purpose) flour	2 TBSP
guinness or stout	440 ML (15 FL OZ)
beef-style stock powder	2 TSP
kecap manis	2 TBSP
vegan worcestershire sauce	2 TBSP
soft brown sugar	1 TBSP
vegemite	1 TSP
unsweetened cocoa powder	½ TSP
chopped thyme leaves	½ TSP
black pepper	½ TSP

To make the pie filling, heat the mushroom stock in a saucepan over medium heat, then tip in the TVP, remove from the heat and set aside for 5 minutes to rehydrate.

Melt the butter in a saucepan over medium heat, add the shallot, mushroom, carrot and celery and sauté for 10 minutes. Mix in the flour and cook for 2 minutes. Add the remaining filling ingredients, stir well and simmer over low heat for 10 minutes or until reduced slightly.

Preheat the oven to 150°C (300°F). Choose two small oval pie dishes or ramekins for the pies.

Cut one of the pastry sheets in half and use it to line the pie dishes or ramekins, trimming any excess pastry. Up-end one dish or ramekin and place on the remaining sheet of pastry. Use a knife to cut out two pie lids. Set aside.

Line the dishes or ramekins with baking paper, then add baking beads and blind bake for 10 minutes. Remove from the oven and lift out the baking paper and beads. Carefully press down any risen pastry.

Increase the oven temperature to 200°C (400°F).

Fill each pastry crust with half the filling, pressing it in to fill up completely. Place the pie lids on top, then use a fork or your fingertips to crimp where the pastry top meets the base and seal the filling inside so it doesn't have any chance of escape.

Cut leaf shapes in varying sizes from the remaining puff pastry scraps, using the knife to etch texture into the leaves. Place them across the top of the pies and press in to decorate and cover evidence of imperfections. Whisk together the olive oil and soy milk, then brush over the top of the pies. Bake for 20–25 minutes, until the pastry is cooked through. Serve with steamed peas, topped with a few mint leaves.

MAKES 2 INDIVIDUAL PIES

Maafé

✴

This beefy West African peanut stew will cure whatever's ailing you, providing it's not a peanut allergy. It freezes well for the perfect repeat weeknight dinner.

INGREDIENTS

vegetable oil	2 TBSP
onion, roughly chopped	1
garlic cloves, roughly chopped	4
minced ginger	2 TBSP
ground turmeric	1½ TSP
fenugreek seeds	1 TSP
chilli powder	HEAPED TSP
ground cumin	1½ TSP
ground cinnamon	1 TSP
tomato paste (concentrated purée)	2 TBSP
large sweet potato, unpeeled, diced	1
carrots, diced	2
diced tomato	300 G (2½ CUPS)
dried shiitake mushrooms	50 G (1½ CUPS)
beef-style stock	1.75 LITRES (60 FL OZ)
bay leaves	2
large eggplant (aubergine), diced	1
red capsicums (bell peppers), thinly sliced	3
large TVP chunks	250 G (9 OZ)
smooth peanut butter	250 G (1 CUP)
black pepper	TO SEASON

TO SERVE

crushed peanuts	–
chilli flakes	–
coriander (cilantro) sprigs	–
lime wedges	–

Heat half the vegetable oil in a large saucepan over medium heat. Add the onion and garlic and cook, stirring occasionally, for 5 minutes. Add the ginger and turmeric, fenugreek, chilli powder, cumin, cinnamon and tomato paste and cook for 3 minutes. Stir in the sweet potato and carrot and cook for 5 minutes. Add the tomato, shiitakes, stock, bay leaves and eggplant and bring to the boil, then reduce the heat to low, cover and simmer for 20 minutes.

Meanwhile, preheat the oven grill (broiler).

Massage the sliced capsicum with the remaining oil, place on a baking tray and grill (broil), tossing frequently, for 20–25 minutes until charred.

Place the TVP chunks in a bowl and ladle over 250 ml (1 cup) of hot broth from the stew and set aside for 10 minutes to soften. While this is happening, remove the bay leaves from the stew, then add the peanut butter and pepper to taste. Use a stick blender to purée the mixture until smooth. Add in the TVP chunks and most of the charred capsicum, then simmer for a further 15 minutes.

Let the stew sit for at least 20 minutes before serving, so the TVP is fully hydrated. Serve your hot bowl of healthy, drinkable peanut sauce with the reserved charred capsicum, a few crushed peanuts, chilli flakes, coriander leaves and a lime wedge or, really, anything else that might help deter you from drinking the whole bowl in one gulp.

SERVES 6-8

You can use beefy seitan chunks (page 237) instead of TVP as an alternative!

Barbecue Beer Brisket

The best way to recreate a smoked slab of meat out of plants is to treat them equally on the barbecue. Smoking seitan low 'n' slow for hours rewards you with the same crisp bark, tender inside and smoky flavour. The process won't feel that brisk, and it may take some time, but hey – you've gotta risk it to get the brisket.

INGREDIENTS

vegetable oil	1 TBSP

BRISKET

Seitan beef from VWG (see page 237)	2 × QUANTITIES
plain (all-purpose) flour	2 TBSP
minced garlic	2 TSP
red yeast rice powder OR	1 TSP
vegan-friendly red food colouring (both optional)	A FEW DROPS

BARBECUE BEER SAUCE

dark beer (stout)	3 TBSP
tomato ketchup	3 TBSP
caramelised onion relish	1 TBSP
molasses	2 TSP
white vinegar	2 TSP
paprika	1 TSP
vegan worcestershire sauce	1 TSP
wholegrain mustard	1 TSP
garlic powder	½ TSP
sea salt	¼ TSP

To start on the brisket, divide the seitan beef dough into six pieces, then use your hands to flatten each portion as much as possible. Lay three pieces on a plate and microwave on High for 45 seconds. Vigorously knead the remaining three pieces for 30 seconds each, then flatten again.

Mix together the flour, garlic and 60 ml (¼ cup) of water to make a garlic paste. Remove one-third and add to it the red yeast rice powder or food colouring (if using).

On a work surface, stack the six pieces of seitan, alternating between the microwaved and non-microwaved pieces and brushing the uncoloured garlic paste between each layer. Allow to rest for 5 minutes, then press and shape the relaxed seitan into a rectangle. Rub the reserved paste into the exterior of the seitan to mimic a pink smoke ring. Cover with plastic wrap or foil and rest in the fridge for anywhere from 1 hour to overnight.

Prepare a smoking box and barbecue or smoker as per the instructions on page 52. Place the smoking box directly above the heat source and place a baking tray underneath the grill, away from direct heat. Lay the brisket on the grill above the tray, then close the barbecue or smoker, leaving a gap for airflow. Smoke for 1 hour, replenishing the wood chips as needed. Turn the brisket over halfway and baste with water.

Whisk together the barbecue beer sauce ingredients and baste the brisket all over. Smoke for a further 2½ hours, basting and turning every 20 minutes as the glaze dries.

Whisk a teaspoon of the remaining glaze with the oil and glaze the entire brisket. Transfer the brisket directly over the heat on the barbecue grill. Cook for 4–5 minutes on each side to create char marks and finish off the brisket. Allow to cool slightly, slice up and serve for the full payoff.

SERVES 8

For a chewier texture, serve the brisket fully cooled or after an overnight stint in the fridge. The brisket is also fantastic sliced and grilled or served as a deli meat!

Beet Tartare

If you look up Julia Child using a blowtorch to make steak tartare on the David Letterman show, you'll find a masterclass on how to improvise a dish; her original goal was hamburgers but the hotplate wouldn't turn on. You'll also find Julia's biggest challenge after all that was convincing David that she was serving up anything but suspicious-looking meat with flamed cheese atop. She's less successful on this front given tartare is literally raw meat.

We're drawing inspiration for this dish from Julia's improvisational approach: for the tartare, we're using earthy beetroot and keeping the standard mix-ins, but the egg yolk is getting upgraded to layers of smoky aioli. Serve with toasted bread.

INGREDIENTS	
beetroot (beets)	500 G (1 LB 2 OZ)
olive oil	1 TBSP
balsamic vinegar	1 TBSP
finely sliced chives, plus extra to scatter	3 TBSP
small white onion, finely chopped	1/3
minced capers, plus extra to scatter	1 TBSP
dijon mustard	3 TSP
minced dill pickles (gherkins)	1 TBSP
hot sauce	SPLASH
vegan worcestershire sauce	1 TSP
tomato ketchup	1 TSP
Smoked aioli (see page 55) in a squeeze bottle	1/2 × QUANTITY
toasted bread	TO SERVE

Preheat the oven to 225°C (440°F).

Coat the beetroot in the olive oil and place in a large casserole dish (Dutch oven). Roast for 1½ hours (less for small, longer for very large beetroot) until the beetroot are fork tender. Allow to cool, then peel and finely dice.

Place the beetroot in a large bowl, stir in the balsamic vinegar, then mix in the chives, onion, capers, mustard, dill pickle, hot sauce, worcestershire sauce and ketchup.

Grab two serving plates and place an egg-ring in the middle of one plate. Spoon in some beetroot mixture to one-third fill the ring, then smooth down. Squeeze a little aioli across the top, then repeat twice to fill the entire ring with a solid patty layered with aioli. Remove the ring and repeat on the other plate.

Generously pipe more aioli on the tartare and scatter the extra capers and chives on top. Store in the fridge to allow the flavours to meld and serve with warm, toasted bread when you've emotionally prepared yourself to fall in love with beetroot all over again.

SERVES 2 AS A STARTER

Lamb Shish Kebab

Balancing the skewers over the rim of a baking tray is a novel way to turn your oven into a miniature, manual rotisserie spit for these skewers. This recipe is the perfect excuse to crack out a bowl of fresh Greek salad: chunkily chop tomatoes, cucumber, red onion and green capsicum (bell pepper), then toss with kalamata olives, dried oregano, dairy-free feta, olive oil, salt and pepper.

INGREDIENTS	
oyster and pearl mushrooms	500 G (1 LB 2 OZ)
red onion, cut into chunks	1
olive oil	1 TSP
sea salt and black pepper	TO SEASON
SPICED YOGHURT	
dairy-free yoghurt	250 G (1 CUP)
lemon juice	2 TBSP
lemon zest	1 TSP
garlic cloves, smashed and peeled	2
extra-virgin olive oil	1 TBSP
dried mint	2 TSP
sweet paprika	1½ TSP
sea salt	¾ TSP
ground cumin	¾ TSP
dried oregano	¾ TSP
ground allspice	½ TSP
black pepper	½ TSP
ground cardamom	½ TSP
TAHINI SAUCE	
tahini	90 G (⅓ CUP)
lemon juice	3 TBSP
olive oil	1 TBSP
chopped flat-leaf parsley	1½ TSP
garlic clove, minced	1
chopped mint (optional)	25 G (½ CUP)
sea salt	PINCH

Place the mushrooms in a large mixing bowl and tear any significantly larger mushrooms into smaller chunks.

Combine the spiced yoghurt ingredients in a bowl, then pour over the mushrooms. Stir to coat, using your hands if needed to make sure the mushrooms are fully covered. Cover and marinate in the fridge for 1–12 hours.

Soak five bamboo skewers in cold water for at least 30 minutes. Preheat the oven to 225°C (440°F).

Coat the red onion with the olive oil, salt and pepper.

Whisk together the tahini sauce ingredients in a bowl, then slowly whisk in 3 tablespoons of water until you have a creamy consistency.

Alternating the marinated mushrooms and red onion, thread the ingredients onto the prepared skewers.

Place the skewers in a small roasting tin, so that the tips are resting on the rim of the tin, suspending the skewers in the air like a rotisserie spit. Bake for 45–50 minutes, using two forks either side of the skewers to lift and rotate occasionally if needed. When the mushrooms are crispy, remove from the oven and serve with the tahini sauce, or continue on to Gozleme (see page 254).

MAKES 5 SKEWERS

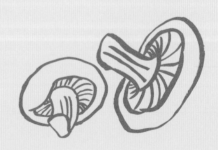

Gozleme

I learned how to make this Turkish stuffed flatbread through my friend Nalin at the Greek-ish Vegan (that's Greek and Turkish!) cooking classes we taught together in Melbourne, Australia. Her top tips were to use the thickest tomato paste you can find, add kalamata olives for extra flavour and say the damn thing right! As Nalin explains: 'The word gozleme has three syllables. The "o" in the first syllable rhymes with the "i" in the word "flirt", but in a short staccato way. Then the two "e"s are both pronounced to rhyme with the "e" in the word "pet". Emphasis is on the first syllable. So it's "GOZ-le-me", not "goz-leem"!'

Thankfully, it's less complicated to make than it is to say. Swap out the fillings for spinach and cheese, other meats from this book or whatever you please.

INGREDIENTS	
Lamb shish kebab (see page 252)	1 × QUANTITY
vegetable oil	FOR SHALLOW-FRYING
tomato paste (concentrated purée)	2 TBSP
dairy-free feta, crumbled	140 G (4½ OZ) PLUS EXTRA TO SERVE
pitted kalamata olives, chopped	80 G (½ CUP)
small red capsicum (bell pepper), finely diced	½
lemon wedges	TO SERVE
DOUGH	
active instant yeast	1 TSP
warm water	200 ML (7 FL OZ)
plain (all-purpose) flour	350 G (12½ OZ) PLUS EXTRA
sea salt	½ TSP
olive oil	3 TBSP PLUS EXTRA

To make the dough, mix the yeast and warm water with a pinch of flour. Allow to sit for 10 minutes to bloom. Combine the remaining flour and the salt in a mixing bowl, then mix through the yeast mixture and oil. Knead in a stand mixer fitted with a dough hook for 3 minutes, adding more flour if needed for the dough to come together in a ball. Place in an oiled bowl, cover and rest for 1 hour for it to rise to the occasion. Divide the dough into quarters.

Slide the mushrooms and red onion off the lamb shish kebab skewers and chop into small pieces.

Coat the base of a large saucepan with the vegetable oil and set over medium–high heat. Flour a work surface and grab one-quarter of the dough. Roll into a thin oval and smear 2 teaspoons of tomato paste over one half, leaving an empty strip around the edge. Scatter over one quarter of the feta, olives and capsicum, then top with some of the mushroom and red onion, making sure everything is evenly distributed. Fold over the other half of the dough and use your fingers to seal the edges tightly.

Place the gozleme in the hot oil and fry for 3–4 minutes each side until golden and black spots are beginning to appear. Replenish the oil between gozleme as you continue to roll and build each one while the previous one is frying.

Place the fried gozleme on a chopping board and cut into even squares. Serve hot with extra feta crumbled over the top and lemon wedges for squeezing.

SERVES 4

Chimichurri Steak Tacos

If you've got a beef with mushrooms, you'll thoroughly enjoy crushing them to death via this method. Brutally collapsing them as they cook allows them to sizzle and brown in their own juices, it'll force the umami out – and quickly! By the time you've put together a lovely, fresh herby chimichurri sauce, you can dress the seared mushroom remains with it and bury them in a taco.

INGREDIENTS

shimeji, oyster, pearl or lion's mane mushrooms (or a mixed medley)	400 G (14 OZ)
sea salt and black pepper	TO SEASON
small corn tortillas	8
avocado, sliced	1
fresh jalapeno, thinly sliced	1
coriander (cilantro) leaves	TO SERVE
lime wedges	TO SERVE

PICKLED RED ONION

small red onion, thinly sliced	1
white vinegar	185 ML (3/4 CUP)
granulated sugar	2 TBSP
sea salt	1 TSP

CHIMICHURRI SAUCE

garlic cloves, smashed and peeled	4
long red chilli, chopped	1
coarse sea salt	1 TSP
olive oil	125 ML (1/2 CUP)
lemon juice	2 TBSP
finely chopped flat-leaf parsley	15 G (1/2 CUP)
finely chopped chives	2 TBSP
dried oregano	1 TBSP
black pepper	TO SEASON

To make the pickled red onion, place the onion in a clean jar. Place the vinegar, sugar, salt and 125 ml (½ cup) of water in a saucepan and bring to the boil. Once the sugar has dissolved, pour the vinegar mixture into the jar. Set aside for 1 hour to pickle.

To make the chimichurri sauce, mash the garlic, chilli and coarse sea salt using a mortar and pestle. Mix in the remaining ingredients to complete the chimichurri.

Grab a large saucepan and place over medium heat. Add the mushrooms and press with the base of a smaller saucepan, following the the guide on page 44. Crack salt and pepper over the mushrooms, then press down again to flatten. They may emit a screaming noise. Don't worry! They're just very cross with you but will soon get over it. Baste heartily with the chimichurri and cook, pressing occasionally and basting frequently, for 10 minutes until beginning to char. Remove from the heat and use a fork to break up if needed.

Microwave the tortillas under a damp cloth in 30-second bursts on High until warmed.

Divide the flattened mushroom among the tortillas and drizzle a little chimichurri sauce on top. Add the avocado, slices of pickled onion, jalapeno and coriander if you're into it. Serve with the lime wedges on the side. Buen provecho!

MAKES 8 TACOS

Meatballs in Sauce

Mushrooms come packing all the flavour and protein you need. Whizzed up with other goodies, then rolled and baked in a simple tomato sauce, they satiate just as well as any meatball could. These tasty mushballs are anything but mushy. Wildly moreish and easy AF to make, they're a top pick for your weeknight dinners.

INGREDIENTS

mixed cherry tomatoes	500 G (1 LB 2 OZ)
onion, sliced	1
minced garlic	2 TBSP
dried basil	2 TSP
olive oil	3 TBSP
sea salt and black pepper	TO SEASON
cooking oil	SPRAY
crusty bread or cooked spaghetti	TO SERVE
basil leaves	TO SERVE

MUSHROOM MEATBALL MINCE

olive oil	1 TBSP
onion, diced	1
mixed mushroom medley, roughly chopped	500 G (1 LB 2 OZ)
garlic cloves, minced	4
flaxseed (linseed) meal	1½ TBSP
soy sauce	1 TBSP
rolled (porridge) oats	75 G (¾ CUP)
dried okara or breadcrumbs	75 G (¾ CUP)
nutritional yeast	2 TBSP
chopped flat-leaf parsley	2 TBSP
rosemary leaves	2 TSP
thyme leaves	2 TSP
liquid smoke	½ TSP
dried oregano	½ TSP
sea salt	½ TSP

Preheat the oven to 180°C (350°F).

Pierce the tomatoes, then place them on a baking tray, along with the onion. Coat the ingredients in the garlic, basil, oil, salt and pepper. Bake for 30 minutes, then transfer to a blender and purée until smooth. Pour the sauce into a baking dish.

Increase the oven temperature to 200°C (400°F). Grease and line a baking tray.

To make the mushroom meatball mince, heat the oil in a saucepan over medium heat. Add the onion and sauté for 10 minutes, then remove from the pan. Add the mushroom and a splash of water to the pan and increase the heat to medium–high. Cook, stirring, for 10–15 minutes until the moisture from the mushroom evaporates. Stir through the garlic and switch off the heat.

Combine the flaxseed meal and soy sauce in a small bowl to form a gel egg. Transfer the mushroom mixture to a food processor, crack in the gel egg, add the remaining mince ingredients and purée for 1 minute until the texture is uniform.

Use your hands to roll the mince mixture into golf ball–sized balls and place on the prepared tray. Spray with cooking oil spray and bake for 15 minutes, rolling occasionally so they crisp up on all sides. Place the meatballs in the sauce and stir to coat. Bake for 5 minutes, then serve with crusty bread or freshly cooked spaghetti with the basil leaves on top.

SERVES 4-5

Mushroom Steak Frites

Mushrooms and potatoes don't need much more than technique to put on a rather convincing impression of steak frites. Read up further on why squashing mushrooms while they cook creates a dense steak in minutes on page 44.

INGREDIENTS

large lion's mane mushrooms	2
sea salt and black pepper	TO SEASON
red wine	60 ML (¼ CUP)
soy sauce	1 TBSP

FRITES

large russet potatoes, unpeeled	1.5 KG (3 LB 5 OZ)
sea salt	TO SEASON
canola oil	FOR DEEP-FRYING

You can also use maitake mushrooms torn into chunks or whole portobello mushrooms to make the steaks.

If you have one, a sandwich press makes quick work of flattening the mushroom steaks.

For the frites, fill a large saucepan with cold water. Slice the potatoes into your desired thickness. Add the fries to the water as you go, replacing with fresh cold water when done. Set aside to soak for at least 4 hours. Drain and place the fries back in the pan, cover with fresh water and season generously with salt. Bring to the boil over high heat and cook until the fries are just soft enough to pierce. Drain in a colander, then dry completely using a clean tea towel. Transfer to the freezer to fully cool and firm back up.

Heat the canola oil in a large heavy-based saucepan over medium–high heat to 150°C (300°F) on a kitchen thermometer. Working in batches, add the fries to the hot oil, turning the heat to high just after they enter the pan. Loosen the fries with a slotted spoon, then fry for 8–10 minutes, until they form a light crust. Transfer the fries to a plate lined with paper towel. When dry, return the fries to the freezer to cool completely (reserve the oil).

Heat the oil in the pan to 190°C (375°F). Working in small batches again, cook the fries for 5 minutes until golden and crisp. Line a large bowl with paper towel and transfer the fries to the bowl. Toss lightly, then discard the paper towel. Immediately throw an obscene amount of salt over the fries and toss everything in the bowl.

Meanwhile, halve each mushroom horizontally through the middle to make thick steak-shaped slabs. Season with a good crack of salt and pepper.

Preheat a large frying pan over medium heat and add the mushroom. Sit a small heavy-based saucepan on the mushroom and press, allowing the mushroom to simmer in its own liquid for 5–8 minutes. Remove them from the pan, leaving any charred pieces behind.

Combine the red wine and soy sauce, then deglaze the pan with it. Allow to bubble for 2 minutes until thickened. Return the mushroom to the pan and coat in the wine glaze for a further 5 minutes. Serve immediately with the frites.

SERVES 4

Rogan Josh

The naan recipe comes from an old friend and kitchen compadre, Megan, who unfortunately damaged her garlic receptors years ago and now compensates with at least one bulb per recipe. In her honour, this garlic naan is a little more garlic than naan and makes the perfect edible bowl for serving the warming, flavour-packed lamb-style rogan josh.

INGREDIENTS

black bean tempeh, cut into 4 cm (1½ in) chunks	600 G (1 LB 5 OZ)
dairy-free butter, plus extra for cooking the naan	60 G (2 OZ)
large onion, thinly sliced	1
bay leaves	2
black peppercorns	1 TSP
passata (puréed tomatoes)	240 ML (8 FL OZ)
dairy-free yoghurt, plus extra to serve	120 G (4½ OZ)
soy sauce	2 TBSP
mint leaves	TO SERVE

ROGAN JOSH PASTE

fennel seeds	1 TSP
mace	1 PIECE
cardamom pods	2 TSP
whole cloves	½ TSP
cumin seeds	1 TSP
tomato paste (concentrated purée)	2 TBSP
minced garlic and ginger	2 TBSP
long red chilli, finely chopped	1
ground coriander	3 TSP
smoked paprika	2 TSP
garam masala	1 TSP
beef-style stock powder	1 TSP
ground turmeric	½ TSP
black pepper	½ TSP
chilli powder	1 TSP

To make the rogan josh paste, toast the fennel seeds, mace, cardamom pods, cloves and cumin seeds in a frying pan over medium heat until fragrant. Transfer to a food processor, along with the remaining paste ingredients and a splash of water and process to a paste. Coat the tempeh in the rogan josh paste, then cover and marinate in the fridge for 1–12 hours.

Heat three-quarters of the butter in a saucepan over high heat. Reserve 2 teaspoons of the paste, then add the tempeh, remaining paste and onion to the pan and sauté for 10–15 minutes. Shove the tempeh to the side and add the bay leaves, peppercorns and remaining butter and cook for 2 minutes. Stir in the passata, then reduce the heat to low and simmer, stirring every now and then, for 45–60 minutes until the sauce is thick. Stir through three-quarters of the yoghurt, the soy sauce, the remaining paste and 150 ml (5 fl oz) of water (if needed) for the last 10 minutes.

To make the naan, combine the flour, sugar, garlic powder and salt in a large bowl. Mix the yeast with 125 ml (½ cup) of warm water in a small bowl. After 5 minutes, add the yoghurt and two-thirds of the butter to the yeast mixture, then stir into the dry ingredients. Knead for 1 minute until a dough ball forms. Cover and allow to rise in a warm place for 1 hour.

Dust a work surface with flour, divide the dough into four portions, then roll out each portion using a rolling pin to make four large round naan. Heat 1 tablespoon of butter in a large frying pan over medium heat. Fry the naan, one at a time, replenishing with more butter as you cook, for 5 minutes each side, until brown spots begin to appear.

NAAN	
self-raising flour, plus extra for dusting	300 G (2 CUPS)
granulated sugar	1 TBSP
garlic powder	2 TSP
sea salt	2 TSP
warm water	125 ML (½ CUP)
active dried yeast	1 TSP
dairy-free yoghurt	2 TBSP
dairy-free butter	90 G (3 OZ)
minced garlic	4 TBSP
chopped flat-leaf parsley	3 TBSP
sea salt	LARGE PINCH

Sauté the remaining butter and the garlic in a saucepan over low heat for 10 minutes. Switch off the heat and stir in the parsley. Use a pastry brush to brush the garlic mixture over both sides of the freshly cooked naan and sprinkle over a hearty amount of salt.

Press the naan into bowls until they sit comfortably and take on the shape. Spoon in the rogan josh, add a dollop of yoghurt and scatter the mint on top.

SERVES 4

Giant Spaghetti-stuffed Meatball

Come and worship at the church of the giant spaghetti monster. As yet, we haven't discovered any living creature that takes the form of a spaghetti-stuffed ball, so for those who prefer fake meat that doesn't look too realistic, you're in for a treat. Ready plant-based mince is easy to source, and if you've got the budget or find a stack on special, this is the perfect shrine to gluttony to turn it into.

INGREDIENTS	
dried spaghetti	175 G (6 OZ)
marinara sauce, plus extra to serve	250 G (1 CUP)
cooking oil	SPRAY
Mushroom meatball mince (see page 258) or store-bought vegan mince	2 × QUANTITIES
grated dairy-free cheese	100 G (1 CUP)
chopped chives	TO SERVE
ARTICHOKE PESTO	
tinned artichoke hearts, drained	150 G (5½ OZ)
chopped flat-leaf parsley leaves	15 G (½ CUP)
chopped basil leaves	3 TBSP
unsalted shelled pistachios	3 TBSP
garlic cloves, smashed and peeled	2
nutritional yeast	2 TBSP
lemon juice	2 TBSP
sea salt and black pepper	GENEROUS AMOUNT
olive oil	60 ML (¼ CUP)

To make the artichoke pesto, place the artichoke hearts, parsley, basil, pistachios, garlic, nutritional yeast, lemon juice and salt and pepper in a food processor and process until smooth. Keep the processor running and slowly pour in the oil. Scrape down the side as needed, taste and adjust, then cover and store in the fridge until ready to use.

Preheat the oven to 200°C (400°F). Grease and line a baking tray.

Cook the spaghetti in plenty of salted boiling water for 8 minutes or until just less than al dente. Drain, then mix with the marinara sauce.

Cover a large mixing bowl with plastic wrap, with extra hanging over the edge. Coat in cooking oil spray. Press the mince mixture in an even layer to line the entire bowl. Sprinkle over the cheese to form a second layer, then tip in the spaghetti. Bring the excess plastic wrap together to fully encase the spaghetti with the mince layer. Remove from the bowl and smooth around the giant meatball. Unwrap the meatball and place on the prepared tray, smoothing the ball into shape. Marvel at your creation. Spray with cooking oil spray and bake for 40–45 minutes until the outside is crisp. Complete your centrepiece by spooning the pesto on top and sprinkling over the chives. Slice up like a cake and serve with extra marinara for good measure.

SERVES 6

It's your turn to eat the blob that ate everything.

Beet Wellington

**Boot the beef for some beet! Serve with your choice of good old gravy,
Shroomy sauce (see page 240) or Olive caramel (see page 270).**

INGREDIENTS

small beetroot (beets)	5–6
olive oil	3 TBSP
frozen dairy-free puff pastry sheets, thawed	2
soy milk	2 TSP
aquafaba	2 TSP

FILLING

French shallots, diced	4
mushrooms, chopped	200 G (7 OZ)
chopped rosemary	1 TBSP
minced garlic	2 TSP
chopped thyme	2 TSP
white wine or sherry	2 TBSP
tempeh	200 G (7 OZ)
brown lentils, cooked	150 G (5½ OZ)
psyllium husk	2 TBSP
vegan worcestershire sauce	1 TBSP
tomato paste (concentrated purée)	1 TBSP
dijon mustard	1 TSP
ground nutmeg	½ TSP
liquid smoke	½ TSP
sea salt and black pepper	TO SEASON

GOOD OLD GRAVY

dairy-free butter	80 G (2¾ OZ)
plain (all-purpose) flour	40 G (1½ OZ)
beef-style stock powder	1 TBSP
dark soy sauce	3 TSP
balsamic vinegar	2 TSP
vegemite or marmite	1 TSP
black pepper	1 TSP

Preheat the oven to 225°C (440°F). Place the beetroot in a casserole dish (Dutch oven). Coat in 1 tablespoon of the oil, then roast for 1 hour, until soft. Peel while warm and set aside.

For the filling, place the shallot and another tablespoon of oil in a saucepan over low heat and gently sauté for 10 minutes. Add the mushroom and cook for 10 minutes, adding splashes of water intermittently so they are sitting in a shallow pool of boiling water until they begin to brown. Add the rosemary, garlic and thyme to the pan, then deglaze with the wine or sherry. Transfer to a food processor, add the remaining filling ingredients and pulse until well combined.

Lay a sheet of plastic wrap on a work surface and place a sheet of puff pastry on top. Evenly spread the filling over the pastry, leaving a 2 cm (¾ in) border. Place the beetroot along the centre of the wellington to fill most of the length. Use the plastic wrap to help you roll the filling and beetroot into a log, rolling the mushroom and pastry around the beetroot until both sides of the pastry meet. Flip the wellington over, then transfer to a baking tray lined with baking paper.

Tuck in the ends of the pastry to seal the log, then cut the remaining puff pastry sheet into thin strips and create a lattice on top of the wellington. Place in the fridge for an hour to firm up. Preheat the oven to 200°C (400°F).

Combine the remaining olive oil, soy milk and aquafaba in a jug, then brush all over the wellington. Transfer to the oven and bake for 35–40 minutes, until lovely and golden.

To make the gravy, heat the butter in a saucepan over medium heat until bubbling. Sift in the flour and stir constantly for 1–2 minutes until you have a roux, then stir through the stock powder. Slowly stir in 500 ml (2 cups) of hot water, then add the soy sauce, vinegar and vegemite and simmer for 5–10 minutes until thickened. Taste and don't skip the pepper as it makes a great difference.

Allow the wellington to rest for 15 minutes, then slice into portions and serve with the good old gravy.

SERVES 6

Herb-crusted Lamb Chops

Despite its deceptive looks and meatiness, this recipe also celebrates all the extra flavours brought to the table by delicious veggies! Get a load of this line up: beautifully spiced and perfectly cooked 'lamb'; a leek bone; soft, marbled eggplant fat; a herby breadcrumb coating; and kalamata olive caramel to drizzle on top. Eyes light up, tastebuds rejoice and minds open to veganism when this dish hits the dinner table. Choose your favourite store-bought plant-based mince to substitute in this recipe for an impressive creation that'll be done quicker than two shakes of a lamb's tail.

You'll want to serve your chops with a potato-centric side dish.

INGREDIENTS	
leek, white part only	1
small eggplants (aubergines)	2
seitan beef mince (see page 236) or use store-bought vegan mince	450 G (1 LB)
chopped mint leaves	3 TBSP
chopped oregano leaves	3 TSP
chopped rosemary leaves	1 TSP
minced garlic	2 TSP
ground sumac	1 TSP
ground cumin	½ TSP
black pepper	½ TSP
dijon mustard	1 TBSP
cooking oil	SPRAY

Cut the leek in half lengthways and wash thoroughly, taking care to keep the leek halves intact. Cut each half lengthways again to create four long 'bones' (1).

Peel the eggplants, then cut a thin slice lengthways off each side of the eggplants to create two flat sides, then halve lengthways to create four roughly rounded 'chop'-shaped slabs (2).

Use a paring knife to carve out the centre and the majority of the eggplant flesh, leaving rough irregular sides to imitate marbled fat. Out of the removed eggplant flesh, carve irregular squiggles (keeping them the same thickness as the eggplant slabs) to make more marbled fat pieces (3).

Cut the smaller end off the eggplants to create a space for the leek 'bone'. Depending on the size of your eggplant, you may need to whittle some of the smaller end to imitate the shape of a lamb chop.

In a large bowl, mash together the mince, herbs and spices. Divide the mince mixture into quarters for each chop and clear a work surface.

Grab an eggplant chop and begin to fill the hole with the mince. Add some of the reserved eggplant marbled fat and secure with more mince mixture (4). Insert a leek bone, white end first, and secure with more mince (5).

CONTINUE ☞

You don't eat meat?
It's OK, we'll make lamb.

LAMB CHOP CRUST

flat-leaf parsley	½ BUNCH
mint	¼ BUNCH
lemon, zest finely grated	1
dry breadcrumbs	50 G (½ CUP)
chopped rosemary leaves	1 BUNCH
olive oil	1½ TBSP

OLIVE CARAMEL

pitted kalamata olives	75 G (2¾ OZ)
kalamata olive brine	125 ML (½ CUP)
black garlic cloves	5
balsamic vinegar	1 TSP
granulated sugar	110 G (½ CUP)

Firmly squeeze and smooth everything into a lamb-chop shape. Level off the mince and smear it over the leek bone to hide it inside, making sure the marbled eggplant is exposed (6). Place on baking paper, then repeat with the remaining eggplant, mince and leek ingredients to make four chops. Transfer to the fridge for an hour to firm up.

Preheat the oven to 200°C (400°F). Grease and line a baking tray.

Blend or combine the lamb chop crust ingredients in a food processor until fine, then tip into a shallow bowl.

Whisk the mustard with 2 tablespoons of water in a separate shallow bowl. Carefully roll the edge of the chops in the mustard, then roll in the crust mixture. Use your hands to firmly secure the crust, then place on the prepared tray. Spray cooking oil over everything and bake for 40 minutes or until cooked through and the eggplant is soft to touch.

Meanwhile, to make the olive caramel, blend together the olives, brine, black garlic and balsamic vinegar. Mix the sugar with 2 tablespoons of water in a saucepan and cook over low heat without stirring. Watch closely and take a meditative moment as it slowly changes colour over the course of 10–15 minutes. Snap out of your reverie just as it reaches a dark amber – it can darken quite rapidly towards the end. Immediately remove from the heat and carefully stir in the olive mixture – be careful as it may splatter. Allow to cool.

To serve, divide the crusted lamb chops among plates and serve with the olive caramel on the side.

Leftover olive caramel will keep in a glass jar in the fridge for up to 2 weeks.

MAKES 4 JUMBO LAMB CHOPS

WHERE'S the BEEF (... and LAMB)?

BURGERS

AND

SANDWICHES

METHYLCELLULOSE • METHYLCELLULOSE AT HOME • FLAVOURED FAT • BASIC METHYLCELLULOSE MINCE
CHICKEN STINGER BURGER • FILLET NO FISH • TUNA SALAD MELT • PULLED-PORK BURGERS
MUFFULETTA • RIBWICH • CHEESEBURGER SLIDERS

BURGER AND SANDWICH BASES

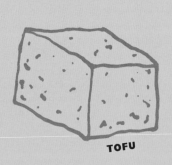

TOFU

WATERMELON HAM

TVP

BANANA BLOSSOMS

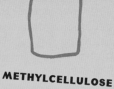

METHYLCELLULOSE

VEGAN SALAMI

VEGAN MORTADELLA

Who can fault a burger or sandwich? There's beauty in the simplicity: sauce, salad and something meaty between bread to hold the lot together. It's a quick meal with breadible packaging that you can pimp out in a million different ways. Of course, this is no secret to the vegan community, who have been enjoying veggie patties, mushroom and tofu burgers for decades. These days, brands of hearty, meaty plant-based patties – pre-formed for your convenience – have broken into the mainstream and aren't hard to find at cheaper price points or as luxury, realistic replacements for whatever your budget and taste.

Elevate those patties with the sauces below and cooking techniques in this chapter for reliable, easy dinners with new, complex flavours every night. Then expand your horizons and make the patties yourself out of loads of different plant-based meat bases, from teeny tiny sliders with homemade mince to a mammoth muffuletta loaded with deli slices and olive salad. Veggie patties better scoot over, because we're living in the renaissance of the vegan burger!

FLAVOUR ADDITIONS AND SAUCES:

STINGER SAUCE • TARTARE SAUCE • CHIPOTLE MAYO • SMOKED AIOLI • BUFFALO SAUCE • GARLIC • MINT
SEAWEED: NORI, KOMBU, DULSE, KELP • WASABI • WHITE WINE

BASES:

TVP • METHYLCELLULOSE • SEITAN • MUSHROOMS • TOFU • JACKFRUIT • BANANA BLOSSOM • BEANS

METHYLCELLULOSE

Methylcellulose is a popular, newfangled binding ingredient that is widely used in commercial plant-based meat products. Chris Maillard is the lead researcher at Unreal, an Australian meat-alternative company pioneering and promoting the properties of eating plant-based foods. He states:

> 'THE EXPLOSION OF THE NEED FOR PLANT-BASED FOODS OVER THE LAST DECADE HAS SEEN COMPANIES RAPIDLY RESEARCHING AND DEVELOPING INGREDIENTS, TECHNIQUES AND PROCESSES TO MIMIC TEXTURE, FLAVOUR AND THE MOUTHFEEL OF MEAT PRODUCTS. METHYLCELLULOSE IS ONE SUCH INGREDIENT, A THERMO-REVERSIBLE HYDROCOLLOID USED TO MIMIC TEXTURE FOR COOKED MEAT ALTERNATIVES.'

This means that at certain temperatures methylcellulose activates and becomes a gel to create a network between all the other ingredients. Fairly new on the block, it's just becoming available to the public and, depending on where you live, may take a little effort to track down. But then again, mother nature took a few billion years to put cows together, so a few weeks waiting for shipping pales in comparison to making one yourself. Your best bet for sourcing food-grade methylcellulose is to search for specialty retailers online.

Food-grade methylcellulose forms a reversible gel that hydrates when cool and solidifies when heated. Once the food drops below each variety's respective gelling temperature range, the gel decays, so when cooking with this ingredient it's important to serve fresh and hot for it to work! Once plant-based meats using methylcellulose are cooled, the product will lose its bite and firmness. This is often why plant-based burgers left to cool end up being mushy. For best results at home, hydrate methylcellulose at cold temperatures by combining with water (50%) and ice (50%), in a food processor or blender before combining with your other ingredients.

WARNING:
SUPER-ADVANCED STUFF!

METHYCELLULOSE AT HOME

As an emerging product, there's no agreed naming convention between different brands and varieties of methylcellulose. To help us navigate, Chris Maillard has put together this guide.

VISCOSITY		YIELD
700 (1)	700cP	(700 × 1)
75X (*Rn X = 10)	750cP	(75 × 10)
4C (*Rn C = 100)	400cP	(4 × 100)
1M (*Rn M = 1000)	1000cP	(1 × 1000)

*Rn = Roman numeral

The two most common naming conventions for methylcellulose are:

① (Grade), (Viscosity) e.g. (K)(4M)
② (Name), (Viscosity) e.g. (Johns)(40,000)

Many different grades are available. The easiest and most suitable to source for home use are the grades K, E, A, MX or HV. The number refers to the viscosity. Here's how to interpret the numbers listed after the grade:

Use this guide to estimate how much methylcellulose to use in your home recipes:

< 500cP = 5-10%
< 1000cP = 2.5-5%
< 5000cP = 1-3%
> 10000cP = 0.5-2%

For example, (A)(4C) - listed commercially as A4C - has a viscosity of 400cP, so using the above at-home guide, the recipes in this book call for it to be used at 5% of the total recipe's weight. A newer, stronger form of methylcellulose (MX) can be used in the same recipes at 1% of the total weight. When in doubt, follow the manufacturer's usage percentage and internal temperature/gelling temperature recommendations to ensure you're getting bang for your buck.

Increasing the percentage of methylcellulose (up to a certain point) will increase the bite strength of your food. The other ingredients in your recipe and the amount of water will also affect the ultimate effectiveness of the methylcellulose. I've included a basic mince recipe (see page 280) in this chapter to show you how to use methylcellulose. If you can only get your hands on a different variety, use the guide above to work out where to start. And join me and the plant-based, food-science revolution in becoming one of the early experimenters helping to discover this ingredient's properties.

FLAVOURED FAT

★ ★ ★

MAKES 180 G (6½ OZ)

Fold fat into plant-based meat mixtures after water or flavoured liquid has had time to properly hydrate the other ingredients. As fat is a great carrier for flavour, I like to add extra ingredients to it before using it in homemade mince recipes.

INGREDIENTS	
sundried tomato oil	100 ML (3½ FL OZ)
refined (flavourless/ odourless) coconut oil	100 ML (3½ FL OZ)
garlic cloves, peeled	30 G (1 OZ)
kombu powder or aonori seaweed flakes	5 G (¼ OZ)
smoked paprika	1 TSP
xanthan gum	¼ TSP

① Combine the sundried tomato oil, coconut oil and garlic in a saucepan and place over very low heat. Cook for 30 minutes to soften the garlic. Remove from the heat if the garlic begins to darken further than a light golden brown.

② Add the remaining ingredients and purée with a stick blender until smooth.

③ Pour the flavoured fat into a freezer-friendly container and freeze until solid. Store in the freezer until needed, then use a fork to scrape through the solid oil to create small flakes for use in recipes.

GET THE LOOK

If you're looking for prominent, unmelted chunks of fat in your finished product, as you get more comfortable using methylcellulose, you may like to experiment and add a small portion to your flavoured fat mix before puréeing with a stick blender.

BURGERS and SANDWICHES

BASIC METHYLCELLULOSE MINCE

★ ★ ★

MAKES 4 X 120 G (4½ OZ) PATTIES

If you're over healthy people acting high and mighty just because they grow their own burgers or whatever, now you can too. Use this recipe to dress up with flavours you love for the perfect stuffing for sausages, or mince to form into Meatballs in sauce (page 258) or beefy burger patties for sliders (page 237).

INGREDIENTS

TVP mince	100 G (3½ OZ)
beef-style stock or mushroom stock	75 ML (2½ FL OZ)
caramelised onion relish	1½ TBSP
liquid smoke	½ TSP
tomato paste (concentrated purée)	1 TBSP
psyllium husk	20 G (¾ OZ)
tapioca flour	2 TSP
red yeast rice powder	1¼ TSP
torula yeast	1 TBSP
porcini powder	2 TSP
dried parsley	2 TSP
liquid aminos	2 TSP
vegemite or marmite	1 TSP
dried thyme	½ TSP
black pepper	½ TSP
flaked flavoured fat (see page 279)	3 TBSP

METHYLCELLULOSE

A4c at 5%:	12.5 G (½ OZ)
plus water	115 ML (4 FL OZ)
plus ice cubes OR	115 G (4 OZ)
MX/HV at 1.5%	4.5 G (¼ OZ)
plus water	100 ML (3½ FL OZ)
plus ice cubes	100 G (3½ OZ)

① Mix together the TVP and stock in a large bowl and allow to sit for 5 minutes to hydrate.

② Stir through the onion relish, liquid smoke and tomato paste. Add the psyllium, tapioca flour, red yeast rice powder, torula yeast, porcini powder, parsley, liquid aminos, vegemite or marmite, thyme and pepper and stir to combine.

③ In a high-powered blender or coffee grinder, pour in the water and ice cubes for the methylcellulose. Add the methylcellulose, seal and blend until the ice is blitzed and you have a cold slurry.

④ Fold this slurry through the ingredients in the bowl and allow to sit for 10 minutes. Sprinkle the fat flakes over the mince and fold them through, too. Cover and place in the fridge for 10 minutes.

⑤ To make burger patties, divide into 120 g (4½ oz) portions and use your hands to mould into smooth patty shapes – a little thicker than desired as you'll press them down while cooking. Once you've mastered that, graduate to using this mince in Meatballs in sauce (see page 258), a Giant spaghetti-stuffed meatball (see page 264), Herb-crusted lamb chops (see page 268) or sausages (see pages 218 and 220).

This is food science at home, so using digital scales is essential for an advanced recipe like this!

Chicken Stinger Burger

Spice, spice baby! Here's a fabulous way to add kick to homemade chicken-style seitan. Substitute with oyster mushrooms or tear the seitan patties into bite-sized pieces to make easy fried chicken-style pieces without pesky accompaniments like 'bread' and 'sauce that might help lessen the pain'.

INGREDIENTS

cornflour (cornstarch)	40 G (⅓ CUP)
vegetable oil	FOR DEEP-FRYING
vegan brioche buns	2
lettuce leaves	4

STINGER MARINADE

chicken-style stock	375 ML (1½ CUPS)
vegan worcestershire sauce	1½ TBSP
vinegar	1 TBSP
mustard powder	1 TSP
chilli powder	1 TSP

CHICKEN SUBSTITUTE

TVP OR	4 LARGE SLICES
Chicken-style seitan patties (see page 64) OR	2
oyster mushrooms	100 G (3½ OZ)

STINGER CRUMB

panko breadcrumbs	35 G (1¼ OZ)
salted corn chips	50 G (1¾ OZ)
chilli powder	1 TSP
garlic powder	½ TSP
sea salt	¼ TSP
MSG	¼ TSP
ground white pepper	⅛ TSP

STINGER SAUCE

vegan mayonnaise	2 TBSP
hot sauce	1 TBSP
tomato ketchup	2 TSP

Combine the stinger marinade ingredients in a bowl. Next, choose your chicken substitute. To prepare the TVP, place the stinger marinade in a small saucepan and bring to the boil. Add the TVP and cook, keeping the slices submerged in the boiling liquid, for 5–10 minutes, until fully softened. Use a fork to stab and press out any bubbles if the TVP slices are too thick to fully hydrate. Squeeze out any excess liquid before proceeding with the recipe. To prepare the seitan patties or mushrooms, soak either ingredient for 10 minutes in the stinger marinade.

Combine the stinger crumb ingredients in a food processor and process to create a fine dust, then tip into a shallow bowl. Using one hand, remove the chicken substitute from the marinade, dust in the cornflour and place on a plate. Whisk the remaining cornflour into the marinade to make a batter. Dip the dusted pieces in the batter, then coat in the stinger crumb, firmly pressing in the crumbs to create a consistent coating. Destroy all uniformity by drizzling the excess batter haphazardly over the pieces and pressing in more crumbs to create folds and irregular shapes.

Heat enough vegetable oil for deep-frying in a large heavy-based saucepan over medium heat. Test if the oil is ready by inserting a wooden skewer or the handle of a wooden spoon into the hot oil; if it begins to bubble quickly, then you're ready to go. Fry the crumbed chicken for 4–5 minutes, until golden and crisp. Drain on paper towel.

Combine the stinger sauce ingredients in a small bowl. Cut the brioche buns in half.

Divide the lettuce leaves between the two bottom buns and top with the stinger chicken. Smother in the stinger sauce, sit the other half of each bun on top and then be on alert for some delicious hurt.

SERVES 2

Opt for the version with two TVP
pieces for extra crunch and chew.

Fillet No Fish

My brow furrows in a unique way when I hear the words 'tofu burger', likely conditioned into my being from the years when a soft hunk of bland tofu in hard bread was the best burger a herbivore could hope for when on the go. We shan't dwell on past atrocities, so let's just say there's no fish in this burger and let the tofu's added flavours and extra textures speak for themselves.

INGREDIENTS

blocks silken–medium tofu, frozen and thawed twice (see page 34)	2 × 300 G (10½ OZ)
lemon juice	2 TBSP
nori flakes	1 TBSP
white miso paste	2 TSP
soy milk	125 ML (½ CUP)
panko breadcrumbs	30 G (½ CUP)
sea salt and black pepper	PINCH
vegetable oil	FOR SHALLOW-FRYING
vegan brioche buns	2
butter lettuce leaves	4
slices vegan cheddar	2

TARTARE SAUCE

vegan Japanese mayonnaise	3 TBSP
dill pickles (gherkins), finely chopped	55 G (2 OZ)
chopped dill	1½ TSP
lemon juice	½ TSP
dijon mustard	¼ TSP
caper brine	¼ TSP

To prepare the fish fillets, use your hands to carefully press out the excess liquid from the tofu. Place the whole blocks in a large bowl, then in a separate bowl combine the lemon juice, nori flakes and miso. You may need to massage the miso into the lemon juice to disperse it. Pour this mixture over the tofu and sit for 10 minutes. Pour the soy milk over the tofu and set aside to thicken as you prepare the rest of the recipe.

To make the tartare sauce, combine the ingredients in a bowl and set aside.

Combine the panko breadcrumbs, salt and pepper in a food processor and process into fine dust, then tip into a shallow bowl.

Heat 2 cm (¾ in) of vegetable oil in a large heavy-based saucepan over medium heat or preheat an air-fryer to 190°C (375°F).

Fish the tofu out of the liquid and coat it in the breadcrumbs, firmly pressing down to adhere as many crumbs as possible before gently shaking off the excess. Test if the oil is ready by inserting a wooden skewer or the handle of a wooden spoon into the hot oil; if it begins to bubble quickly, then you're ready to go. Fry the crumbed tofu in the oil or air-fryer (spray the tofu with a little oil if using this method) for 6 minutes or until golden and a crispy crust forms. Do not flip or agitate until cooked three-quarters of the way through, as the fillets will be very fragile. Transfer to paper towel to drain.

To build the burgers, slice the brioche buns in half and divide the lettuce between the bottom bun halves. Top with the fried fish and a slice of cheese, followed by dollops of tartare sauce. Finish with the bun tops to complete the glow up from basic forgettable tofu to a burger everyone will be very impressed by at its high-school reunion.

SERVES 2

Tuna Salad Melt

This tuna salad recipe is super versatile. Here, it plays the star role in a comforting tuna melt, but it is equally at home as a cold sandwich filling, atop a Buddha bowl or as a cracker accompaniment for all occasions. Go on, get the nice mayo for this one. Or make it yourself!

INGREDIENTS

VEGAN MAYO

soy milk	60 ML (¼ CUP)
apple cider vinegar or white vinegar	¾ TSP
American or dijon mustard	¼ TSP
garlic powder	¼ TSP
sea salt	¼ TSP
canola oil or other neutral-flavoured oil	185 ML (¾ CUP)

TUNA SALAD

boiling water	125 ML (½ CUP)
dulse flakes	1¼ TBSP
lemon, juiced	½
MSG	PINCH
TVP mince	75 G (¾ CUP)
sea salt	¼ TSP
chilli flakes	¼ TSP
celery stalk, finely chopped	½
dijon mustard	½ TSP
chopped dill	2 TSP
chopped flat-leaf parsley	2 TSP
diced red onion	2 TBSP

TUNA MELT

dairy-free butter or vegan mayonnaise	3 TBSP
bread	8 SLICES
vegan cheddar	8 SLICES
tomatoes, sliced	2
dill pickles (gherkins), sliced	4

To make the mayo, place all the ingredients, except the oil, in the bowl of a stick blender or plastic jug. Blend with a stick blender for 20 seconds or so, until frothy. With the stick blender running, slowly pour in the oil in a steady stream for 1–2 minutes, until you have an emulsified and thick mayonnaise. Taste, and adjust the seasoning if necessary. The mayo will keep in an airtight container in the fridge for up to 1 month.

To make the tuna salad, combine the boiling water, dulse flakes, lemon juice and MSG in a bowl. Add the TVP and let it sit for 15 minutes. Add 60 g (¼ cup) of the mayo and the remaining tuna salad ingredients and mix well. Refrigerate for 1 hour to let the flavours meld. Serve cold as is, or continue on to make a mean tuna melt.

Spread the butter or mayonnaise over one side of each bread slice. To build the melts, place the bread buttered-side-down, then top four slices with a cheese slice, one quarter of the tuna salad, the tomato, dill pickle and another cheese slice. Top with the remaining bread slices, buttered-side-up.

Preheat a grill (broiler) to high and grill the melts on both sides, keeping a close eye on them to ensure they don't burn, for about 6 minutes, until the cheese has melted and the outside is golden brown.

MAKES 4 MELTS OR TUNA SALAD FOR 2

Pulled-pork Burgers

The perk of picking something to pull that isn't pork is that jackfruit, banana peel, blossom florets or king oyster mushrooms all do a stand-up job; some even come naturally pre-pulled for your pleasure. I've used banana blossom florets in this recipe, but packaged jackfruit in sauce is readily available and can be reheated rapidly for minimum prep and wait time.

INGREDIENTS

Banana blossom floret pulled pork (see page 182)	1 × QUANTITY
vegan bread buns	2
dairy-free butter	1 TBSP
hot sauce (optional)	TO SERVE

FARMHOUSE SLAW

shredded mixed red and white cabbage	75 G (1 CUP)
green apple, shredded	1/4
small handful flat-leaf parsley leaves, chopped	1
sweetcorn kernels	2 TBSP
dill pickle (gherkin), cut into long thin strips	1
diced red onion	1 TBSP
vegan mayonnaise	1 1/2 TBSP
sea salt and black pepper	TO SEASON

Have the pulled pork hot and ready to go.

To make the farmhouse slaw, combine the cabbage, apple, parsley, sweetcorn, pickle and onion in a bowl. Stir through the mayonnaise, plus salt and pepper to taste. Halve the bread buns and butter the insides. Toast or grill (broil) until crispy to contrast the texture of the pulled pork.

Divide the slaw between the two bottom buns, then top with the hot pulled pork. Add a splash of hot sauce if you can handle a kick, then pop the tops on and go to town on it.

SERVES 2

Muffuletta

★ ★ ★

This cake-sized sandwich could feed an army, but alas, vegans are pacifists, so you'll have to down this on your own. This muffuletta improves over time, so don't be afraid to consume the behemoth over several eating sessions, keeping it in the fridge in the meantime.

INGREDIENTS

Smoked ham roast slices (see page 210)	300 G (10½ OZ)
Mortadella (see page 226)	300 G (10½ OZ)
Seitan salami (see page 228)	175 G (6 OZ)
Italian round loaf or cob loaf	1
dijon mustard	2 TBSP
jarred roasted red capsicums (bell peppers)	100 G (3½ OZ)
vegan mozzarella/tangy cheese mix, sliced	300 G (10 ½ OZ)

TAPENADE

capers, drained	2 TBSP
pitted green olives	125 G (1 CUP)
giardiniera mix	180 G (1 CUP)
pitted black olives	30 G (¼ CUP)
garlic cloves, peeled	2
red wine vinegar	2 TBSP
olive oil	3 TBSP
chopped flat-leaf parsley	3 TBSP
dried oregano	1 TBSP
smoked salt and black pepper	LOTS OF

Add the tapenade ingredients to a food processor and pulse five or six times until coarsely chopped.

Slice the various meats as thinly as possible.

Halve the loaf hemispherically and scoop out some of the bread to leave a 2.5 cm (1 in) shell. (Reserve the bread for another recipe, such as croutons in the Caesar salad on page 95 or blitz into fresh breadcrumbs.) Spread the mustard over the insides of the loaf.

Now, build the muffuletta. Spread half the tapenade on the base of the loaf. Next layer on half the smoked ham, covering the tapenade. Repeat with half the mortadella, then add all the capsicum, followed by all the cheese. Use your hands to make smooth layers of each flavour that cover the entire centre of the muffuletta.

Add layers of the remaining ham and mortadella, then layer on the salami. Carefully balance the rest of the tapenade on top and finish with the loaf top. Gently press down to secure everything, then bundle the muffuletta in plastic wrap. Sit a few tins on top to compress further for 1 hour, or use force from your hands to make a snugly pressed loaf. Store the muffuletta wrapped and unsliced in the fridge for a few hours or up to 2 days, before cutting into portions and basking in the glory of your creation.

MAKES I PLANET-SIZED SANDWICH

You can swap in any store-bought sliced or deli-style vegan meats if you don't want to make them yourself. The more variety the better — so load up the sandwich like an edible, twisted Noah's ark.

Ribwich

This is a no limited-time offer. We start with authentic, letter-graded meat before we process the hell out of it. Serve it to your friends once, never make it again and ascend to the stuff of legends. Now without lettuce and guaranteed early death!

INGREDIENTS

Korean barbecue ribs dough (see page 192)	1 × QUANTITY
barbecue rub	2 TBSP
canola oil	FOR FRYING AND COATING
smoky barbecue sauce	185 G (¾ CUP)
vegan bread buns	4
dijon mustard	1 TBSP
dill pickles (gherkins), sliced lengthways	2

ONION RINGS

soy milk	125 ML (½ CUP)
lemon juice or white vinegar	2 TSP
hot sauce (optional)	1 TSP
plain (all-purpose) flour	75 G (½ CUP)
sea salt and black pepper	TO SEASON
dry breadcrumbs	50 G (½ CUP)
large onion, sliced into 1–2 cm (½–¾ in) thick rings	½

Add a serve of farmhouse slaw (see page 288) on the side for a full meal.

Make the Korean barbecue ribs dough, resting for 10 minutes, then shape into four rectangular patties and set aside.

To start on the onion rings, make a basic buttermilk by combining the soy milk and lemon juice or vinegar in a large bowl. Set aside for a few minutes to thicken. This is also your cue to add hot sauce if you're using it. Place the flour in a shallow bowl and season with salt and pepper. Get out another bowl and tip in the breadcrumbs.

Heat 2 cm (¾ in) canola oil in a large heavy-based saucepan over medium–high heat.

Separate the onion rings and toss in the seasoned flour. Transfer the onion rings to a plate and tip the rest of the flour into the buttermilk, stirring until smooth. Dip each ring into the buttermilk batter until fully coated, then lightly press into the breadcrumbs, shaking off the excess.

Lower the onion rings into the hot oil and fry for 2 minutes, flipping halfway through. Transfer to a plate lined with paper towel to drain and immediately sprinkle with salt. Set aside until needed.

Rub 1½ teaspoons of barbecue rub into the exterior of each patty, add a little canola oil and microwave on High in two 1-minute bursts. Heat 1 tablespoon of canola oil in a frying pan over medium heat and sear the patties for 8–10 minutes per side until starting to char up. Remove from the pan and spread 1½ tablespoons of smoky barbecue sauce on each patty. Microwave for 1 minute, flip over and spread the remaining barbecue sauce on the other side. Microwave for 1 more minute.

Halve the bread buns and spread the mustard on the bottom halves. Place the rib patties on top, add the pickle and onion rings and cover with the bun top to finish. It's vegan magic and now YOU are the Rib Witch.

SERVES 4

Cheeseburger Sliders

Modern vegan burgers are loads healthier than the original vegan-friendly burger option: a double serve of large fries if you could confirm they had been cooked in a separate fryer. This platter of cheeseburgers is perfect for game day and can be warmed in the oven for whenever you're ready to feed a crowd. Brian Watson, aka Thee Burger Dude, who has nobly taken it upon himself to veganise every conceivable burger and then some, comes with extra tips on the side: 'Vegan cheese is 1000 times more resilient than dairy cheese. Immediately add your cheese after flipping the burger, then splash a little water into the pan and cover as quickly as possible to steam and melt the cheese.'

INGREDIENTS

Basic methylcellulose mince (see page 280) OR	1 × QUANTITY
mini store-bought patties	12–14
canola oil	FOR GRILLING
vegan pull-apart burger bun loaf OR	1
small dinner rolls	12–14
dairy-free cheddar slices	12–14
small onion, diced	1
dill pickles (gherkins), sliced into thin rounds	6
dijon mustard and tomato ketchup	TO TASTE

If using methylcellulose mince, use your hands to shape the mince into patties to match your burger buns.

Heat a barbecue grill to medium or place a frying pan over medium heat. Brush the grill or pan with a light coating of canola oil.

Working in batches, add the patties to the barbecue grill or pan and cook, pressing down with a spatula, for about 5 minutes each side, until beginning to char and the internal temperature is more than 80°C (175°F) on a kitchen thermometer. As the patties are cooking, preheat the oven to 150°C (300°F).

Use a serrated knife to slice horizontally through the middle of your chosen buns or rolls (if using the pull-apart loaf, keep the buns attached so you have two slabs: a top loaf half and bottom loaf half). Transfer the bottom loaf half or the bottom of the rolls to a baking tray and place a cheese slice on each bun. Top with the onion and pickles, followed by the just-grilled patties. Grab the mustard and ketchup and douse the patties in both. Cover with the top loaf half or tops of the rolls and bake for 10 minutes to lightly toast the bread and encourage the cheese to melt.

Tear off individual burgers from the slab or serve up the rolls on individual plates when you're ready to feast, and rest easy knowing there's another right behind it, ready for seconds.

SERVES A CROWD

Try Brian's smash burger tip instead of hand-forming your patties. 'Roll the vegan beef into a ball, place it in a hot cast-iron skillet, then smash it down with a large spatula. Use baking paper so the burger doesn't stick to the spatula.'

ACKNOWLEDGEMENTS

This book is dedicated to Chickadee, my pet chicken and good childhood friend, who would ride to school with me in my backpack each day and, in turn, set me on my path to veganism and this book.

Thanks to Megan, Mum and Dad, Sven and my other friends and family who allow me to force-feed them recipe tests, as well as Lucy, Megan, Emily, Meryl, Lee, Evi, Paul and the team at Smith Street Books who helped tie these dishes into a beautiful behemoth of a book.

A huge bucket of gratitude to the idols of mine who are evolving the modern plant-based meat industry and have kindly contributed insight within these chapters: Seth Tibbott, Chris Maillard, Richard Makin, Lauren Toyota, Simon Toohey, Thanh Truong, Oncle Hu, Kasper Schramm, Jim Fuller, Nalin Arileo and Watson, aka, Thee Burger Dude.

Finally, thanks to the people throughout human history who have dreamed up, experimented with and perfected the dozens of techniques and resulting meat alternatives you can find the legacy of throughout the pages in this book.

INDEX

Smith
Street
Books

Published in 2021 by Smith Street Books
Naarm | Melbourne | Australia
smithstreetbooks.com

ISBN: 978-1-922417-32-9

All rights reserved. No part of this book may be reproduced or transmitted by any person or entity, in any form or by any means, electronic or mechanical, including photocopying, recording, scanning or by any storage and retrieval system, without the prior written permission of the publishers and copyright holders.

Copyright text © Zacchary Bird
Copyright photography © Emily Weaving
Copyright design © Smith Street Books

Publisher: Lucy Heaver
Editor: Megan Johnston
Designer: Evi O. Studio | Susan Le, Wilson Leung and Evi O.
Illustrator: Evi-O. Studio | Susan Le, Wilson Leung and Evi O.
Typesetter: Heather Menzies, Studio 31 Graphics
Photographer: Emily Weaving
Food stylist: Lee Blaylock
Food preparation: Zacchary Bird, Meryl Batlle and Megan Beatrice Jackson
Proofreader: Ariana Klepac
Indexer: Helena Holmgren

Printed & bound in China by C&C Offset Printing Co., Ltd.

Book 185
10 9 8 7 6 5 4 3 2 1